The
DISTRIBUTED
LEADERSHIP
TOOLBOX

Essential Practices
for Successful Schools

Mark E. McBeth

CORWIN PRESS
A SAGE Company
Thousand Oaks, CA 91320

For information:

Corwin Press
A SAGE Company
2455 Teller Road
Thousand Oaks, California 91320
www.corwinpress.com

SAGE Ltd.
1 Oliver's Yard
55 City Road
London EC1Y 1SP
United Kingdom

SAGE India Pvt. Ltd.
B 1/I 1 Mohan Cooperative
   Industrial Area
Mathura Road, New Delhi 110 044
India

SAGE Asia-Pacific Pte. Ltd.
33 Pekin Street #02–01
Far East Square
Singapore 048763

Printed in the United States of America.

Library of Congress Cataloging-in-Publication Data

McBeth, Mark E.
The distributed leadership toolbox: essential practices for successful schools/
Mark E. McBeth.
     p. cm.
Includes bibliographical references and index.
ISBN 978-1-4129-5716-8 (cloth)
ISBN 978-1-4129-5717-5 (pbk.)
   1. Educational leadership—United States. 2. School management and organization—United States. I. Title.

LB2805.M332 2008
371.200973—dc22   2007033103

This book is printed on acid-free paper.

07   08   09   10   11   10 9 8 7 6 5 4 3 2 1

Acquisitions Editor:	Hudson Perigo
Editorial Assistants:	Cassandra Harris, Lesley Blake
Production Editor:	Eric Garner
Copy Editor:	Edward Meidenbauer
Typesetter:	C&M Digitals (P) Ltd.
Proofreader:	Cheryl Rivard
Indexer:	Sheila Bodell
Cover Designer:	Karine Hovsepian

Contents

Preface

Contemporary educational reform places a great premium upon the relationship between leadership and school improvement. Research findings from diverse countries and different school contexts have revealed the powerful impact of leadership in securing school development and change. The evidence from the international research base is unequivocal—effective leaders exercise an indirect but powerful influence on the effectiveness of the school and on the achievement of students. The research shows that although the quality of teaching has a powerful influence upon pupil motivation and achievement, the quality of leadership determines the motivation of teachers and the quality of teaching in the classroom. In summary, the contribution of leadership to school effectiveness and school improvement is significant.

—Alma Harris (2002)

PURPOSE OF THIS BOOK

Distributed leadership is a method for engaging educational practitioners in meaningful and timely dialogue about the effectiveness of their leadership practices as they relate to enhancing and changing classroom practices. This, in turn, enhances student learning. A distributed perspective on leadership is best thought of as a framework for thinking about and analyzing leadership (Spillane, 2006a; Spillane, Halverson, & Diamond, 2001, 2004). It proposes an ideology that predicts success in the purposeful creation of leadership and classroom practices on the basis of situationally interdependent interactions between leaders and followers.

The Distributed Leadership Toolbox provides routines and tools for a school's formal leaders and building-level teams that allow them *to diagnose* and *design* leadership practices. These tools help leaders to stop leading by default. Leadership practice is defined as the interactions among the leader(s), followers, and the situation stretched over time (Spillane,

2004a, 2006a). The most important task is to help leaders perfect their performance of these routines and use tools in practice on the basis of observation and reflection. The intent is to give school teams a new way of thinking about the relationship between leadership practice, classroom practice, and student performance.

This book tackles present-day leadership research, which is often on distributed leadership, and transforms it into a precision leadership toolbox for practitioners. Converting research to application has historically been difficult for practicing educators, and the research associated with distributed leadership isn't any different. For most leaders, viewing leadership from a distributed perspective has been, up until now, like trying to read a foreign textbook. Deciphering this research and putting it into practice is a challenge. Therefore, I have worked extensively with several leadership researchers in an effort to translate their research into practical applications for school leaders. It has become clear, as a result of facilitating several leadership teams focused on distributed leadership, that there is a need to have a toolbox of leadership practice diagnosis and design tools.

ADOPTING AND CREATING A REPERTOIRE OF PRACTICES

By no means should this set of tools be perceived as the fix-all for school improvement. Use the tools in this book to begin the process of diagnosing your present practice and to design effective ways to enhance and change teachers' classroom practice. It is important that the tools within this book *don't* become the sole source for evaluation and design of leadership practices. That would be a mistake and I would not have met my objectives of establishing the uniqueness of each school. Leaders must become skilled designers of their own routines and tools. This toolbox was designed to cultivate a "distributed mind-set" in school leaders to move them beyond an exclusive reliance on school leader superheroes and shared leadership.

Different forms of leadership are needed in different stages of a project or an organization's development. No one person can be a leader in every situation. Effective organizations allow the natural leader to emerge as needs require.

—Kathy Kolbe (2004b)

Many schools that have adopted the use of these tools have reported to me that they have necessitated redesigning some tools to fit their situation. In other words, they have used the tools in different ways than their original intention and have redesigned them to meet their unique needs. I celebrate this, because this means they get it. They are adapting and creating their own tools to meet their needs and situations. Leithwood and colleagues (Leithwood, Louis, Anderson, & Wahlstrom, 2004) say we must develop leaders with large repertoires of practices and the capacity to choose from that repertoire as needed. Without fail, schools who have adopted these tools have said the toolbox gave them a framework to work from. They used the tools from the toolbox and created new ones to meet the objectives outlined in the distributed leadership school improvement framework. The toolbox has provided them with a starting point, and they have adapted their use to fit their particular situation.

DO NOT FEAR

As many of you reading this preface can testify, teachers and administrators already have so many federally mandated programs to adhere to, not to even mention the testing that is required, that it is a major challenge to find the time to plan challenging diversified curriculum that the students deserve. Readers who have read this book mostly agree with the philosophy of distributed leadership; however, a normal reaction is a hesitation to implement the underpinnings. Practitioners do not want another program, and even more so, one that would require so much time. The tools within this book lay out a framework and a foundation for your work within distributed leadership; it is not meant to be the composition of reform. In fact, the framework I offer within this toolbox is a complement to your present practices and reform efforts. Use the tools as needed, when needed. Use the tools once or twice and then adopt the theories and philosophies that shape the very purpose of the tools and discard the tool. Although I have a plethora of tools on which to draw, I use only one or two of them when I facilitate individuals and teams. Instead, I use a series of critical questions to identify the issue and then choose a few tools to use as mediating devices, enabling the individual and teams to reflect on their own practice and to help them design new practices.

ABOUT THE BOOK

Given the current conditions of most schools and my experience in working closely with school leaders struggling to make sense of the collective demands put on them in an era of high leadership accountability, I present this book as a leadership practice toolbox used to focus and guide practitioners through a leadership team's collaboration inquiry, diagnosis, and design.

The book is written to support readers new to the distributed perspective as well as for those who have read prior research. To my knowledge, this is the first resource made available in a practitioner's perspective. Therefore, I made efforts to build a set of guiding principles associated with the uniqueness of taking a distributed leadership perspective and, more important, to offer practical field-tested tools, facilitator tips, and an improvement model.

If deliberately implemented, the tools and the model presented here will increase the awareness school leaders have on teachers teaching and students learning. The facilitator tips will provide guidance and increase the confidence and skills of those who choose to engage other leaders in this valuable process. The tools and model will increase the leadership capacity of your school, which in turn will positively influence the learning potential of each child.

Remove the Blinders so You Can See

Efforts to improve leadership should build upon the foundation of well-documented and well-accepted knowledge about leadership that already exists. We know that leadership is most successful when it is focused on instruction and learning. Yet leaders struggle to move beyond the knowing to the doing.

> It is possible to find schools all over the country that don't listen to those who say what they are doing is impossible.
>
> —Karin Chenoweth (2007)

It is imperative that you as a reader remove your blinders and open up your historical-experience filter to allow for a new way of thinking about leadership. Doing the same thing over and over again gets us the same results. Practitioners and users of this field guide need to understand the unique differences associated with the various aspects of leadership. Why is it so important? Because we are creatures of habit and we will fall back on old ways, it is critical for us to understand the framework of leadership we will be using.

What It Looks Like

The book is organized in a way that enables the readers to start with the current condition of leadership and a rationale for looking at leadership differently (Chapter 1). Chapters 2 and 3 are the foundation research and theories that give shape to the uniqueness of distributed leadership. Chapter 4 is the supportive framework for inquiry into the distributed perspective of leadership. Chapter 5 presents tools that can be used during the Information Cycle of the distributed leadership framework, and

Chapter 6 presents the tools that can be used during the Practice Cycle of the distributed leadership framework. Chapter 7 discusses the reflective tools used to analyze the team's effectiveness in using the routines and tools within the previous two chapters.

Brief Description of Each Chapter

Chapter 1: Traditional Thinking/New Opportunities

Chapter 1 is an overview of the traditional views of school leadership, school change, and analysis of classroom practice. It also provides a foundation of thinking about leadership practice as it is stretched across leaders, followers, and their situations. Accounts of leadership often dwell exclusively on building principal attributes and roles as well as school structures. Principals have been put into a superhero limelight as the so-called action-orientated "instructional leaders" of everything. In recent years, schools have become data critiques of classroom practice but have not been critiqued on the other essential contributing factors in student learning such as leadership practice (Leithwood et al., 2004). The challenges facing practitioners in converting distributed leadership research into useful practice is made easy through a series of examples and case studies. Informed by the latest distributed leadership research and by case studies from my work with schools around the Midwest, this chapter illuminates school practitioner pitfalls as well as the potential for effective changes.

Chapter 2: A Distributed Perspective on Leadership

When looking at leadership from a distributed perspective, it becomes more than counting up all the actions taken by individual leaders to describe leadership—it is more about the practices (Spillane, 2005b; 2006a). Chapter 2 challenges readers to look at leadership from a new perspective composed of interactions between leaders, followers, and their situations. A foundation of support is built around the essential role that followers play in how leadership is practiced within a school. The uniqueness of the situation shapes how leadership is practiced in direct relationship to teachers' classroom practices. The situation, the leader, and follower interactions are explored and defined within a complex system of leadership practices. What is leadership practice? What is distributed leadership, or what is it not? These central questions are answered by connecting research to practitioner examples. This chapter will explore the role of reform models and professional learning communities and the relationship school leaders have on their success and failures.

Distributed leadership is categorically not a reform model and is not the same as professional learning communities; however, it is not in conflict with either of them.

Chapter 3: The Impact of Leadership on Successful Schools

Chapter 3 explores four distinctive leadership aspects and the impact they have on school improvement efforts when deployed. All four of the aspects can produce effective results, but only one will create a cohesive maturity among its leaders, which in turn will produce communities of practice. One aspect will produce a series of unwanted outcomes across multiple leadership and organizational factors, including school culture and instructional focus of the teaching staff. The other two aspects of leadership can produce positive enhancements and changes to the organization and student performance. However, if school leaders linger too long in one of these two aspects, they may begin to produce undesirable results.

This chapter also constructs and transcribes a vision for developing facilitative conversations within the distributed perspective of leadership. *How do we know our leadership practices are enhancing and changing teachers' classroom practice?* This question will be surveyed often through a set of essential critical questions for facilitating conversations with school improvement leadership teams. In addition, we will learn about the three vital leadership functions that all successful schools adequately incorporate into their leadership practices. The importance of structuring collaborative inquiry into leadership practice is central; therefore, a provocative leadership impact survey is introduced within this chapter.

Chapter 4: The Framework of Success: A Model for Leadership Inquiry

Distributed leadership is a description of how leadership is at present and what it can become (Spillane, 2006a). A multiphase school leadership improvement outline, "The Distributed Leadership Improvement Framework," is presented as a means for thinking about leadership practice by design. The framework is broken down into three improvement cycles interwoven in partnership with leadership practice and classroom practice. The Distributed Leadership Improvement Framework is a tool that provides the means for practitioners to use a distributed leadership perspective within their present school improvement efforts. The framework takes the reader from diagnosis, to design, to new practice, and finally to the results and analysis of school leadership practices. The framework serves as a foundational tool for all the tools that are explored in the remaining chapters.

Chapter 5: Information Cycle: Effective–Efficiency Process

Chapter 5 is broken into seven sections (labeled A through G). This chapter provides practitioners the opportunity to explore the lived reality of their leadership practices and to put new or reworked practices in place by design. This chapter is devoted to guiding leaders through the Information Cycle in preparation for the Practice Cycle. A wide array of diagnostic tools for teams, each with stories, examples, facilitator instructions, and rationales, are explored.

Section A helps identify a starting point, the Dimension of Practice, which serves as the foundation for diagnosis of a school leadership and classroom practice. Section B tools are used to determine which leaders are influencing which classroom teachers in direct association with the identified Dimension of Practice. Sections C, D, and E tools are designed to give guidance to practitioners as they diagnose and analyze their leadership practice in association with classroom practice. The tools are created for the purpose of helping practitioners make purposeful application in direct relationship with distributed leadership. Sections F and G are a set of design tools used to assist leaders in their efforts to enhance and change their leadership practices, including routines, tools, and structures. Sometimes teams hesitate to undertake a major leadership initiative because they fear the potential difficulties and negative repercussions that might ensue from innovative actions. The tools within this section facilitate alternative solutions to practices while using the unique talents of an array of formal and informal leaders. The tools make it possible for teams to move beyond good intentions to meaningful action. The anecdotes and strategies constructed within this chapter serve as a practical resource for the novice as well as the experienced practitioner.

Chapter 6: Practice Cycle: Practice Improvement Process

Chapter 6 tools assist leaders as they move from the Information Cycle to the Practice Cycle. A series of new practices and data tools for teams, each with stories, examples, facilitator instructions, and rationales, are investigated. Chapter 6 is divided into three sections (labeled A through C). The tools are designed to give guidance to practitioners as they design and monitor leadership practices that enhance and change teachers' classroom practice. Only when practices are put in place by design can they be evaluated for their effectiveness in enhancing and changing classroom practices, which in turn may boost student learning. Section A is intended to help bridge the gap between design and new practice. Section B exposes leaders to planning templates that are uniquely designed to address the interactions of leaders and followers in association with their identified situation. The tools in Section C provide teams with a means for evaluating the results that are produced from their new leadership practices.

Chapter 7: Tools for Reflective Practice

Teams habitually move from one practice diagnosis to another without processing the tools and course of action the team used. It is essential that teams review the tools and processes used for the diagnosis to determine what should be repeated, revised, or deleted. This chapter explores the collaborative successes and struggles of the team as they use a number of different Information and Practice Cycle tools. Teams identify the impact of their practices, distill a formula for improving the use of the routines and tools, and examine how to apply this knowledge to future leadership practice reviews.

Reproducible Blank Templates

Many of the tools you are exposed to in the various chapters have reproducible templates. The templates can be accessed from the section immediately following Chapter 7, and they are arranged in alphabetical order. Maximize your facilitation of leadership teams, faculty meetings, and workshops by reproducing the templates for handouts or overheads. These templates have also conveniently been provided electronically on the provided CD.

Reproducible Resources

Many of the concepts and visual tools used throughout the chapters have been reproduced for your convenience in a handout form. In addition, a list of terms associated with distributed leadership has been created for facilitators and leaders during inquiry sessions with leadership teams and faculties. These templates have also conveniently been provided electronically on the provided CD.

DISTRIBUTED LEADERSHIP TOOLS FOR SCHOOL IMPROVEMENT

Tools	Reproducible templates	Page #	Cycle	Facilitator tips	Page #
Leadership Impact Survey	✓	232–236	Dialogue	✓	59–62
A Vertical Leadership Component Map	✓	238	Information	✓	94–96
Advice Network Map	✓	243	Information	✓	109–111
Identified Leadership Practices	✓	244–245	Information	✓	117–119
Routine Microanalysis Chart	✓	246	Information	✓	124–126
Microanalysis Chart Reflection	✓	247	Information		
Systems of Practice	✓	249	Information	✓	138–141
Directional Intentions of Leadership Practices	✓	268	Information	✓	157–160
Competing Dimensions of Practice	✓	269	Information	✓	153
Common Dimensions of Practice	✓	270	Information	✓	155
Multiple Leaders Practice Diagnosis	✓	250	Information	✓	146–148
Practice-to-Practice Vertical	✓	251	Information	✓	170–172
Practice-to-Practice Horizontal	✓	252	Information	✓	170–172
Shaping of Leadership Functions Form	✓	253–254	Information	✓	164–166
Side-by-Side Content Comparison	✓	255	Information	✓	174–176
Side-by-Side Building Comparison	✓	256	Information		
Practice Gap Summary	✓	257	Information	✓	179–181
Practice Bridge Dialogue Questions	✓	258	Information	✓	181
Forecasting Leadership Initiatives Grid	✓	259	Information	✓	185–187
Alternative Solutions Applied Chart	✓	260	Information	✓	191–194
Leadership Function Support Analysis Form	✓	261	Information	✓	196–197
Intentions Versus Action	✓	262–263	Practice	✓	203–205
New Practice Action-Planning Chart	✓	264	Practice	✓	208–210
Stakeholder Analysis Support Chart	✓	266	Practice	✓	213–215
Tally Log			Practice	✓	216–218
Data Collection Chart	✓	265	Practice	✓	218–219
Verbal Flow			Practice	✓	220–221
Reflection Worksheet	✓	241	Reflective	✓	229
Lessons Learned Questionnaire	✓	240	Reflective	✓	228
Post-Leadership Routine Reflection	✓	237	Reflective		
Shaping Our Reflection	✓	239	Reflective	✓	229
Systems of Tools: Circle Reflection	✓	248	Reflective	✓	229
Leadership and Classroom Practice Worksheet	✓	242	Reflective	✓	229
Example 6 Person Placemat	✓	267	Decision Making		

Acknowledgments

Writing this book could be one of the greatest personal triumphs I have ever had the pleasure to suffer through. My successful goal attainment has come about as a result of so many people's support and input.

I owe my greatest gratitude first and foremost to my best friend and daily inspiration, my wife, Jeri McBeth. She never stopped believing in me, even through the most challenging times. She was my early encourager to start the book, and she remained my personal motivational coach and sounding board throughout the process. Her patience and understanding of my creative sharpness and crushing compassion for students' learning can at times leave me dumbfounded. She has sacrificed so much for the welfare of others and has asked for so little in return. She is my true hero.

My exposure to the distributed perspective first came about when Larry Wheeles, a coworker, gave me an article written about the distributed leadership perspective. Five months later, Larry and I were launching the Kansas Distributed Leadership Academy. I can't thank Larry enough for serving as my mentor, intellectual and psychological support, cognitive coach, and friend. His knowledge and vast experience have enhanced and changed my practices.

My first meeting with Dr. James (Jim) Spillane was in a coffee shop in Chicago. On that day, Jim, Larry, and I mapped out a practitioner's perspective of his innovative research. Jim's support and insight make my role in the circle of distributed leadership possible and the work I do credible. My life as an educator has forever changed as a result of my interactions with him.

This book would not be possible without the contribution of an outstanding network of coworkers. I am especially grateful to Howard Shular, Gary Manford, Judi Miller, and Bill Hagerman for their intellectual challenges and extensive insight from years of field experience as school leaders. Sometimes one is fortunate to have friends who go beyond their role of merely being friends. I wish to acknowledge those friends who endured the editing role of my multiple versions of this book. I know reviewing my early work was dreadfully challenging. This book has benefited greatly from the thoughtful critiques of Linda Brooks, Lynn Bechtal, Dee Lewis, and Diane DeBacker.

I must give special thanks to the following people for their contributions to the distributed leadership research and invaluable feedback they offered prior to my manuscript work and during: Richard Halverson, Eric Camburn, and Alma Harris. This book also would not have been possible without the generous feedback of so many quality people. I would like to acknowledge the people who have taken the time to read early drafts of my work and provide feedback that contributed to the shaping of this manuscript. These significant people are Diana Wieland, Tim Wies, Kathy Boyer, Linda Gieger, Kevin Case, Kelly Tolman, Dr. Andy Tompkins, Bill Wilson, Bonita Duran, Melissa Tillman, and Dr. Jaque Wilson.

To know one's own talents can truly be validating and rewarding. Thanks to the brilliant insight of Kathy Kolbe, I am able to trust my instincts. To seek advice from those who have paved the path before you can be a true blessing and significant asset. One such blessing for me were my conversations with Richard Deems, an author of 14 books and a nationally recognized expert on organizational change and leadership.

Special thanks go to the teachers and school leaders who have directly or indirectly contributed to this book. Their dedication to student learning has given purpose to my efforts and to my dedication to the field of education. Many have opened their doors and allowed me to see the great things they are doing and, in some cases, their challenges.

I owe a huge thanks to the Corwin Press staff for their guidance and acceptance of my work.

The contributions of the following reviewers are gratefully acknowledged:

Carrie Carpenter
Grant Coordinator
Deschutes Edge Charter School
Redmond, Oregon

Bruce Deterding
Principal
Wichita Heights High School
Wichita, Kansas

Mary K. Culver
Clinical Assistant Professor
Northern Arizona University
Flagstaff, Arizona

Kathryn Harwell Kee
Professional Coach and Consultant
Coaching School Results, Inc.
Shady Shores, Texas

Rachel McMillan
School Improvement Specialist
Corporate Landing Middle School
Virginia Beach Public Schools
Virginia Beach, Virginia

Steven R. Thompson
Coordinator, School Leadership
   Program
Miami University
Oxford, Ohio

Jerry Vaughn
Elementary Principal
Cabot Public Schools
Cabot, Arkansas

Kim E. Vogel
Principal
Parkdale Elementary School
Hood River County School District
Parkdale, Oregon

About the Author

 **Mark E. McBeth** has been an educator for the past 17 years at the elementary, secondary, and university levels, as well as an independent consultant and a consultant with a state department of education. His experience as an educator has led him to teach both nationally and internationally.

He has chaired and served on numerous statewide leadership committees and has presented at national and statewide conferences on his cutting-edge leadership perspective. In addition, he has presented on a number of other topics including instinctual talents, student engagement, high-quality professional development, effective synergistic teams, classroom instruction that works, and school-related student resiliency and leadership facilitation. His passion and experience in distributed leadership are shaping school, district, and statewide leadership initiatives directed at providing educators with the knowledge and tools needed to enhance and change practices.

Recently an Educational Program Consultant in the Learning Service Division at the Kansas State Department of Education, Mr. McBeth has worked extensively in four major statewide leadership initiatives in Kansas. He designed and directed the Kansas Distributed Leadership Academy, a high-quality, professional development, district-level leadership program. His experience includes providing intensive technical support to districts and schools in need of improvement. He trains and coaches administrators on distributed leadership, instinctual talents leading to creativity and problem solving, team goal attainment, student engagement data collection systems, high-quality professional development, student resiliency, federal No Child Left Behind Act (2001) regulations, and choice implications.

Presently Mr. McBeth is applying the principles of distributed leadership as a contracted turnaround principal, independent speaker, trainer and consultant.

Mr. McBeth received his master's degree in Educational Administration and Supervision, and an Educational Specialist degree in Educational Administration and Supervision from Western Illinois University.

Traditional Thinking/New Opportunities

The history of failure in war can be summed up in two words: too late. Too late in comprehending the deadly purpose of a potential enemy; too late in realizing the mortal danger; too late in preparedness; too late in uniting all possible forces for resistance; too late in standing with one's friends.

—General Douglas MacArthur

When Baker, a small rural school and Kansas Distributed Leadership Academy participant, was asked to identify the leadership practices they used associated with reading pedagogical strategies, no one knew the discoveries that would be made. The team discovered nearly 50 different leadership practices. At first, the team was impressed, and then they became somewhat perplexed. "How did all these practices come about?"

A superficial analysis revealed that some of these subconscious practices were the filtrate of past administrators and had been around for years. Many of these practices created a facade of being unique, but in actuality, they were mere replicas of each other. Teachers, to fill in the perceived gaps that existed in fruitless practices, created some of their own. Consequently, the staff just added to the plethora of already existing long-standing practices. The most surprising discovery was that the team could identify only one practice that enhanced and changed teachers' classroom practices that in turn positively impacted student learning.

Critical Thought

If, as a leader within your school, you knew that a leadership practice you were using was going to have an impact on student learning, would you not want to know?

What if your practices were not going to affect the outcome of your students' learning? Would you not want to know that as well?

One practice out of 50! Do you think the Baker team felt that they had properly allocated their time, energy, and capital to enhance student learning? Baker found this discovery to be titanic in nature, and the ship was sinking. Baker, like so many other schools, would have continued to plod along with their daily routines and never have discovered why they were working so hard, never knowing if they were making a difference.

We are what we repeatedly do.

—Aristotle

By using a few of the tools within this toolbox, Baker was able to discover the lived reality of their practices as well as the formal structure of their school. Prior to this leadership practice diagnosis, Baker was oblivious to the fact that they were expending so much capital on reading pedagogy with a minuscule outcome. This discovery was a step in the right direction for Baker's efforts to improve students' ability to read proficiently.

Baker was able to rethink their leadership practices; thus, they kept their one impact practice, enhanced a few others, deleted 40-plus ineffective practices, and added a few additional ones. Baker created a meaningful system of leadership practices to monitor their ability to enhance and change classroom practices.

Folks often ask me, "What was the one thing?" The short answer to this question is, "It doesn't really matter." The purpose of the story is to point out that they were able to discover what practices were enhancing teachers' classroom practices and which ones were not. As a result of this discovery, the school was able to reduce wasted resources and energy and was able to focus attention on a few well-intentioned and soundly designed leadership practices, monitored for their effectiveness.

The total direct and indirect effects of leadership on student learning account for about a quarter of total school effects.

—Leithwood, Louis, Anderson, and Wahlstrom (2004, p. 5)

Thus, leadership practices that were effective at enhancing classroom practices that improved student learning were kept, and all others were reworked or thrown out.

HAVE YOU HEARD THE NEWS?

Have you heard the news? Researchers have recently documented that school leadership makes a vast contribution to student learning. The review of research done by Leithwood, Louis, Anderson, and Wahlstrom (2004) has made it very clear that leadership contributes significantly to school conditions that lead to high student academic performance. "You make a difference" is the newest battle cry of educational reform specialists.

In reality, it is not anything new; after all, these educational reform specialists have been telling their loyal followers this for years. The greats like Linda Lambert, Victoria Bernhardt, Richard Elmore, Larry Lezotte, Peter Senge, Richard DuFour, Mike Schomoker, Doug Reeves, and so many more have urged school leaders to reform their practices. Other reform specialists have erected a picture of education in a time of major

> *Effective educational leadership makes a difference in improving learning.*
> —Leithwood and colleagues (2004, p. 3)

crisis that advocates that we do not have a choice but to change. Michael Fullan (2001) refers to this as the "Moral Imperative."

HOT LIGHTS!

The interrogation light shines fiercely on those in education today and on none more than those who serve as instructional leaders. As pressure for improving student performance in the current accountability environment swells and test results are scrutinized, school leaders are being urged to focus their efforts on how teachers perform in their classrooms. This focus is essential as educators are now looking at how they teach each student, ensuring that each learns. However, this accountability for performance does not mean that leaders need only to work harder; instead, they must learn to work smarter and more efficiently. School leaders should practice their craft with a precise and purposeful intention to enhance classroom teachers' practices, which in turn will boost student learning.

CENTER STAGE

Clearly, so many great educational reformers cannot be wrong. We are in a time of crisis and we know that effective leadership enhances student performance, so we need to buck up and face this challenge head-on. To do so, we need new analytical or diagnostic leadership tools that enable us to think about school leaders in a new way (Leithwood et al., 2004). The tools within the Distributed Leadership Toolbox enable us to approach school leadership in new ways that put "how we practice leadership" center stage.

Before we can truly gauge the value of these tools, we must understand the purpose and value of the distributed leadership perspective (Spillane, 2006a). We must understand the present conditions of education, and we must understand the theoretical base that gives shape to the distributed leadership perspective. Note: *Distributed leadership perspective* is a term used by Dr. James Spillane and colleagues (Spillane, 2006a; Spillane et al., 2001) to differentiate leadership involving acts of single leaders from that involving interactions of leaders and followers.

Distributed leadership is a relatively new topic on the school leader's radar, and as such, most practitioners know very little or nothing about its true uniqueness.

"HOW" DO YOU KNOW "WHO'S" ON FIRST?

The great Abbott and Costello baseball skit describing "Who" is on first and "What" is on second makes people laugh every time they hear it. Do you remember who was on third base? No, you are right that "Who" is on first, but "I Don't Know" is on third base! In reality, not knowing "who" (or in this example, "I don't know") is on third base is not a laughing matter. Given some thought, you may notice that a key name is missing from the ballgame: *How.* Studying *how* leaders interact with followers, as well as the "who" and "what," is essential when thinking about leadership (Halverson, 2005a; Spillane, 2006a; Spillane et al., 2001). The skit is funny and we laugh at Costello, who is not aware of his name blunders and remains clueless throughout the entire episode. Educators often end up as confused as Costello does. Accounts of school leadership often dwell exclusively on the organizational structures and the actions and roles of individual leaders (Spillane, 2006a). Educators think about leadership in the facet of who the leaders are and what they do to others. As a result, "the day-to-day leadership practice falls through the cracks" (Spillane, 2006a, p. 7). When thinking about leadership practice from a distributed perspective, we will need to ensure that "How" is in the ballgame to ensure that the practice of leadership is addressed.

GROWING UP A SUPERHERO

Were you one of those people who grew up watching Saturday morning superhero cartoons and reading the latest comic strip in your tree house? As your teacher was in her second hour of lectures on Monday morning, did you space out and drift into superhero comic-strip land? Were you one of those students who were going to save the world so everyone would look up to you as the hero? For most of us, it is a culturally ingrained state of mind and therefore becomes an answer of "Yes." These illusions of being the superhero did not disappear as we entered high school, where we were compelled to be the biggest and strongest athlete or the smartest kid in the class.

As educators, from the first day we entered our classrooms, our school administrators expected us to know our subjects, cover the material, maintain student behavior, be entertaining, and raise student assessment scores. With these expectations upon us, we find ourselves once again put into a situation to be superhuman.

In our principal preparation programs, we learned that we were knighted "The Instructional Leader." Many principals have stood in front of their staffs and given the declaration of "I am your Instructional Leader." All they were missing was a superhero cape with the embroidered letters "IL"! A proclamation of being the sole instructional leader and having that superhero cape with "IL" on it is like returning to our childhood of being a cartoon superhero.

> *For many years, principals have been told that they need to be instructional leaders. Defining instructional leadership can be problematic as well. This term, however, has remained a vague concept.*
>
> —Waters, Marzano, and McNulty (2004)

Many educational leaders carry a conviction that they must keep instruction front and center, yet they struggle to fulfill the false expectations of superhero heroics and the external prospect of being the champion of all related to instruction. Leaders caught in this quandary expend countless amounts of energy being unproductive, which leads to high tension. We must be willing to let go of the superhero mentality we place on positional leaders, mainly on building principals. If school staffs are to meet the needs of every child, to have perseverance to put each child first, and to create a combined wisdom (Kolbe, 2004a) of all stakeholders for the betterment of our students, then schools cannot rely on a single heroic person (Elmore, 2000; Reeves, 2006b; Spillane, 2004a, 2005c, 2006a).

WITHOUT A DOUBT

I just stated above that we need to remove the principal from the superhero mentality, but without a doubt, the principal is crucial to this leadership perspective. The principal cannot or should not be perceived as the sole leader just because of the positional power that goes along with such a title. Louis and Kruse (1995) identified the supportive leadership of principals as one of the necessary human resources for school-based professional communities, referring to them as, "post-heroic leaders who do not view themselves as the architects of school effectiveness" (p. 234). The role of the principal is essential (Elmore, 2000; Halverson, 2005a; Harris & Chapman, 2002; Spillane, 2004a, 2006a), and sometimes temporarily it includes acting as a superhero (Harris & Chapman, 2002). We will explore this concept further in this chapter and in Chapters 2 and 3.

WHO LEADS AND WHAT THEY LEAD

There are large quantities of books that expose us to the heroics of building leaders. We read books on being a team player and collaborative leader, but these accounts of leadership still center on the context of the positional leader's actions. There are volumes of evidence-based research to provide clues about what educational leaders should be doing within their schools. In fact, we struggle to count up all the actions we, as instructional leaders, are to manage (Spillane, 2006a; Spillane et al., 2001, 2004).

> *The hard part is letting go of the myth of individualism . . . even when leadership tales venture beyond the single hero or heroine to acknowledge the part played by two or more supporting players.*
>
> —Spillane (2006a, p. 2)

Many principals often do not feel their day or week is successful unless they are in every classroom every day or week. Principals who believe this should try to answer the following questions. First, how do you practice this routine of being in the classroom? Second, how do you know you are enhancing or changing classroom practice as a result of being in the classroom? When asked these questions, most principals cannot answer both, and rarely the second, with any assurance of fact.

So why would we not work harder? Working harder to save our schools often further erodes the possibility of productive improvement. The reality is that these superheroes want teaching and learning to be the central focus, but instead can find themselves managing the daily order of the school with an unconscious awareness of their actions' impact on student performance. Leader Superheroes maintain traditional structures in order to manage the standard practices of highly prescriptive cultures (Spillane, 2004a). See Chart 1.1.

As I will share in Chapter 3, the Leader Superhero aspect of being highly descriptive (Spillane, 2005b) is what is needed for schools who struggle to meet student needs. This aspect of leadership can be necessary to build a capacity to sustain efficient professional communities for schools that are struggling to meet the needs of all children.

As Spillane and colleagues (Spillane, 2006a; Spillane, Halverson, & Diamond, 2001, 2004) point out, most research puts emphasis on the actions,

Chart 1.1   Leader Superhero Aspect

> - Leadership Focus: Designated formal leader
> - Research: Primarily principal—focused on actions, attributes, styles, behaviors of the individual
> - Instructional Focus: Teaching and learning—should be the central focus (reality: this is not likely)
> - Teacher Leader: Positional or veteran teacher—opportunities should be situational (reality: it may be role-oriented)
> - Practice: Highly prescriptive—most likely traditional in approach
> - Questions: Who? What?

Source: Created by McBeth & Wheeles (2005a). Revised by McBeth for this book.

attributes, styles, and behaviors of the individual who is in a leadership position. All these characteristics of leadership are important components to consider, but they can also be problematic if that is where we stop. Low student performance and ineffective classroom practice will continue to exist as long as we ignore or avoid leadership practice; we must know how leadership is practiced in order to meaningfully attend to all educational factors that contribute to student learning (Blase & Blase, 1999; Leithwood et al., 2004; Spillane, 2004a).

Do we as educational leaders want to look like cartoon characters? If not, we must let go of the Leader Superhero mind-set. We must move beyond "doing leadership" on others. We must give due attention to how leadership is practiced through the interactions of leaders, followers, and their situations (Spillane, 2004a, 2005b, 2006a; Spillane et al., 2004). As educators, we need to know not only the actions but also the interactions of leadership practice. We should not interpret an emphasis here on how we practice leadership as devaluing who leaders are and what they do. That would be far from the truth. Instead, we need to think about another aspect of leadership: that of leadership practice. Gronn (2000) and Bryant (2003) encourage us to "de-center" the leader and to not solely view leadership as something that resides within the individual at the top. Leadership resides in every person who, in one way or another, acts as a leader (Goleman, 2002; Spillane et al., 2001, 2004).

> *No institution can survive if it needs geniuses or supermen to manage it. It must be organized to get along under a leadership of average beings.*
>
> —Peter Drucker

25/75: IMPACT OF SCHOOL-RELATED FACTORS

One must always be able to map the factors associated with leadership practice to that of classroom practice (Spillane, 2005c). Due to the accountability of high-stakes testing dictated by federal policy, we have spent an exhausting amount of time and effort talking about classroom practice. Do not take this wrong, but if that is all we do, then we continue to miss the passing boat.

Ken Leithwood and associates (2004) have recognized that the total direct and indirect effects of leadership on student learning account for about a quarter of the total school effects, whereas the other 75% can be tied to classroom practice (see Figure 1.1). The effects of successful leadership are considerably greater in schools that are in more difficult circumstances (see Figure 1.2). I interpret this to mean that the percentage of leadership effort may need to increase when schools are in "high need." Leadership is the catalyst in the turnaround stories of troubled schools. We must give serious consideration to the fact that existing theories, concepts, and constructs of leadership have largely failed to deliver instructional improvement. The dominant model of leadership, which has been chiefly concerned with the skills, abilities, and capabilities of one person, has been proven severely limited in generating and sustaining school- and classroom-level change (Fullan, 2001). Thus, leadership

Figure 1.1

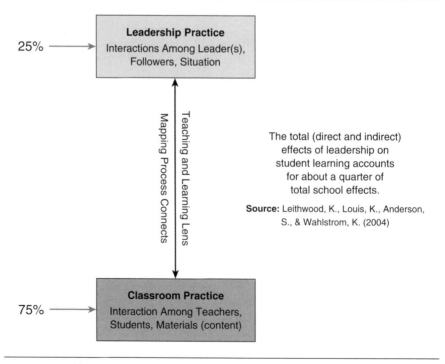

Source: Created by McBeth & Wheeles (2005b).

Figure 1.2

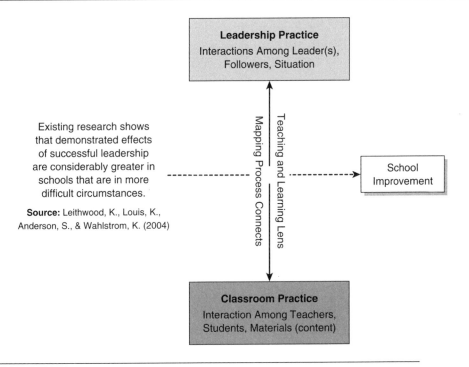

Source: Created by McBeth & Wheeles (2005b).

as it is today needs to be questioned in view of what we know about leadership (Fullan, 2001; Leithwood et al., 2004; Spillane et al., 2001, 2004). The distributed leadership perspective could be part of the answer to the leadership question.

The fact is that leadership practice analysis needs to be an important piece of the school improvement puzzle. However, it is rarely done and really has not received much attention until Gronn brought it to light in 2000. Spillane, Halverson, and Diamond published their research findings in 2001, which described leadership practice within the context of distributed leadership as an essential way of thinking about leadership.

The Distributed Leadership Toolbox provides a set of routines and tools for diagnosing and designing essential practices for successful schools. The intent is to give school teams a new way of thinking about the relationship between leadership practice, classroom practice, and student performance. My task with this book is to help leaders perfect their performance of these routines and use of these tools. The steps listed in this book are not meant to be the fix-all, cure-all medical prescription for school academic illness. However, the steps do create the means for schools to self-diagnose their present health and to prescribe solutions that can be monitored for intended results.

Chapter Reflection

As a result of reading this chapter, what has become apparent to me?

What connections have I made to my present situation?

What questions do I still have unanswered?

As a result of reading this chapter, what actions am I going to take?

A Distributed Perspective on Leadership

> Distributed leadership is not a blueprint for practicing school leadership more effectively.
>
> —Spillane (2006a, p. 9)

Have you ever had that lightbulb effect? You know the one, when something so powerful hits you and the future all of a sudden seems brighter. That is what happened when a coworker, Larry Wheeles, suggested I read an article written by Dr. James Spillane, Rich Halverson, and John Diamond titled "Towards a Theory of Leadership Practice: A Distributed Perspective" (2004). This was my first introduction to the theories of distributed leadership and its underpinning perspective of practice. An overnight trip to Northwestern University in Chicago by Larry and me to visit with Spillane illuminated that lightbulb, and somehow his theories filled in the missing pieces to the leadership puzzle. Spillane taught us that leadership was more than an effort to have people follow. It was more than actions, and it clearly was more than the structures one might put in place. Spillane explained that leadership from a distributed perspective becomes more than just counting up all the actions we as school leaders take; it is more about the practices we employ as leaders. This flew in the face of the administrative leadership training I received in my advanced degrees at the university. Yet it made so much sense.

During that meeting, the three of us created the framework for the Kansas Distributed Leadership Academy. The concept was to take

Spillane's innovative research on leadership practice (distributed leadership) and place it into the context of practitioners. Although the framework of the academy changed over time and many more researchers contributed to the outcome of our work and the work outlined in this leadership toolbox, Spillane's theories, ideologies, and research have remained the foundation for Kansas's and my work with distributed leadership.

This chapter lays out the underpinnings of distributed leadership. It builds the foundation needed by the reader to use the tools within this toolbox. Although more and more researchers are beginning to explore distributed leadership and its premiums of leadership practice, Spillane's work is arguably the institution of distributed leadership. For this reason, in this chapter I may appear to address Spillane's work more than that of other reputable researchers. This is not to devalue or discredit the work of other researchers; it is merely a fact of this work. However, the theories and ideology in this book have been refined to define distributed leadership in a practitioner's perspective and the metamorphosis that has ensued as a result of the practical experiences of working in the field to bring distributed leadership theories to fruition.

> *The distributed leadership perspective moves beyond the Superman and Wonder Woman view of school leadership.*
>
> —Spillane (2005d)

LEADERSHIP PRACTICE FROM A DISTRIBUTED PERSPECTIVE (SPILLANE)

The distributed leadership perspective does not remove instructional leadership from the radar; rather, this perspective helps identify instructional leadership (Halverson & Clifford, 2005; Spillane, Halverson, & Diamond, 2001). As you will discover as you progress through this book, leadership practice is framed by the interactions of school leaders, followers, and the aspects of their situation stretched across time (Spillane, 2006a; Spillane et al., 2001). See Figure 2.1. As we will discover, leadership practice is essential when considering all factors that contribute to student learning. Leadership practice will be further defined as we go along.

Figure 2.1 Leadership Practice From a Distributed Perspective

Leaders	Followers	Situation

Stretched Over Time

Source: Spillane (2005c; 2006a)

THE OFTEN OVERLOOKED "FOLLOWER"

Leadership practice is shaped by the follower's reaction to the leader's practice, which in turn shapes the practice of leadership (Leithwood & Jantzi, 2000; Spillane, 2006a; Spillane et al., 2001). This becomes a repeated cycle of interactions between the leader and follower. Therefore, the follower or followership role becomes an essential piece of the perspective of distributed leadership. Researchers have observed that leaders not only influence followers but are also influenced by them (Cuban, 1988; Dahl, 1961; Leithwood & Jantzi, 2000; Spillane, 2006a).

To describe the concept, let us look at a teacher's classroom practice. As the lesson progresses, a teacher senses, based on student facial expressions, that the students do not understand the concept being taught, and as a result, the teacher changes her approach and reteaches the concept in another manner. This may continue until the teacher perceives the students have grasped the concept. The teacher created a system of observing facial and verbal cues for monitoring the students' abilities to understand the information. When the monitoring system identified an issue, the practice was reframed into a new practice. This cycle of interaction interplay is further visualized in Figure 2.2. In the scenario I just described, the teacher is the leader and the students are the followers. The students clearly shaped how

Figure 2.2   Teacher–Student Interaction Model

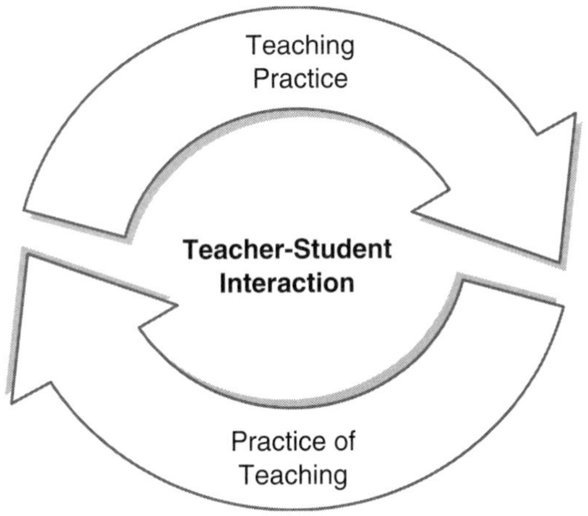

the teacher taught her lesson. The same can then be said of the interactions between adult leaders and followers in the school. Leadership practice is shaped by the follower's (teacher) reaction to the leader's practice, which in turn shapes the practice of leadership (Leithwood & Jantzi, 2000; Spillane et al., 2001). Let us explore this just a little more.

Not only are researchers beginning to cast followers in a new light, they are also advocating that feedback from followers is an essential element of leadership practice. From a distributed perspective, Spillane (2006a) has defined leadership as not simply something that is *done to* followers; it is more about leaders and followers *in interaction* with each other. Thus, the actions of the leader and the actions of the followers give shape to leadership practice, similar to that of the teacher-student interaction. The right-hand side of Figure 2.3 further demonstrates this. In addition to interacting with followers, leaders also interact with aspects of the situation including tools, routines, small tasks (microtasks), and structures (Halverson, 2005b; Spillane, 2005b; Spillane et al., 2001). School leaders work with tools, routines, and microtasks similarly to how a teacher uses his or her tools with students. It might be stating the obvious, but a unique difference between the two is that the teacher has a captive audience, whereas the school leaders have noncaptive audiences.

Figure 2.3   Infinity Practice Process

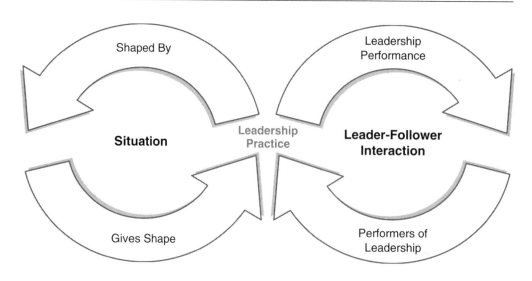

SITUATION AND LEADERSHIP PRACTICE

Situation

The situation is a unique set of content and dimensional criteria for which routines, tools, and structures create the interaction associated with leadership practice (Spillane, Diamond, & Jita, 2003). For an example, let us pick a content area such as mathematics. Mathematics is a huge topic to lump all leadership practices within, although we do so when we think from a Leader Superhero mentality. So, let us look at the multiple situations associated with this content area. There are content knowledge, pedagogical strategies, student engagement, content standards, and more. Let us pick pedagogical strategies for this example. To use different pedagogical strategies at different grade levels, we will need to narrow our focus. In this example, let us pick fifth grade.

> The situation defines the interactions and is defined through them. Change is ongoing through the design/redesign process.
>
> —Spillane (2006a)

The situation is now more narrowly defined by fifth-grade mathematical pedagogical strategies, and we can see that leadership practice then will need to respond to this narrow focus. Otherwise, we have classroom practice with no aligned leadership practice. The leader would pass the follower as they head in two very different directions. Let us be sensible here, though; not every classroom practice will have a direct correlation with a leadership practice. That just is not feasible or reasonable. In Figure 2.3, on the left side you can see that the situation is centered between two rotating arrows. This model represents how the situation defines and gives shape to leadership practice and, in turn, how it is shaped by the practice of leadership (Spillane, 2004a, 2005d, 2006a, 2006b; Spillane et al., 2001).

Let us pull this together with the right side of the model discussed earlier. If we would step back and look at the larger picture, we can see that change is ongoing through the design and redesign of practice, as defined by the interactions (Spillane, 2006a). In addition, the situation is shaped *by* and gives shape *to* the practice. The situation defines the interactions and is defined through them (Halverson & Gomez, 2001; Spillane et al., 2001). Thus, we can see that the revolving circles in the model actually create a sideways figure eight, or an "Infinity Practice Process" (McBeth & Wheeles, 2005b). The situation can become complex and is clearly influential, but we can now also see how the interactions among leaders and followers interweave within the intricacies of leadership practice.

Leadership Tools

In the context of the Distributed Leadership Toolbox, a *tool* is a mediating device that shapes interactions between two or more people; it is something tangible that can represent policy and required procedures (Gronn, 2002b; Halverson, 2005a; Spillane, 2004b). Tools may include student assessment data, observation protocols for evaluating teachers, improvement plans, lesson plans, and student academic work, among other things (Gronn, 2002b; Halverson, 2005a; Spillane, 2004b, 2005b). Student engagement data is another example of a leadership tool. Spillane (2006a) warns us that leaders at times think of tools as by-products of their work and do not identify them as something that allows them to work more effectively. We must be careful when sidelining the true value of leadership tools that bring routines to fruition (see routines below). This would miss the fact that tools, when deployed in interaction with leaders and followers, can fundamentally shape the practice of leadership (Halverson, 2005a; Spillane, 2006a). Tools, like teacher evaluation templates and processes, help shape a leader's practice when interacting with teachers (Halverson & Clifford, 2005). Tools become necessary components when thinking about leadership from a distributed perspective.

Routines

Routines involve two or more actors in "a repetitive, recognizable pattern of interdependent actions" (Feldman & Pentland, 2003; Spillane, 2006a). A school's Monday morning late arrival data meeting could serve as an example of a routine. It happens every Monday morning and has a recognizable pattern of addressing the school data. Like tools, leaders often overlook routines as valuable contributions to their leadership practice. As educators, we participate in numerous staff meetings, but rarely do we consider them a part of our leadership practice. We consider them . . . well . . . meetings! Routine practice is something that happens repetitively. Therefore, we would consider this weekly meeting a routine.

Another example would be an instructional coach's monthly collection of student formal writing from the tenth-grade teachers and then analyzing them to see if the teachers are using comprehensive strategies with the students. The coach discovers this information from the students' work and from the teachers' written comments to the students. The coach then uses the opportunity to write comments to the teachers on their successes and possible methods of improving their practices.

Microtasks

Smaller tasks within the routine are referred to here as *microtasks* (Halverson, 2005b; Spillane et al., 2001). In subsequent chapters, I will share in more depth about Pleasanton Middle School's weekly Standards in

Practice staff meetings to discuss a teacher's lesson plan. The staff met with the intention of expanding their knowledge on teaching reading standards-based lessons by reviewing lesson plans. The routine of discussing a teacher's lesson plan involved seven interdependent steps, including analysis of a teacher's lesson plan, written analyses of the teacher dialogue, and monitoring the teacher's new knowledge. Microtasks often engage multiple parties including teacher leaders, principals, and instructional coaches. Using a microtask analysis enables us to define interactions that characterize routines (Halverson, 2005b). Without the microtask analysis, leadership diagnosis often leads to the description of events only, such as a staff meeting. In other words, we fall back on "who" and "what," but we do not get to the root interactions that really shape "how" the leadership routines are practiced. The distributed leadership perspective is about the interactions of leaders and followers; however, we cannot make meaning of the interactions without identifying the actions as well.

From a distributed perspective, leadership practice stretches over tools, routines, and microtasks. Taking a distributed perspective involves more than simply acknowledging the importance of tools and routines. These aspects of the situation are integral in that they give shape to leadership practice (Gronn, 2002b; Halverson, 2005a; Spillane, 2005c, 2006a).

Section Reflection

As a result of reading this section, what has become apparent to me?

What connections have I made to my present situation?

What professional questions do I still have unanswered?

As a result of reading this section, what actions am I going to take now?

TWO-MINUTE STORY

Take a moment to reflect on your school. How might you describe it to someone else? Now take two minutes and tell me about your school.

Next, answer the following questions:

1. What was the subject of your description?

2. Who were the characters in the description?

3. Did you address how something is done at your school?

Structure

My guess is that you described the large structures that give shape to your organization, such as the size of your school population (staff or students), urban versus rural, eight-period day, reading blocks, and so on. You may have brought key characters into play in your description, such as who the positional leaders are within your school. Structures are defined as modules, properties, or systems (Spillane, 2004c). For most people, deciphering the "how" from the structures within an organization can sometimes be difficult. In recent years, schools have begun to implement meetings or early release times for professional development. Chances are that if given the opportunity to tell a two-minute story about a school's late arrival to allow teachers to meet, a structural description would be given. An additional description of the original purpose, or the philosophy behind the late arrival might be given. I challenge you to think about how much weight we as educators give to the structures within our organizations, versus that given to leadership or classroom practices.

Do you remember the opening case study of 50 leadership practices? Ouch! School structures, tools, and routines create packages of possibilities that shape leadership practice under certain circumstances but that can also be reshaped by that practice. After all, tools, routines, and structures can be made, remade, and reappropriated for purposes for which they were not designed (Spillane, 2006a).

Although I have given caution to structures, I must agree with Halverson when he argues that leaders are able to create the conditions for strong professional communities by building or adapting structures. By leaders creating structures, he argues, they are able to create the means for interaction, facilitate mutual expectations, and provide opportunity for expectation feedback.

Reform Efforts Lack Practice

Answer the following question by reflecting on the two-minute description of your school. If you were to write up the description word for word and hand it to another school, could they replicate the successes you have had within your school? The odds are not very likely. The traditional way of describing our successes in our schools doesn't go much more in-depth than what you described in your two-minute story, even if given more time.

Researchers have written countless articles explaining why they think reform efforts have failed our instructional efforts. One concern is that there is often a lack of fit between the innovation design and classroom practice (Cohen & Ball, 2000) and leadership practice (Spillane, 2006a). Another concern is that educators often adopt reform structurally, but only at a superficial level. Reform models can become facades of teaching and learning when they are about putting structures in place that address nonacademic related functions. We must not give false value to these reform efforts.

Reflective Questions

We must ask ourselves why some schools are having success.

Why does the model not work when an influential teacher or principal leaves?

We might ask why these models cannot always be replicated from one school to the next.

Why, if a school adopts a reform model, does it not perform at the same level as the school it was adopted from?

Carver: A Neighborly Visit

Carver (a suburban high school), as a result of their data analysis, developed a school improvement plan that clearly stated each core academic teacher would engage students in higher-order learning. As part of the planning process, a leadership team went to visit a neighboring school that was having great success in engaging their students in higher-order thinking skills. You guessed it—the Carver team listened to the neighboring school's story and reported to their staff that there were two initiatives needed to increase student engagement in higher-order thinking. One initiative was to have professional development days throughout the year for teachers to learn the new skills and strategies they needed. Second, they needed to implement the Instructional Practice Inventory (IPI) developed by Painter and Valentine at the University of Missouri (Valentine, 2005), a tool introduced to this school through the Kansas Distributed Leadership Academy. The Carver staff agreed and adopted these two initiatives for their two-year plan.

> The Instructional Practices Inventory (IPI) was designed by Painter and Valentine. The purpose of the IPI data-collection profile system is to establish processes for accurately measuring the nature of student-engaged learning from various instructional practices across an entire school. Such information, when gathered according to the IPI protocols for data collection, provides a valid picture of learning and instruction across a school or school system. Researchers and practitioners can also use the IPI data-collection process to analyze the relationships among learning experiences, instructional practices, and other school variables.
>
> —Valentine (2005)

Over the course of a year, teachers participated in four one-day training sessions on student engagement. During the year, they collected data from an external, trained IPI observer. The neighboring school had their principal trained to do the IPI observations. The teachers and principals met in a learning community team to discuss the results only once each semester. A year later, student engagement scores were down. Why was Carver not able to replicate the same results as the neighboring school? The school personnel participated in the professional development workshops and the IPI data collection. When properly utilized in conjunction with other supporting leadership practices, the IPI is an **extremely powerful** tool. So, why did Carver struggle to get students engaged in higher-order thinking skills?

The Lived Interactions (Spillane)

The answer to Carver's dilemma may lie within its leadership practice or lack thereof. The Carver staff did not bring back an analysis of the neighboring school's practices; rather, they brought the initiatives or structures. The problem is, theories and programs, like reform initiatives, often fall short in setting direction on how to diagnose the "lived" interactions of leaders and followers (Ch. 1). Reform models fall short in interpreting the situation. They also fall short of identifying how the interactions between leaders and followers change drastically. Structures do give shape to our classroom and leadership practices (Cohen & Ball, 2000; Silva, Gimbert, & Nolan, 2000; Spillane, 2004b), but they cannot be the only aspect we choose to acknowledge when thinking about reform model implementation. Practices bring life to an otherwise lifeless entity. Many of these reform models have not attended to an essential ingredient of leadership practice; therefore, most have become impossible to replicate from one school to the other (Elmore, Peterson, & McCarthy, 1996).

Richard Elmore and colleagues (1996) explained that there is a difference between reform schools in which teaching changed and those in which it did not change. In schools that had extensive planning opportunities for teachers to learn how to make connections with instructional content, they did. In others without such opportunities, teaching changed very little. In other words, by deploying leadership practices to enhance and change classroom practices, reform models are successful, but when not deployed, there is very little, if any, change. The failure to establish sustainable leadership practice within a reform model often leaves staffs talking about them years later as "that thing we did."

The Carver leadership team failed to capture the lived interactions between the leaders and followers at the neighboring school. Carver is a school where a learning community is more of a declaration than an organization of de-privatized classroom practice. The team went through the motions of meeting and discussing the IPI data, but they did not have a meaningful dialogue that would lead to enhanced or changed classroom practice. Teachers discussed the data results of the IPI, but the neighboring school used dialogue-driven tools, such as Valentine's "Effective Strategies Worksheet." The IPI dialogue tool helped to de-privatize classroom practice by giving the teachers a deep, reflective activity necessary for improving student-engaged learning. Teachers who were the early adopters and had documented success in the school became human resources for teachers who were still trying to grow.

Carver's failure to enhance student engagement should not be interpreted as the result of misplaced structure alone. Although the adoption of the structure from the neighboring school set a course for failure, we must acknowledge that leadership practices were missing from the Carver improvement plan. Therefore, the structure gave shape to Carver's leadership efforts. However, the practices, or lack of, shaped the lived reality* of their inadequate performance. Let us take a closer look at the system of leadership practices Carver deployed.

SYSTEMS OF PRACTICE (HALVERSON)

As represented in Example 2.1, "A Side-by-Side Building Comparison," Carver used three routines, and the neighboring school used five. Subsequently, Carver adopted two tools, as opposed to the several adopted by the neighboring school. However, more does not necessarily mean better. The

---

* The term *lived reality* is a term used by Dr. James Spillane to describe the actual practice.

Example 2.1	A Side-by-Side Building Comparison			
Leadership Dimension: Student engagement in higher-order thinking				
Routine	**Building 1**	**Building 2**	**Similarities**	**Differences**
	Carver	Neighboring School		
Building Action Plan	X	X	Both schools created district action plans.	
Professional Development Days (4 per year)	X	X	Both set 4 days aside for professional training.	Neighboring school created individual action plans associated with training.
IPI Data Collection	X	X	Both used the IPI observations; staff reviewed IPI data charts.	Neighboring school trained internal observers, Carver did not; neighboring school used the IPI Effective Strategies Worksheet; IPI critical questions for faculty consideration; also used the IPI self-assessment record.
Walkthrough Observations		X		Observation tool used to observe student engagement as identified in building action plan.
Faculty Meeting		X		Devoted time during every meeting for early adopters to share effective lesson plans.

Note: IPI = Instructional Practice Inventory

neighboring school put together a highly effective system of routines and tools. The variation in their systems of practice may explain why tools developed and implemented successfully in one setting may marginalize, or purge, when implanted in another (Cuban, 1986, 1990; Halverson, 2006; Powell, Farrar, & Cohen, 1985). Halverson (2005b) encourages us to consider a system of practice as being composed of tools and routines (*artifacts*) that leaders use to influence teaching and learning. Leaders develop and use artifacts (policies, programs, and procedures) to enable teachers to engage in the key tasks of teaching and learning. In addition, Halverson and colleagues (Halverson, Grigg, Prichett, & Thomas, 2005) point to the success of various schools across the nation that are having gains in student learning in large part due to factors designed by school leaders to work together in shaping complex instructional systems. In particular, they point to a system of practice directly associated with student data-driven instruction.

> *A system of practice is defined as a network of routines, tools, and structures comprising a single dimension of practice to influence the practice of others.*
>
> —Mark E. McBeth

In the present state of education, few school leaders scrutinize the effectiveness of their practices, but even fewer think about the interrelatedness of their practices (Halverson, 2003, 2006). We will look at the Carver case more in-depth in Chapter 5 when we explore the "Side-by-Side Building Comparison" tool.

Section Reflection

As a result of reading this section, what has become apparent to me?

What connections have I made to my present situation?

What am I still curious about?

As a result of reading this section, I know I need to . . .

NOT SHARED LEADERSHIP

Many people read the words "distributed leadership" and prematurely jump to the conclusion that it is all about shared leadership. Dr. Leithwood and associates (Leithwood et al., 2004) warn us that using the term *distributed leadership* in this context is pragmatic at best. Spillane (2004a) warns us that although shared and delegated leadership is essential, it is not sufficient to capture the complexities of leadership practice. Spillane (2004b, 2005c, 2006a) refers to this shared-leadership concept as the Leader-Plus aspect, defined in detail in Chapter 3.

Reform models often bring the mental image of shared-leadership teachers coming together and working for the common good of the school. Shared leadership often refers to the disbursement of responsibilities. As mentioned earlier, if the principal is to be perceived as the instructional leader, he will need to give up some of his managerial responsibilities. Shared-decision-making schools use a system of committees that take responsibility for research and making recommendations about the approaches needed within the school (Bernhardt, 1999, 2002; Halverson, 2005b, 2006). Often teams are formed to implement the actions needed as outlined in

The c ... dership is under-standable. ... ated" or "sharing of respons ... ltiple individuals taking resp ... the complexity of the practic ... ame time, distrib-uted leader ... p in which teach-ers develop ... et al., 2001). The distributed ... ects. The Leader Superhero ... ter 1, will receive further exp ...

Leadersh

The se ... ader-Plus aspect (Spillane, 2005c), which recognizes that leading schools requires multiple leaders. As Elmore (2000) points out, in a knowledge-intensive enterprise like teaching and learning, there is no way a single leader can perform all of the complex tasks without extensively distributing the responsibility for leadership among roles in the organization. This aspect is vital to the overall leadership framework for school improvement. By creating these collaborative relationships within a school, learning communities can be physically formed (Halverson, 2005b). This collaborative effort is a move in the right direction for schools that are moving away from the Leader Superhero aspect. Shared or collaborative leadership is valued and vital, but this aspect alone is insufficient as a leadership framework (Spillane, 2006a).

Leadership Practice Aspect (Spillane)

The third and most vital part of the distributed leadership perspective is the Leadership Practice aspect. Within this aspect lies the distributed framework that extends the thinking of leadership actions to the inter-actions among leaders, followers, and their situations (Spillane, 2004a, 2006a; Spillane et al., 2001). The relationship between the Leadership-Plus aspect and the Leadership Practice aspect will receive further exploration in Chapter 3.

Classroom Practice (Cohen & Ball)

Most people think of instruction as what teachers do (Cohen & Ball, 2000), but in reality, instruction should be defined as the interactions among the teacher, student, and content or material. Cohen and Ball (2000) further support this: "Instruction is not created by teachers alone, or students, or content, but in their interactions" (p. 3). In addition, they remind us that "interaction" does not necessarily refer to a particular form of conversation, but to the connected work of teachers and students on content.

If students and teachers are not focused on the same task, learning is likely to suffer in various ways (Cohen & Ball, 2000). The same could be said that if teachers (followers) and leaders are not focused on the same task, learning could suffer. If, as earlier described in "The Often Overlooked Follower" section, the teacher had not changed her response to the students' distressed looks of confusion and merely continued with her lecture, she would have had a different lesson with a clearly different outcome. The teacher was able to change her teaching practice by monitoring the students' learning. Most likely, this teacher did so as part of a larger picture of understanding that the students needed to master the concept prior to being able to handle the next concept or assignment. Yet, when we look at the Carver story, we see teachers that do not get retaught or are not given an opportunity to deepen their knowledge to enhance and change their classroom practices. The bigger picture of what was truly expected appeared to be missing.

CONNECTING CLASSROOM PRACTICE WITH LEADERSHIP PRACTICE

With recent research supporting the impact of leadership on student learning, we must move the conversations beyond teachers and classroom practice alone to leadership practice (Leithwood, Louis, Anderson, & Wahlstrom, 2004; Spillane, 2006a, 2006b; Spillane et al., 2001; Waters, Marzano, & McNulty, 2004). Most schools talk about classroom practice, but few do so in connection to leadership practice (Spillane, 2004b). In years past, the walls of the classroom were rigid and impenetrable, much like a medieval fort, but those walls have come down within recent years.

After all, classroom instruction is one of the most widely experienced and public activities about which virtually anyone can talk from personal experience (Fullan, Hill, & Crevola, 2006). This is not to say that we know everything about classroom practice.

> Leaders want to know how others are doing, but rarely do they ask how they are doing.
>
> —Kouzes and Posner (2006)

In recent years, and with the thrust of professional learning communities upon us, we have begun to de-privatize our classrooms; thus, we actually talk about classroom practice. Educators talk about and analyze classroom practices much more extensively than they do that of leadership practices. Cohesiveness is often missing from the talk and analysis of supporting leadership practices (Halverson, 2005a, 2005b; Spillane, 2004c, 2006a). Unlike the short walls of teachers talking to teachers about classroom practice, the walls still stand tall and rigid when describing talk associated with leadership practice (see Figure 2.4). Unmistakably, leadership is the neglected practice. We must first admit this is true before we can successfully move forward; after all, the very premise of this book is about improving our leadership practice capacity.

The main contribution to leadership research, as mentioned earlier, comes from the Leader Superhero mentality of *fixing* classroom practice. We must not forget that leadership practice and classroom practice are the most influential school factors in the process of improving student achievement (Leithwood et al., 2004). Therefore, we cannot look at classroom practice or leadership practice in isolation of each other (Spillane,

Figure 2.4

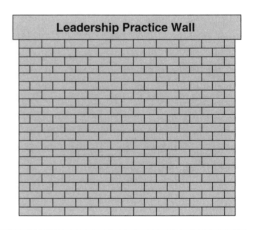

2004b); nor can we afford not to acquiesce to them as influential student learning partners.

In Figure 2.5, you will see that there are two circles representing a lens (Bennett, Wise, Woods, & Harvey, 2003; Spillane et al., 2004) that connects leadership practice and classroom practice. Two arrows represent the practice in connection to a common denominator (i.e., content and dimensions of practice). Through this lens, we are able to discover common links between classroom practice and leadership. The links identify the practices that influence one another and can serve as the target for practice designs that lead to student learning.

Shared leadership is essential for the overall success of school reform. Research over the past several years and the contributions of professional learning communities have provided evidence to the success of effective leadership deployment (Halverson et al., 2005). We must diagnose how leadership is practiced (Spillane, 2006a) and how it enhances and changes classroom practice, or how it does not. To do so, we need to begin to remove the bricks associated with the leadership wall. We must look at leadership from a completely new perspective and shift our thinking of dictatorial fixes to explanatory leadership practice and data-driven decisions (Halverson et al., 2005; Spillane, 2006a). In other words, we need to take a distributed perspective on leadership. Look at this book as the frame that holds the lens enabling you to see leadership in a new and clearer way.

> *A distributed perspective on leadership is best thought of as a framework for thinking about and analyzing leadership. . . . A distributed perspective on leadership then is neither friend nor foe.*
>
> —Spillane (2006a, p. 10)

Figure 2.5

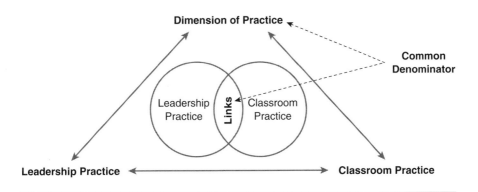

Section Reflection

As a result of reading this section, what has become apparent to me?

What connections have I made to my present situation?

What questions do I still have unanswered?

As a result of reading this section, what actions am I going to take?

The Impact of Leadership on Successful Schools

> *The achievements of an organization are the results of the combined efforts of each individual.*
>
> —Vince Lombardi

High-performing schools know their success depends on securing timely, accurate information about circumstances that could affect their performance. All schools are confronted with confusing and ever-changing challenges. Some schools melt down during these challenges, whereas others embrace them and somehow create remarkable miracles. How do these schools embrace these challenges and excel through them like an Indy racecar on the downtown bypass, whereas other schools participate in the county demolition derby? The answer is relatively simple: leadership.

These miracle schools have a multitude of formal and informal leaders who are attentive to their thoughtfully designed practices. Although informal leaders play an essential role in these schools, research clearly identifies principals as an essential pivot point between the system and student success. Formal leaders are more likely to influence the school's culture and improvement practices than informal leaders

> *Leadership is second only to classroom instruction among all school-related factors that contribute to what students learn at school.*
>
> —Leithwood (Leithwood, Louis, Anderson, & Wahlstrom, 2004, p. 1)

(Leithwood & Riehl, 2003). These school leaders, whether formal or informal, are not creating miracles; they are approaching the school improvement process as a never-ending perpetuity (Wenger, 2000). They are doing this by willfully and purposefully engaging their practices in essential leadership functions that produce impactive results. Why, then, do other schools struggle?

Sometimes it becomes vital to temporarily step back from the daily pandemonium to obtain an objective and unobstructed picture of the school's lived reality. Consider a school whose student performance has been deteriorating.

Three essential leadership functions:

- Setting direction
- Human development
- Organizational development

—Leithwood and colleagues (2004)

Perhaps the school has allowed its learning focus to be cheapened to the point that state test standards are taught quickly and ineffectively. Many may argue that the federal mandates of high-stakes testing have become a detriment to many schools. This is especially so for schools who have placed testing results as their core mission. The problem may be the result of other factors, such as the inability of a district to retain quality formal leaders within the school, or perhaps the initiative-model-of-the-month mentality is causing cultural instability.

Being able to spot the overt symptoms of our performance problems is one thing; it's quite another to determine the underlying causes of those problems. We must discover the root cause of our shortcomings. Paul Preuss, in his book *School Leader's Guide to Root Cause Analysis* (2003), defines root cause as "the deepest underlying cause, or causes, of positive or negative symptoms within any process that, if dissolved, would result in elimination, or substantial reduction, of the symptom" (p. 3). No longer can we afford to do surface reviews when it involves leadership. Therefore, we must spend some quality time with introspection into the impacting factors of our present leadership practices.

School staff can blame many external factors for their performance, and in doing so, they acquire a hard-shelled insect appearance. Much like insects, we might need to shed our protective exoskeleton to allow for new growth. As stated in the introduction, school leaders need to have a large repertoire of practices and the capacity to choose from that repertoire as needed (Leithwood et al., 2004). For leaders to be able to build a repertoire of practices, they need to understand who is involved, what they do, why they do it, and the practice of leadership (Spillane, Halverson, & Diamond, 2001).

In this chapter, we will explore three leadership functions that have significant impact on enhancing and changing teachers' classroom practice. A school metamorphoses into a cognizant and accomplished organism when all three functions purposefully apply to a system of practice and are monitored for results.

In addition, we will explore Spillane's three leadership aspects in-depth to determine the pros and cons of each. The aspect that leaders choose to address in their schools also determines the organization's culture, communication, instructional focus, and decision-making processes. In addition, there is a strong correlation to student academic performance. We will explore these correlations with the "Leadership Impact Survey."

MORE THAN ONE WAY TO LEAD

Clearly, there is more than one way to think about leadership. For our purposes here, these three aspects of leadership define school leadership: Leader Superhero (Gronn, 2002b; Spillane, 2004a), Leader-Plus, and Leadership Practice (Spillane, 2005b, 2005c, 2006a). In the following paragraphs we will explore the *pros* of schools functioning within each aspect, the possible *cons* schools may face while functioning within each aspect, and what efforts (*change practice*) the school leaders need to take if the school finds itself stuck within a particular aspect or in a particular aspect for a prolonged period of time. Highly successful schools address the essential components associated with the Leadership Practice aspect.

The "Leadership Triplex" can be found in the reproducible resource section and can be used as a visual tool for you and for sharing this perspective with other staff members. The Triplex outlines the strengths and weaknesses of each of the leadership aspects.

NO NOTICEABLE LEADERSHIP

A school could have a situation in which there is no noticeable leadership aspect. Although it goes unsaid, I will say it anyway. A school with no noticeable leadership is **not functioning** in a manner in which teachers' classroom practices are being positively enhanced and changed, which in turn **will not positively** impact student learning. Communication in a school like this will be nonexistent, and staff will be pointing fingers at the formal leaders for the struggles and failures of the school. Leader and follower decision making is made out of respect for the teaching profession and will not be focused on student learning. The culture will be in a state of continual flux, which in turn will drive professional development to be a hit-and-miss·process. The school may be orderly, but there will not be a comprehensive reform effort driven by the multiple academic situations that give shape to the school.

LEADER SUPERHERO ASPECT

As mentioned in Chapters 1 and 2, the heroics of leadership can be problematic (Spillane, 2006a), but the heroics aspect can also be extremely valuable, especially in high-need schools (Fullan, Hill, & Crevola, 2006; Gronn, 2002b; Harris, 2002).

Pro: Turnaround Leadership

Schools that function within the Leader Superhero aspect can reap many rewards. One advantage for a staff functioning within this aspect is the fact that they know who is in charge. There is a formal leader, usually a principal, who takes on the sole, or at least the predominant, management and leading of the school. In turn, the formal leader is able to be directive in nature and can make decisions relatively quickly with limited input from others. The leader designs the school improvement plans. The physical structures and written policies (i.e., class schedule, 55-minute class period, preparation-time arrangements for teachers, meeting frequency) give shape to teacher practices, which in turn establish expectations. Research within the heroics genre is very prevalent and provides support for the actions, attributes, and styles of the formal leader.

Schools that are in high need of improvement can benefit greatly from a well-trained turnaround principal. Many large districts with struggling schools are hiring these turnaround principals to perform heroic feats. They are paid to make hard-line decisions in order to move the school from point A to point B. Thus, the school improvement and professional development

> *Leadership effects are usually largest where and when they are needed most.*
> —Leithwood and colleagues (2004, p. 3)

efforts are prescriptive in nature. Schools that are in high need with poor student performance more often than not necessitate a direct push to move out of their slump. This aspect lends itself as a great starting point for struggling organizations. Fullan and his coauthors (2006), in their book *Breakthrough*, state that in the early stages of reform, the principal is key, often in association with one other internal "change agent." However, rarely does such an authoritarian approach take the school from point A to point Z (see Chart 3.1). At best, school leaders functioning within the Leader Superhero aspect are able to launch the improvement efforts of the school.

In a study of successful school leadership done by Harris and Chapman (2002), the majority of schools in the study emerged from being on the state improvement list, were suffering from serious weaknesses, or both. All the school leaders acknowledged that they adopted a more autocratic leadership style during the early phases of improvement.

Chart 3.1   A to Z Leadership Impact

Leadership Aspect			
Limited noticeable leadership	Leader Superhero aspect	Leader-Plus aspect	Leadership Practice aspect
School Improvement Practice			
Stable standard practice	Structure-driven Practice	Adaptive practice	Infinity of practice

A	B	C	D	E	F	G	H	I	J	K	L	M	N	O	P	Q	R	S	T	U	V	W	X	Y	Z

This included paying special attention to issues such as policy implementation and consistent standards of instruction. However, they also agreed that this leadership approach was least likely to lead to sustained school improvement.

Con: Limited Staff Engagement

Stories of the heroics of leadership genre are problematic for a number of reasons, but none more than the idea that the role of leader is the sole responsibility of a building principal (Fullan et al., 2006; Spillane, 2006a). Epic stories, in general, equate school leadership with school principals and their valiant actions, but at times, other leaders are featured in these accounts. Still, more often than not, they are cast in minor, supporting roles. Whereas the school principal is critical to school leadership, leadership does not begin and end with the individual in the principal's office. Although we ask these superheroes to be the instructional leaders for their buildings, they often fall short in keeping teaching and learning as the central focus.

*The task of the **leader is to get his people** from where they are to where they have not been.*

—Henry Kissinger

Within the Leader Superhero aspect, teachers can be given responsibilities. What researchers have discovered within this aspect of leadership is that teachers are given formal positions to supervise or give direction to other teachers. This can be best described as leadership acts of "doing" to others. Teachers do not engage in the most important decisions that impact classroom practice and student performance (Leithwood & Jantzi, 2000). Many of these teachers earned their positions as a result of the test of time. In other words, they were the veteran teachers of the school and therefore got the positions. This is not to say they are poor leaders; it is merely a description of the positional leadership role. Leithwood and Jantzi (2000) stated that principal and teacher leadership had significant influence on schools, but not on classroom conditions, when functioning within this aspect of leadership. The leadership involvement of these teachers from a distributed perspective should be situational but often remains role-oriented (Spillane, 2006a). For example, teachers are promoted to department chair (a formal role) and expected to be the expert at resource providing, pedagogical skills, technology implementation, and content knowledge. Whereas teachers might not perceive this formal teacher as a vital source of expertise for their advice networks, they might seek these four expertises spread across two or more informal leaders. In fact, researchers have found this to be true: The situations (i.e., content, pedagogy), not position, define who teachers perceive as their experts.

Practice within the Leader Superhero aspect is prescriptive in nature and draws upon the traditional thinking of school leadership (Spillane, 2005b). It involves the orderly management of the school building; thus, instructional leadership is limited or nonexistent. Schools that linger for very long in this aspect rarely, if ever, create systemic leadership maturity. They do not meet the high expectations of every child's learning needs at an elevated

Change P

Acknow   ond the school
principal in   cipal in school
leadership, l   ollective, rather
than individ   r as we analyze
leadership p   ake leadership
responsibiliti   positions, such
as principals,   nal leadership
over the past   onal manager.
Autocratic pr   to find ways to
improve instr   ncipal can no
longer manag

Researchers have advocated that teachers can help fill this educational leadership void (Reeves, 2006a, 2006b). To ensure sustainable reform, focus must be on the instructional activities rather than people's attributes or styles. Defining ways in which teachers may share in these responsibilities can help move instruction and learning to the forefront. After all, teachers are engaged in instructional practices on a daily basis compared to formal leaders, who are trying to balance daily managerial responsibilities with that of instruction.

Leaders must become aware of their impact on student performance. However, turnaround leaders in particular need to understand that their structure-driven practices are best suited for the short term. They need to progress toward an adaptive approach according to the academic situation. Focus needs to be on establishing leadership routines for teachers to participate in the growth of their school. The leaders and engaged followers will need to muster the courage to move student learning to the top of their priorities list. Over time, the turnaround leaders must be willing to let go of their directive styles of communication and move teachers and other stakeholders to collaborative discussions. Leaders must be aware of their present practices if they are ever to accomplish the aforementioned. Then, with conscious intention, they must put newly designed practices into place. The intention of the tools within this Distributed Leadership Toolbox is to assist leaders in that process.

Section Reflection

What challenges will I face if I try to make school improvement progress by working alone? Why might these be challenges?

What advantages are there in making school improvement progress by learning and working together? What challenges might working together with others cause me?

I have noticed the following about my situation . . .

I am curious about . . .

LEADERSHIP-PLUS ASPECT

Pro: Learning Organizations

Spillane's (2005b, 2005c, 2006a) Leader-Plus aspect recognizes that leading schools can involve multiple individuals, not just those in formal leadership positions. School leadership does not reside exclusively in the principal's administrative center. Specifically, individuals who are not formally designated leaders also provide leadership and management in the distributed leadership paradigm. Teachers are more likely to contribute to the effectiveness of their schools by working collaboratively on instructional matters that relate to student learning.

> In the past a leader was a boss. Today's leaders must be **partners with their people** . . . they no longer can lead solely based on positional power.
>
> —Ken Blanchard, American Businessman, Author

By having multiple leaders involved in the decision making of the school, individuals take possession of their decisions, which leads to increased productivity. Shared leadership displaces the sole responsibly of all leadership on one individual, and as a result, leaders are able to put more time and effort into leading activities. Thus, there is a sense of a common goal as the staff reaches self-actualization, which in turn may ultimately lead to an organizational mission to help others. Kathy Kolbe (2004a) said in her book *Powered by Instinct* that if you aspire to make a difference in the world, to be socially responsible, you must first become passionate. Then, and only then, can you move to be compassionate for others.

When school teams become compassionate for others, professional development is student- and staff-centered and linked to an improvement plan developed by all staff. In addition, the school's leadership decision-making process focuses on inspiring followers to lead. Leadership, although arranged within the Leadership-Plus aspect, still produces prescriptive solutions with incomplete academic situational considerations (Spillane, 2006a). Prescriptions within this aspect often take on the appearance of comprehensive reform models. Research contributions to the Leadership-Plus aspect focus mainly on the actions of multiple leaders, not the interactions associated with practice (Spillane, 2006a, 2006b).

> Teachers need **better leadership** that provides more powerful collaborative learning with each other **focused** on improving their **practice**.
>
> —Mark E. McBeth

Con: Lacks Practice

As Blanchard clearly stated, leaders must be part of a partnership. This too, like the Leader Superhero, can be problematic if thought of in isolation. This is because when we look at the Leader-Plus aspect, we are conversing about the operation of leaders merely because they are employees of the school. We tend not to think about their leadership practice expertise within instruction.

The distributed leadership perspective attempts to acknowledge and incorporate the work of those individuals who have a hand in leadership practice. Educators can become temporarily self-congratulatory when they have shared decision making, even if it is not directly affecting student performance, and as such, they can become complacent.

Issues arise if shared structured systems are implemented and there is a dearth of clear, purposefully defined interactions. Time for staff to have meaningful dialogue is essential; thus, staff common time devoted to dialogue is unmistakably a best practice. Yet, one may argue that student late arrivals and early release times (teacher conference or collaboration time without students) have become one of the most abused "best practices" of the past decade. Often within these get-togethers, staffs meet with limited purpose, and they do not use mediating tools within a comprehensibly designed routine for interaction.

When there is a declaration of professional learning communities within the school, but the support for the leadership practices are systemically missing, issues arise. DuFour, Eaker, and DuFour (2005), in their book *On Common Ground*, give further support to this perspective: "Many schools and districts that proudly proclaim they are Professional Learning Communities have shown little evidence of either understanding the core concept or implementing the practices" (p. 9).

Instead of evaluating whether their leadership practices are enhancing and changing classroom practices, school leaders might find themselves adding up the teams as a means of measuring success within a professional learning community. At times, a leader still needs to be a leader among leaders. "If a team does not have a leader who takes responsibility for influencing its members to strive towards achieving common goals, the rest of the process can be for naught" (Kolbe, 2004b, p. 292). Only the interactions of leaders and followers can ever bring school structures to life (Leithwood & Jantzi, 2000). Extensive leadership practices, including routines and tools, must exist for schools to become true professional learning communities (Halverson, 2005a).

Change Practice: Leadership Practice Is Paramount

For schools to become legitimately functional communities of practice, they need to discern how their leadership practices impact student performance. To discern our practices, we must investigate our "*leadership by design*" (Spillane, 2005b, 2005c). The Leadership Practice aspect within this chapter, and throughout this book, diagrams behaviors for enhancing and changing our leadership practices. The tools within this book can point you in the right direction, but ultimately each leader and each school must chart their own course.

LEADERSHIP PRACTICE ASPECT

Distributed leadership is unmistakably more than adding up all of the responsibilities for leadership in a school and examining who is responsible for which leadership function or activity (Spillane et al., 2001). It is more important that we aggrandize our thinking to, *How does leadership get practiced, and how do followers play a role within leadership practice?* Leadership practice is a construct of interactions, rather than in and by acts of individuals or groups of leaders (Spillane et al., 2001). In this way, the distributed leadership framework extends the Leader-Plus aspect by putting leadership practice at the center (Spillane, 2006a). A distributed perspective frames leadership practice as it is stretched out over individuals who have responsibility for leadership functions and their interactions with followers within a particular situation (Spillane, 2006a; Spillane et al., 2001).

> *Only those who demonstrate . . . compassion for others . . . become **authentic leaders***.
>
> —Kolbe (2004a, p. 222)

Pro: Student Learning Enhanced by Designed Practice

The interactions of leaders and followers are designed with the intention of enhancing and changing classroom practice, which in turn enhances student performance. Schools that want to be on the verge of breakthrough communities of practice must recognize that discussion always follows highly engaged dialogue. (Please see box below for an explanation of the difference between *discussion* and *dialogue*.)

Wellman and Lipton, in their book *Data-Driven Dialogue* (2004), refer to dialogue as more than the exchange of words. It is the art of thinking together and embracing different points of view. It is a conversation with a center and no walls. It is a way of conversing about a topic while suspending judgment. They refer to dialogue as a precursor to discussion, which, when defined, means "to cut off"—or in this case, to end the conversation.

Interdependency

Leaders and followers come together with an interdependency of what is needed for students' success. Within the Leadership Practice aspect, there is a combined wisdom of all stakeholders for each child. By creating leadership practices that shape and structure a spirit of sustained collective inquiry within and between leaders and followers, school teams are able to create a sense of interdependency; they are able to create an inquiry into their effectiveness of their own leadership and classroom practices. The employed leadership practices become part of the group, not of the individuals in the group. By creating a conscious awareness of the interactions needed between leaders and followers in association within a variety of academic situations, leadership teams become more mindful.

> *True spiritual practice calls for persistently renewed* **mindfulness***.*
>
> —Scott Thompson (2004)

Density

The Leadership Practice aspect of the distributed framework takes us deeper into the complexities of leadership, beyond the questions of who the leaders are and what they do to others and about the responsibilities within these actions (Spillane et al., 2001). The interactions are an important aspect to understanding leadership practice. The Leadership Practice aspect then moves the focus from aggregating the actions of individual leaders or of the shared actions to clearer interaction among leaders, followers, and their situations.

Con: Complexity of Change

If there are cons in the Leadership Practice aspect (which I would dispute there are few), they would be included in the following. Working from a Leadership Practice perspective could create a change in role responsibilities among formal and informal leaders. Change can cause a disruption to individuals who instinctually try to stay away from the unknown. The change might feel risky to some, and indeed, there is risk in exposing one's leadership practice to analysis, change, observation, and evaluation. This aspect is systemically much more complex than traditional approaches and, therefore, may cause additional time for diagnoses and design. An argument, however, could be made that the Leadership Practice aspect saves time as well. No matter what leadership style is predominant, a lack of time

> *Teaching and learning must remain our* **central focus***.*
>
> —Statement of Leading Educational Experts

is the most prevalent complaint heard from practitioners. Categorically educators have a hard time pulling themselves away from their traditional ways of doing their work in order to enhance their practices. Reflection upon Baker's situation, as outlined in Chapter 1, gives credence to the value of taking a distributed perspective as a time-saver.

Change Practice: Situational

Teams that take the time to use the distributed leadership framework will find themselves saving time and getting additional returns for their efforts. Therefore, it becomes essential to put the distributed leadership framework into our repertoire of improvement efforts. If we want to increase student learning performance, we must change our present ways of doing our work.

Bottom Line

Although the Leader Superhero and Leader-Plus aspects may have an impact, only when the Leadership Practice aspect is effectively used will the energy and resources of the organization be fully utilized. Only then will true systemic innovation take place to meet and to exceed high-stakes accountability expectations, and, more important, only then will student learning be maximized.

Section Reflection

As a result of reading this section, what has become apparent to me?

What connections have I made to my present situation?

What questions do I still have unanswered?

Given what I know now, I will change . . .

CORE LEADERSHIP FUNCTIONS

As stated earlier, leadership contributions are vital to the overall success of schools. However, the mere presence of leadership does not constitute successful schools. "We know the leadership is most successful when it is focused on teaching and learning" (Leithwood & Riehl, 2003, p. 7). All leadership practices need to stem from a single set of leadership functions.

There have been several attempts at identifying key leadership standards or functions for formal leaders such as principals; however, few have truly defined them in a manner that addresses leadership practices and their relationship to classroom practices. Recently, I came across an article that "cross-walked" several different leadership standards (i.e., the Interstate School Leaders Licensure Consortium [ISLLC], the Educational Leadership Constituent Council [ELCC], the National Association of Elementary School Principals [NAESP], the Southern Regional Education Board [SREB], and the Mid-continent for Education and Learning [McREL]) in an attempt to fit all the standards within a few distinct categories. A discovery was made that each set of standards defined a highly qualified leader slightly differently. One significant issue or concern within these organizations' leadership standards is that they all try to address the heroics of the principal. The pure volume of the number of standards can become overwhelming to practitioners.

Leithwood and colleagues (2004), in my estimation, have unmistakably identified a set of core leadership functions that constitute the basis of successful schools, and they are valuable in almost all educational contexts. There are three broad leadership functions identified as important for leadership success in all schools. They are setting direction, human development, and organizational development (see Chart 3.2). Each category encompasses specific competencies, orientations, and considerations (Leithwood et al., 2004).

These three leadership functions serve us well within a distributed leadership perspective. They address leadership practice and not simply actions of leaders. They do not pinpoint the practices of a single leader, but instead they subjectively imply multiple leaders. All academic leadership practices nestle themselves within each of these three leadership functions. In addition, there are only three functions. I can remember three functions, and when I say "setting direction," vision, mission, goals, and expectations immediately come to mind. The leadership functions are accurate and simple to understand. That is what I like about them.

Chart 3.2   Essential Leadership Functions

Setting Direction

- Constructing, selling, and sustaining a *vision*.
- Getting cooperative commitment for organizational *goals*.
- Setting and maintaining *high expectations*.

Human Development

- Monitoring instruction and progress.
- Developing teachers' knowledge and skill, both individually and collectively.
- Providing encouragement, recognition, and support.
- Developing a sense of accountability for performance.

Organizational Development

- Adapting and modifying standard operating procedures (routines, tools, structure) to support instructional improvement.
- Building a culture that de-privatizes classroom practice, supports collaboration among teachers, and maintains high expectations.
- Procuring and distributing resources.
- Handling disturbances/creating and maintaining an orderly work environment.

—Leithwood, Louis, Anderson, & Wahlstrom (2004)

Setting Direction

Evidence suggests that those leadership practices included in *setting direction* account for the largest proportion of a leader's impact (Leithwood et al., 2004). This leadership function includes actions and interactions intended to develop mutually agreed-upon goals inspiring others with a sense of purpose and vision of the future. It addresses the setting and maintaining of high expectations for teaching and student learning, thus giving teachers meaning and identity for their classroom practices.

Human Development

Although setting direction has been identified as the most impactive of the three leadership functions, by no means can it be considered adequate as a stand-alone function. Nor does direction setting contribute to the human scholarly muscle needed to move schools in that direction. Most work in schools is, of course, accomplished through the efforts of people. Effective educational leaders influence the development of human resources in their schools, enabling them to excel within the unified expectations set upon them. Leadership practices that significantly and positively change and enhance the competence of teachers to boost their classroom practices include monitoring and supporting best practices, developing the teachers' knowledge and skills through high-quality professional development, providing intellectual motivational support, and developing a sense of accountability for performance.

Developing the Organization

School leaders attend to aspects of the school as an organization and a community, with consideration to internal processes and external relationships. Effective leaders within this function build a culture that de-privatizes classroom practices and enables the school to function as a professional community that supports and sustains the performance of teachers as well as students. Leaders create and maintain an orderly work environment void of classroom disturbances. They procure and distribute the necessary resources needed for teachers to change and enhance their classroom practices.

> *Successful educational **leaders develop** their schools as effective organizations that support and sustain the performance of teachers, as well as students.*
>
> —Leithwood and colleagues (2004, p. 7)

Most important, these effective leaders modify standard operating procedures to support advancements in best practices and instructional improvement. Richard Halverson (2005a) said,

> leaders and teachers need to constantly struggle to maintain professional community by repurposing *tools and routines*, shifting discussions to novel problems and time consuming trouble shooting in order to avoid a relapse into the status-quo of loosely-coupled school organizations. (p. 28)

Relevancy: Title I Distinguished Award-Winning School

During a flight home from the 2007 National Title I Conference, I was fortunate to sit next to an exceptional principal of a Title I Distinguished Award-Winning School. The principal and the multiple teacher leaders were functioning within the Leadership Practice aspect of the school and student learning paralleled their practice, as documented on state assessments. However, the principal told me that he was going to lay out a new direction with firm expectations for the staff next week. I asked him why he would pursue such an effort when the school team was doing noticeably well. His response was,

> I sometimes need to shake up things to prevent my leaders and teachers from becoming complacent. They need to revisit the

purpose once in a while in order to grow and develop. It will only be a few weeks until they take the lead again.

This principal effectively modified the teachers' standard operating procedures to support advancements in best practices and instructional improvement by revisiting the setting direction function.

Relevancy Reflection

What is your initial reaction to this principal's statement about needing to "shake up things"?

What are you going to take away from this relevancy story?

APPLICATION TO OUR PRACTICE

It is vital for effective schools to address all three of the core leadership functions. All instructionally related leadership practices can and need to be defined within each of these three core functions. The three leadership functions can serve as a foundation tool for diagnosing and designing leadership practices within our schools. As an organization, we must identify the functions as they are manifested in our daily lived practices, the tools used to mediate leadership routines, and the formal and informal leaders that are involved.

Typical Example: Functional Professional Learning Communities

"Welcome to our learning community." Recently, when working with a middle school, I was welcomed with this statement. It is a statement heard more and more as school leaders continue to move their buildings toward a professional learning community concept. I thought, "Great, they are really into the Leadership-Plus aspect and have a good foundation for the work we are about to do," but I soon found myself in search of a professional learning community. There were a few strong isolated dimensions of practice focused on teaching reading content, but an organizational professional learning community did not exist. A search for pedagogical strategies in reading and mathematics came up short.

A system within the dimension of practice needs to address all three leadership functions. If leaders address only one or two functions, there is a sizable void within the professional learning community. Even if all three functions were being addressed, but not with true conviction and purposeful intention, there can be voids.

Typical Example Reflection

What is your initial reaction to this statement: *"Welcome to our learning community"*?

What are you going to take away from this example story?

Objective Lesson: The One-Function Wonder

Tim Quick, a K–12 principal in a small northeastern Kansas rural school, and I were dialoguing about an afterschool initiative he and his staff were working on. Through the use of the practice-to-practice tool (see Chapter 5), we discovered Tim was doing an outstanding job sustaining the school's mission, vision, and goals as outlined in the building improvement plan, and he was also maintaining high expectations for student learning. In essence, Tim was leading his school by setting a comprehensive direction for staff and students.

Mr. Quick's staff respect him—he does fantastic work within his building—and so do others throughout the state, but at times, he can be the one-function wonder. Tim cannot do it all, and at times his own instinctual talents become the very barrier to creating a system of practice that would address necessary and critical leadership functions.

He is cognitively astute and unequivocally intelligent about organizational education leadership initiatives such as professional learning communities. He is highly motivated and has a desire to do what is best for students and staff. He also has a creative talent for taking action that is very intuitive, visionary, and highly original. He has a knack for finding alternatives and discovering unique ways to get things done. So, how do these great talents place barriers to Mr. Quick's ability to create a meaningful system of practice?

In the past, the majority of Mr. Quick's energy was spent on the *setting direction* function. He spent countless faculty and grade-level meetings selling and sustaining a zero–student failure policy, vision, and mission. He set the goals for his staff and maintained a sense of high expectations for student learning and engagement. In fact, while observing a faculty meeting, Mr. Quick mentioned the mission of the "Attention" program (the Attention program is further outlined in Chapter 5) and his expectation for student results no less than three times (see Tally Log in Chapter 6). It was a surprise and a breakthrough to discover that no attention had been given to the *human development* leadership function. Tim was able to see an area he and his school staff needed to address, and he was able to set a course to put new leadership practices in place by design that addressed the human development function. We will continue to explore Mr. Quick's case study in greater depth in later chapters.

Objective Lesson Reflection

What is your initial reaction to this question? *How can Mr. Quick be so knowledgeable about professional learning communities, be motivated to make a difference, and have such great talent and still be a one-function wonder?*

What are you going to take away from this objective lesson?

I cannot emphasize enough the value of consciously addressing these three leadership functions. We can quickly view what functions we are addressing, and which ones we are not, through a set of tools within this distributed leadership toolbox. The first of the tools we will explore is the Leadership Impact Survey, which follows this section.

Section Reflection

As a result of reading this section, what has become clear to me?

What connections have I made to my present situation?

I realize that I need to know more about . . .

As a result of reading this section, what actions am I going to take?

TOOL: The Leadership Impact Survey

Introduction: Impact

How do you know you are enhancing and changing teachers' classroom practices? This has to be the most challenging question I ask school leaders today. The aspect of practice that leaders consciously or unconsciously choose has far-reaching impacts, whether positively or negatively, on their schools' culture, structures, and professional development. It influences the type of leadership deployment, communication, decision making, and the school improvement practices. The chosen aspect gives shape to the instructional focus of the teaching community, and most important, it determines the impact and influence on student learning.

Purpose: Dialogue

The Leadership Impact Survey tool is designed to amass qualitative data on the deployed leadership aspect of your school. More important, its purpose is as a collaborative or self-talk dialogue data tool. The tool, if taken with integrity, will brandish the lived reality of a school's leadership practices across the three leadership functions and their impact across 13 leadership and organizational-related factors. The survey makes an excellent formative instrument to measure your leadership effort progress.

Philosophy: Correlational in Nature

Making correlations between multiple leadership and school-related factors sometimes can be difficult to swallow, but it is sometimes necessary. The research is compelling for the reciprocal relationship between the factors within the Leadership Impact Survey. A persuasive research correlation can be made that if leadership communication is nonexistent, there will be limited noticeable leadership. If a school leads from a practitioner's perspective, the school improvement efforts will be adaptive in nature. If there is a cohesive maturity among the school's leaders, there will be a looping, or never-ending, improvement process. This in turn produces collaborative dialogue among stakeholders focused on each child's learning.

> *Correlational: A causal, complementary, parallel, or reciprocal relationship, especially a structural, functional, or qualitative correspondence between two or more comparable entities*
>
> —Dictionary.com

These 13 interrelated factors (see Chart 3.3) have rarely been compared to each other in such a reciprocal relationship as they are here. You will find a prominent parallel and causal relationship between each

Chart 3.3 13 Interrelated Leadership and Organizational Factors

1. Leadership aspect
2. Leadership type
3. Awareness of leadership impact on student performance
4. Essential leadership questions addressed
5. School improvement practice
6. Improvement from a leadership practice perspective
7. Organizational culture
8. Professional development criteria
9. Leadership communication
10. Instructional focus
11. Structure
12. School decision making
13. Leadership decision making

of the factors, which should lead to provocative dialogue about your school's leadership practices and their impact. Let us explore two unique but somewhat successful case studies. In both cases, the schools were functioning with limited noticeable leadership and academically performing poorly on state assessments prior to their intentional leadership interventions.

Case Study: Pleasanton Middle School

Pleasanton Middle School, a large Kansas urban school, could be considered a success story in some people's opinion. Historically, Pleasanton Middle School was an all-White school, but in the late eighties and early nineties, the school's demographic shifted to a 40% mixed minority population. There was a noticeable increase in students of low socioeconomic status. Student performance on state exams plummeted, aided in part by the mass departure of teachers seeking affluent White-populated schools. Fifteen years later, 44% of the students were Hispanic; 38% were White; and 18% were African American, Asian, and Native American. Eighty-three percent (83%) of the students came from low socioeconomic-status families.

In 2000, 39.7% of the students scored proficient or above on the state reading assessment, whereas 31.4% scored proficient or above on the state mathematics assessment. In 2001, the school was added to the state's Needs Improvement list as a result of not making Annual Yearly Progress (AYP) in Mathematics. Pleasanton Middle School had been on the state's low-performing school list for mathematics for 2 consecutive years when, in 2003, Markus Long became Pleasanton's principal. In 2005, 64.7% of the students scored proficient or above on the state reading assessment, an increase of 24.9%, whereas 53.2% of the students scored proficient or above on the state mathematics assessment, an increase of 21.2% (see Figure 3.1).

Figure 3.1   Pleasanton Middle School Assessment Results

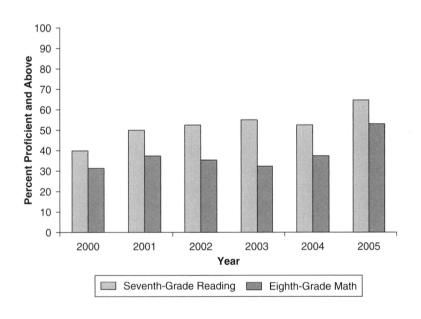

Markus Long is a 6-foot 4-inch, self-assured, African American man in his mid-thirties. He is a sharply dressed, buttoned-up-suit type of person who gives a resolute physical appearance of professionalism 24/7.

In 2004, Pleasanton Middle School participated in the Kansas Distributed Leadership Academy. It was during the first year of the academy that teachers and administrators at Pleasanton Middle School shared their story. The crux of the story centered on their principal, Markus, who was depicted as the authoritarian leader who accepted nothing less than perfection from his staff, parents, and students. The teachers described, in detail, the new policies and program structures put in place not only for students but for the teachers as well. Teaching and learning were always the central focus under his leadership. Teachers would often refer to making connections between one routine and the next and felt there was meaningful instruction under Markus's leadership. Some of these routines will be explored in further detail in later chapters. When Markus shared about what the school was doing to improve student performance, he would address a bounty of collaborative actions the staff was taking to improve their instructional practices. When asked about his leadership methodologies, Markus would go into explicit detail about his deliberate actions and interactions to ensure that teachers were indeed improving their instructional practices.

Markus was hired to take the helm of Pleasanton Middle School as a turnaround principal, and that is exactly what he did. To do so, he took a Leader Superhero aspect approach. The staff was ready for someone to step forward and make some essential decisions. Like many schools that end up on the state improvement list, there is anger and embarrassment at the distinction, and later on a sense of urgency. After a thorough analysis of both qualitative and quantitative data, Markus, by design, took the following actions and interactions:

- shared his vision and mission with his staff;
- set the goals for improvement with input from the staff;
- created a relentless culture of high expectations for teaching and learning;
- established routines and tools to monitor instruction and student progress;
- created a routine and tool that held teachers to a strong sense of accountability;
- established highly focused professional development with intensive in-class support;
- revised the students' academic schedules to ensure uninterrupted instruction;
- created opportunities for staff instructional collaboration;
- secured grant funds to ensure that teachers were adequately resourced;
- used an assistant principal extensively to create an orderly work environment.

List Reflection

What leadership functions did Markus address in his list of actions and interactions?

What aspect of leadership do you believe Markus was embarking on? (*Leader Superhero, Leader-Plus, Leadership Practice*)

Why do you believe it was important for Markus to take the lead?

When the list of Markus's actions and interactions is compared to the list of the three essential leadership functions for successful schools, one can see a strong correlation between the two. It is obvious that Markus had given serious thought and considerable attention to improving the school's culture and focus on teaching and learning. His leadership communication style was directive in nature, yet he created opportunities for staff input. Like many turnaround principals, Markus trusted his gut and outlined the priorities needed for success.

Figure 3.2 is a scoring sheet that accompanies the Leadership Impact Survey. This figure displays the 2001 and 2005 leadership impact upon the 13 leadership and organizational factors as a result of the deployed leadership aspect. The 2001 score (1.21) shows that there was Limited Noticeable Leadership (Leadership Aspect); however, Markus deployed a Leader Superhero aspect approach. By 2005, the score (2.71) on the Leadership Impact Survey depicts a school functioning in the early stages of the Leader-Plus aspect. A quick review of the Pleasanton Middle School assessment data (Figure 3.1) set side by side with the deployed leadership aspects (Example 3.1) reveals a correlation between leadership and student performance.

Pleasanton has reaped the satisfaction of student success as a result of Markus's purposeful Leader Superhero aspect approach. In following this approach, Markus was able to take the school from an aspect of limited noticeable leadership to one in the early stages of a professional learning community. I would argue that as a result of such practices, student performance was enhanced. Although successful, the school

Example 3.1 Pleasanton Middle School's 2001 Estimated Score of 1.2 Compared With the 2005 Score of 2.71

Pleasanton Middle School Leadership Impact Survey

1.0	1.2	1.4	1.6	1.8	2.0	2.2	2.4	2.6	2.8	3.0	3.2	3.4	3.6	3.8	4.0

Leadership Aspect

Limited noticeable leadership	Leader Superhero aspect	Leader-Plus aspect	Leadership Practice aspect

Leadership Type

Manager	Turnaround leaders	Practitioners	Systemic maturity

Awareness of Leadership Impact on Student Performance

Nonacademic management	Unconscious leadership	Mindful leadership	Leadership by design

Essential Leadership Question Addressed

Who	Who and *what*	Who, what, and *why*	Who, what, why, and *how*

School Improvement Practice

Status quo	Structure-driven practice	Adaptive practice	Infinity of practice

Improvement From a Leadership Practice Perspective

Design	*Analysis*; design	Analysis; design; *monitors results*	Analysis; design; *new practice*; monitor results

Organizational Culture

Continual flux	Stable standard practice	Systems thinking	Breakthrough routine

Professional Development Criteria

Hit and miss	*Content*	Content and *context*	Content, context, and *process*

Leadership Communication

Nonexistent	Directive	Discussion	Dialogue

Instructional Focus

Instruction and learning should be the central focus (*Reality: not likely*)	*Instruction* and learning is the central focus	*Teaching* and learning is the central focus

Structure

Management practice (orderly)	Comprehensive reform	Situational: Leadership practice is paramount

School Decision Making

Respect for teaching	Ambition to try	Courage to put student learning first	Perseverance for each child	Wisdom of all stakeholders for each child

Leadership Decision Making

Interest in education	Involves followers	Engages followers	Convinces followers to take action	Inspires followers to lead

1.0	1.2	1.4	1.6	1.8	2.0	2.2	2.4	2.6	2.8	3.0	3.2	3.4	3.6	3.8	4.0

has not yet met the needs of all its students. To do so, Markus and his staff would need to change their leadership approach to one more suited to that of the Leader-Plus aspect.

Case Study: Learning Point: Value

Without a leadership tool like the Leadership Impact Survey, a school may try to stay the course in its leadership efforts after seeing positive changes in student performance. By reviewing survey results, a school like Pleasanton Middle School could easily visualize where they are on the continuum and could choose a new course of leadership practices to take them to a state of cohesive maturity. As mentioned earlier, schools will not reach a state of sustained leadership capacity by functioning for very long within the Leader Superhero aspect. Because there would be a reliance on Markus's leadership approach, the school staff could fall back on the ways of the past if he were to leave the building. If used properly and leadership practices are deployed by design, the Leader Superhero aspect is used as an organizational turnaround approach.

The Western School leadership impact is uniquely different from that of the Pleasanton case study. In this case, we will explore how the school's leadership team was able to diagnose their present leadership practices, and more important, how they purposely used designed leadership practices to improve their school.

Case Study: Western School

The leadership team made up of teachers from a small rural school in western Kansas sat at the table reflecting on yet another administrative turnover and contemplating their future. The teachers hung their heads low as they shared their story. This past year, as were many before, was an emotional roller coaster. On the Leadership Impact Survey, the team scored a 1.4 (see Example 3.2). The teachers unanimously proclaimed there had not been a single ounce of noticeable leadership for the past year, nor in years prior, for that matter.

The one bright spot was their devotion to the professional development they had received from the Kansas Distributed Leadership Academy over the past few years. Not unlike prior Februarys, the school was facing the resignations of their principal and superintendent. Just days prior to this meeting, the team of teachers, absent their formal leaders, requested that their school board allow them the opportunity to

Example 3.2 Western School (Example) Score: Beginning Score 1.4 and Later 2.2

Western Leadership Impact Survey

1.0	1.2	1.4	1.6	1.8	2.0	2.2	2.4	2.6	2.8	3.0	3.2	3.4	3.6	3.8	4.0

Leadership Aspect

1.0–1.6	1.8–2.4	2.6–3.2	3.4–4.0
Limited noticeable leadership	Leader Superhero	Leader-Plus aspect	Leadership Practice aspect

Leadership Type

1.0–1.6	1.8–2.4	2.6–3.2	3.4–4.0
Manager	Turnaround leaders	Practitioner	Systemic maturity

Awareness of Leadership Impact On Student Performance

1.0–1.6	1.8–2.4	2.6–3.2	3.4–4.0
Nonacademic management	Unconscious leadership	Mindful leadership	Leadership by design

Essential Leadership Question

1.0–1.6	1.8–2.4	2.6–3.2	3.4–4.0
Who	Who and *what*	Who, what and *why*	Who, what, why, and *how*

School Improvement

1.0–1.6	1.8–2.4	2.6–3.2	3.4–4.0
Status quo	Structure-driven practice	Adaptive practice	Infinity of practice

Improvement From a Leadership Practice Perspective

1.0–1.6	1.8–2.4	2.6–3.2	3.4–4.0
Design	*Analysis*; design	Analysis; design; *monitors results*	Analysis; design; *new practice*; monitor results

Organizational Culture

1.0–1.6	1.8–2.4	2.6–3.2	3.4–4.0
Continual flux	Stable standard practice	Systems thinking	Breakthrough routine

Professional Development Criteria

1.0–1.6	1.8–2.4	2.6–3.2	3.4–4.0
Hit and miss	*Content*	Content and *context*	Content, context and *process*

Leadership Communication

1.0–1.6	1.8–2.4	2.6–3.2	3.4–4.0
Nonexistent	Directive	Discussion	Dialogue

Instructional Focus

Instruction & Learning should be the central focus (*Reality: not likely*)	*Instruction* and learning is the central focus	*Teaching* and learning is the *central focus*

Structure

Management practice (orderly)	Comprehensive reform	Situational: Leadership practice is paramount

School Decision Making

Respect for teaching	Ambition to try	Courage to put student learning first	Perseverance for each child	Wisdom of all stakeholders for each child

Leader Decision Making

Interest in education	Involves followers	Engages followers	Convinces followers to take action	Inspires followers to lead

1.0	1.2	1.4	1.6	1.8	2.0	2.2	2.4	2.6	2.8	3.0	3.2	3.4	3.6	3.8	4.0

stay the course with their professional development within the academy. Their request was granted by the board. The school was clearly struggling, and if it were not for the resiliently devoted teachers, Western students would have been totally lost. Using some of the tools within this book, and others they created on their own, the Western leadership team was able to diagnose their leadership practices. Chart 3.4 gives a summary of the picture these teachers painted for their school board only days prior.

Reflection Questions

If you were a teacher on this team, what might be some of your options to enhance the leadership impacts within your school?

Do you have recommendations for this team?

What might a formal leader do in a school like this to stop the unproductive cycle?

The Western leadership team, under the authority of the school board and the outside support of an exceptionally trained distributed leadership facilitator, set a course for systemic improvement. To do so they knew they would have to represent a visual leadership presence to the other staff members. Functioning as a single entity, the team outlined the school's mission, vision, and goals for the next two years. They asked staff for input, but ultimately they made the final decision and then shared the results of their decision. They clearly let teachers know that their leadership team was in charge and what role they would be playing. The team held weekly meetings to hear staff concerns and to update the staff on the next available professional development opportunity. The professional development opportunities were directly tied to reading and literacy content.

Chart 3.4   Western School Leadership Impact Explanation

Leadership Factor	Explanation
Leadership aspect	There was very limited noticeable leadership, but there was a sense of management of the daily functions of the school.
Leadership type	Administrators devoted an enormous amount of time to student discipline and the management of the building.
Awareness of leadership impact of student performance	Formal leaders had little time left to practice instructional leadership as a result of devoting themselves to the nonacademic management responsibilities.
Essential leadership question	Who is the next principal and is he or she going to do something this time?
	Who was . . . ? Teachers pointing fingers at formal leaders and formal leaders pointing at teaching staff. Formal leaders (principal and superintendent) were the only recognized people who could make decisions.
School improvement	Teachers fell back on the classroom practices that had passed the test of time and what they knew to be true.
Improvement from a leadership perspective	In an attempt to fix the school's system disparities, each new administrator brought a new design concept. Little or no formal analysis of leadership practice was measured.
Organizational culture	A high turnover of formal leaders and yearly design shifts left the school's culture in continual flux.
Professional development	New designs brought about new professional developments with limited connectedness to the teachers' classrooms. Professional development appeared to be the flavor of the month or year.
Leadership communication	Vision and mission of the school were missing from the daily instructional expectations.
Instructional focus	There was little to no instructional focus by the formal leaders. Some teaching staff had not been evaluated for years.
Structure	Formal leaders created policy changes to create order among teachers and often rearranged the daily schedule of the school. Faculty meetings were being used to inform teachers of policy and daily management responsibilities (i.e., discipline referral use and daily attendance logs).
School decision making	Formal and informal leaders worked hard to teach. Self-contained classrooms were the norm with limited collaborative time to talk about instructional issues. The academy finally gave them this time, but it was limited to only a few staff.
Leadership decision making	Proclamations of the value of teaching were made by formal leaders with limited or no involvement in instructional decisions.

In addition, the team was able to convince the school board to allow them to have influence on the hiring of the new principal and superintendent. The team's leader, Jake (who was also the school's music instructor), applied for the principal position. Ironically, Jake was not hired, but the team was able to convince the new principal and the board that an assistant principal was needed to manage the discipline, academic schedules, and other managerial responsibilities to ensure that the principal could focus his time and energy on teaching- and learning-related issues. Jake was hired into this position on a part-time basis. At this point, the school's Leadership Impact Survey score was a 2.2.

Reflection Questions

What is your reaction to this team's leadership effort?

What aspect of leadership do you believe the Western leadership team was embarking on? (*Leader Superhero, Leader-Plus, Leadership Practice*)

Why was it important for the team to have input on the new administrative hires?

What leadership functions did the Western leadership team purposefully address?

Although not an ideal situation, the Western leadership team became the school's turnaround leader. They had the ambition to try to move teaching and learning to the forefront. They involved their staff by using their human and social capital (see the section "Theory: Capital Influence" in "Section B: Identify Advice Network" in Chapter 5) yet made decisive decisions that left little room for negotiation and falling back on old habits. The teachers within the building were starving for some recognizable leadership; as such, they followed the leadership team's directives. These informal teacher leaders were able to bring much-needed stabilization to the school's culture. This leadership team was able to reduce the potential to regress to a culture of unrest by focusing their leadership practices on the immediate needs of the school and by taking a Leader Superhero aspect stance. Time will tell whether their efforts will create a systemic maturity. Nevertheless, clearly their wisdom of leadership practice and the concept of leadership analysis and design played a huge role in their ability to impact teacher practices

LEADERSHIP IMPACT SURVEY

Purpose of Tool:

The tool amasses qualitative data on the deployed leadership aspect of your school. It serves as a collaborative or self-talk dialogue data tool that will brandish a lived reality of the school's leadership practices across the three leadership functions. It shows the impact of the practices across 13 leadership and organizational-related factors. The survey serves as a formative instrument that can shape new and retooled leadership practices.

Facilitator Help:

1. Supply each member of your leadership team with the Leadership Impact Survey. Instruct them to take 10 minutes to complete the 14 questions, which may be done by following the directions on the template.

2. Upon completing the survey, have members add up their subtotal for each of the leadership functions and the total for all three. Instruct members to transfer their scores to "Scoring Sheet 1" following the instructions provided.

3. Add all team members' scores for each function and total, and divide by the number of participating team members. Have each member record their team's score in the "Team Average" column.

4. Distribute copies of the Leadership Functions From a Distributed Leadership handout (see the *Reproducible Resources Section*). Give the members a few minutes to read over the handout and then ask them to answer the five questions following the scoring section of

Scoring Sheet 1. Have them work in small groups of three to four depending on the size of the team (10 to 15 minutes).

5. The dialogue created by the results are far more important than filling in the blanks. Encourage honest and open dialogue among the participants. If there are discrepancies between individual and team scores, share them with their individual rationales. Share with the group as a whole.

6. Have members transfer their team score to Scoring Sheet 2 and follow the directions.

7. Give the members a few minutes to read over Scoring Sheet 2 and then ask them to answer the eight questions following the scoring. Have them work in small groups of three to four depending on the size of the team (10 to 15 minutes). Share with the group as a whole.

8. Lead a discussion about the deployed leadership aspect within the school and its relationship and impact across the other identified factors.

It is the facilitator's responsibility to use this tool to identify the lived reality of the school and to use it as a launching pad for the team's exploration of their leadership practices.

Tips:	**Resources:**
This tool may be your team's first exposure to the distributed leadership aspect. Therefore, it is essential that you encourage and maintain open dialogue. Formal leaders need to be cautious not to become defensive or hard-lined.	• Copies of the Leadership Impact Survey • Copies of the Leadership Functions From a Distributed Perspective handout • At least two different-colored highlighters for each participant
Variations and Applications:	**Sample Critical Questions:**

Have your staff take the survey during a faculty meeting. Caution: If you believe the staff score will be 1.0 to 1.6, it might not be worth the verbal thumping that often comes from staff who believe there is no noticeable leadership.	Knowledge Questions
	    – What are the pressing issues your school is facing?
	    – What are we doing?
	
	Comprehension Questions
	    – How do you know?
	
	Analysis Questions
	    – What evidence supports . . . ?

LEADERSHIP IMPACT SURVEY

Instructions:

1. Use the five-point scale from **Continually (4)** to **Rarely/Never (1)** to describe how regularly the leadership statements apply to your school's leadership practices. Select **Insufficient Information (−1)** if you do not have sufficient information to respond. Circle your responses in the columns. Add subtotals for each of the three leadership functions (Setting Direction, Human Development, and Organizational Development) and total scores.

2. Transfer subtotal scores from the Leadership Impact Survey for each leadership function into the score columns. To do so you will need to add the scores from each function and then divide the total by the number of questions for each: Setting Direction (*3 questions*); Human Development (*5 questions*); and Organizational Development (*6 questions*).

3. Individually or as a team answer the five questions that follow the scoring. It is more important to dialogue about your score than to fill in the blanks.

4. Transfer and highlight your score from the Leadership Impact Survey to the numbered score bars at the top and the bottom of the scoring sheet. Draw a highlighted connection between the top and bottom scores. Draw a highlighted connection on either side of the previous scored line.

5. The highlighted area represents your score; the two outside highlights refer to outliers. A school's leadership impact score does not represent a straight absolute from one factor to the other; however, rarely does a school have a factor score outside of the outliers.

6. Individually or as a team answer the eight questions that follow the scoring.

Example:

Leadership Impact Survey						
	Continually	Frequently	Sometimes	Rarely/Never	Insufficient Information	What were your thoughts that contributed to your score?
Setting Direction						
Formal leaders sell and sustain the school's *collaboratively* developed vision and mission through a number of means (i.e., ongoing staff conversations, collaborative development, achievement student data reviews, and school improvement plans collaboratively developed and monitored for student performance results).	4	③	2	1	−1	Principal shares vision in staff memos, during evaluations, and during staff meetings. Staff had input on mission and vision during the staff inservice in Aug.

Why do you think that a "−1" was given to *Insufficient Information* scores?

Leadership Impact Survey: Scoring Sheet 1			
Leadership Function	**Individual Score**	**Team Average**	**Comments**
Setting Direction	2.2	2.5	Collaborative vision
Human Development	1.8	1.7	
Organizational Development	2.5	2.6	An orderly environment has been created. Lots of resources over the last year.
Total:	2.21	2.27	

In which of the three leadership functions did you score the *highest*? What might be the factors associated with the *high* score?

 – Organizational Development: New discipline policy, instructional coach has been finding good resources for our classrooms.
 – Principal won't let the vision drop.

Leadership Impact Survey: Scoring Sheet 2															
1.0	1.2	1.4	1.6	1.8	2.0	2.2	2.4	2.6	2.8	3.0	3.2	3.4	3.6	3.8	4.0
Leadership Aspect															
Limited noticeable leadership				Leader Superhero aspect				Leader-Plus aspect				Leadership Practice aspect			
Leadership Type															
Manager				Turnaround leader				Practitioner				Systemic maturity			
Awareness of Leadership Impact on Student Performance															
Nonacademic management				Unconscious leadership				Mindful leadership				Focused leadership			

Templates: Pages 232–236

LEADERSHIP IMPACT SURVEY

Use the five-point scale from **Continually (4)** to **Rarely/Never (1)** to describe how regularly the following statements apply to your school leadership practices. Select **Insufficient Information (−1)** if you do not have sufficient information to respond. Circle your responses in the columns. Add subtotals and totals scores.

	Continually	Frequently	Sometimes	Rarely/Never	Insufficient Information	What were your thoughts that contributed to your score?
Setting Direction						
Formal leaders sell and sustain the school's *collaboratively* developed vision and mission through a number of means (i.e., ongoing staff conversations, collaborative development, achievement student data reviews, and school improvement plans collaboratively developed and monitored for student performance results).	4	3	2	1	−1	
Formal leaders get cooperative commitment for school goals (i.e., ongoing staff conversations, collaborative development, achievement student data reviews).	4	3	2	1	−1	
Formal leaders maintain high expectations of staff and students alike. This is visible through the leader's actions and interactions with instructional staff.	4	3	2	1	−1	
Add up subtotals for each column						
Human Development						
Leaders monitor instructional progress (i.e., regularly engages [several times a week] in learning walkthroughs or classroom visits, student work evaluation, multiple formative and summative data sources are shared and analyzed with staff).	4	3	2	1	−1	
Leaders develop teachers' *content knowledge* (i.e., recognized as an instructional leader in the school, consistently sought out for content knowledge, offer professional development with extensive classroom practice and support, provide direct classroom support by modeling lessons).	4	3	2	1	−1	
Leaders develop teachers' *pedagogical skills* (i.e., recognized as an instructional leader in the school, consistently is sought out for their instructional teaching strategies knowledge, offer professional development with extensive classroom practice and support, provide direct classroom support by modeling lessons).	4	3	2	1	−1	
Formal leaders provide encouragement, recognition, and support (i.e., teachers with expertise are encouraged to share with others, incentive systems exist to reward teacher progress toward schoolwide goals).	4	3	2	1	−1	
Add up subtotals for each column						

	Continually	Frequently	Sometimes	Rarely/Never	Insufficient Information	What were your thoughts that contributed to your score?
Organizational Development						
Formal leaders adapt and modify procedures, policy, and tools as needed to improve instruction with collaborative input from staff (i.e., has a method for engaging the entire staff in analyzing and designing new practices based on prior initiatives, as well as a way to monitor the results of the school improvement effort; has cross-disciplinary faculty committees with decision-making responsibility).	4	3	2	1	−1	
Formal leaders support and maintain high expectations of collaboration among teachers (i.e., design opportunities for staff participation in curricular design and school improvement; provides time for faculty, grade, and/or department meetings; encourages cross-disciplinary efforts, faculty committees with decision-making responsibility, and professional learning communities).	4	3	2	1	−1	
Leaders procure resources for teachers (i.e., supportive teacher induction programs are maintained within the school; subject matter instructional tools are distributed and mirror the school improvement efforts; differentiated support for teachers based on need, feedback, and observations).	4	3	2	1	−1	
Leaders distribute resources to teachers (i.e., base decisions about budget, school improvement, and professional learning on schoolwide goals for student learning).	4	3	2	1	−1	
Leaders handle disturbances that interrupt teaching practices (i.e., teachers, students, and leaders work together to ensure fair enforcement of rules; they identify and maximize student talents when offering assistance both academically and behaviorally; they use mentors and community support; nonacademic announcements that might interrupt instruction are extremely rare).	4	3	2	1	−1	
Leaders create and maintain an orderly work environment (i.e., teachers, community, and leaders use data on student conduct and achievement to review and adjust policies; leaders maintain a visible presence during passing and instructional times; uninterrupted instructional time is provided for core instruction; collaborative efforts are continually made to improve attendance, student engagement, dropout, and graduation rates for students).	4	3	2	1	−1	
Add up subtotals for each column						
Add up scores from each column Total(s):						
Add the totals from each column together _____ and divide by 14. **Total Score:** _____						

LEADERSHIP IMPACT SURVEY: SCORING SHEET (1 OF 3)

Transfer subtotal scores from the Leadership Impact Survey for each leadership function into the score columns. To do so you will need to add the scores from each function and then divide the total by the number of questions for each: Setting Direction (*3 questions*); Human Development (*5 questions*); and Organizational Development (*6 questions*).

Leadership Function	Individual Score	Team Average	Comments
Setting Direction			
Human Development			
Organizational Development			
Total:			

In which of the three leadership functions did you score the *highest*? What might be the factors associated with the *high* score?

In which of the three leadership functions did you score the *lowest*? What might be the factors associated with the *low* score?

What is the single most alarming aspect of your score? Why?

What is the single most rewarding or pleasing aspect of your score? Why and what would you want to keep the same to ensure your successes?

What one change could you make to help the school perform even more effectively to enhance student performance? *Caution: This is a hypothetical question. More analysis should be given to leadership practices prior to jumping to a new design.*

LEADERSHIP IMPACT SURVEY: SCORING SHEET (2 OF 3)

Transfer and highlight your score from the Leadership Impact Survey to the numbered score bars at the top and the bottom of the scoring sheet. Draw a highlighted connection between the top and bottom scores. Draw a highlighted connection on either side of the previous scored line.

1.0	1.2	1.4	1.6	1.8	2.0	2.2	2.4	2.6	2.8	3.0	3.2	3.4	3.6	3.8	4.0

Leadership Aspect

Limited noticeable leadership	Leader Superhero aspect	Leader-Plus aspect	Leadership Practice aspect

Leadership Type

Manager	Turnaround leader	Practitioner	Cohesive maturity

Awareness of Leadership Impact on Student Performance

Nonacademic management	Unconscious leadership	Mindful leadership	Focused leadership

Essential Leadership Question

Who	Who and *what*	Who, what, and *why*	Who, what, why, and *how*

School Improvement

Status quo	Structure-driven practice	Adaptive practice	Infinity of practice

Improvement From a Leadership Practice Perspective

Design	*Analysis*; design	Analysis; design; *monitors results*	Analysis; design; *new practice*; monitor results

Organizational Culture

Continual flux	Stable standard practice	Professional learning community	Community of practice

Professional Development Criteria

Hit and miss	*Content*	Content and *context*	Content, context, and *process*

Leadership Communication

Nonexistent	Directive	Discussion	Dialogue

Instructional Focus

Instruction and learning should be the central focus (*Reality: not likely*)	*Instruction* and learning are the central focus	*Teaching* and learning are the central focus

Structure

Management practice (orderly)	Comprehensive reform	Situational: Leadership practice is paramount

School Decision Making

Respect for teaching	Ambition to try	Courage to put student learning first	Perseverance for each child	Wisdom of all stakeholders for each child

Leader Decision Making

Interest in education	Involves followers	Engages followers	Convinces followers to take action	Inspires followers to lead

1.0	1.2	1.4	1.6	1.8	2.0	2.2	2.4	2.6	2.8	3.0	3.2	3.4	3.6	3.8	4.0

LEADERSHIP IMPACT SURVEY: SCORING SHEET (3 OF 3)

Which impacting factor (i.e., school improvement, structure) did you find to be the *most alarming*? Why?

Which impacting factor did you find to be the *most accurate* in describing your school's present status? Why?

What is the single most alarming aspect of your score? Why?

What is the single most rewarding or pleasing aspect of your score? Why and what would you want to keep the same to ensure your successes?

How might the score change if we did not address leadership within the school across all content areas? For example, if you had taken the survey for leadership associated with the content reading only or mathematics or another content area.

What one change could you make to help the school enhance student performance even more effectively? *Caution: This is a hypothetical question. More analysis should be given to leadership practices prior to jumping to new design.*

What question(s) would you like to have answered?

The Framework
of Success

A Model for Leadership Inquiry

> *Sustainable leadership goes beyond temporary gains in achievement scores to create lasting, meaningful improvement in learning.*
>
> —Andy Hargreaves and Dean Fink (2004, p. 10)

There was a scientific experiment in which a mouse was placed in a maze with food at the end of one passage. Through trial and error, the mouse finally arrived at the food. When he had run the same course several times, the mouse no longer hesitated or turned down wrong corridors, but went directly down the correct path that led to the food. After a few more runs like this, the food was removed from the previous corridor and placed at the end of another passage. At first the mouse went to the old place. Finding nothing there, he retraced his path and investigated other passages until he found the newly placed food. Thereafter, he had no trouble accommodating himself to the new route that brought the reward.

The journey of a thousand miles begins beneath your feet.

—Lao-Tzu in the *Tao Te Ching*

Now, the point of this story is that it shows the basic difference between mice and leaders. Eventually, the mouse will learn to seek other paths when the one he has always followed is no longer productive, whereas school leaders often keep going down the same unproductive pathway forever. This parable may be overexaggerated, but there is a chilling truth in that anecdote. We will want to revisit this parable later in this chapter as we explore how we as leaders trace our path through an ever changing leadership maze.

THE DISTRIBUTED LEADERSHIP IMPROVEMENT FRAMEWORK

As leaders, we must understand our practices of today to be able to lead tomorrow. We must diagnose the effectiveness of these practices at enhancing and changing classroom practice, which in turn enhances student learning. If it works for us, then that is fine, and we must hold on to these practices and even share them with our colleagues. If some of the practices we are currently using no longer work, even though they may have worked in the past, then let us take a close, hard look at them and see if there are other passageways we can explore that *will* work and that *will* bring about our desired goals. By diagnosing the effectiveness of our practices, we will

---

Critical Thoughts

As Leaders . . .

- How often do we continue to do things in a certain manner just because they have always been done that way?
- Haven't we ever felt that our actions were not bringing the results we desired? Yet we continue to persist in our actions.
- Do we analyze our practices' effectiveness in meeting our students' learning needs?
- Do we retrace our action to see how they might have gone awry?
- Are we looking for new paths to our desired results?
- Are we prepared to revisit our chosen paths routinely?
- Do we accommodate new practices based on our ever-changing situations to ensure we meet the needs of all children?
- Can we answer all these questions with confidence and assurance that we are doing each of them? If not, then read on.

not throw out practices simply because they are old, but because they don't work. We should not adopt a practice because it is new, but because it works.

How do we know if the new practice works? We know because we engage in the new practice by design, with an intentional method to measure its intended results. We then analyze the results and take one of two paths (see Figure 4.1). On one path, we stay the course and continue to monitor the results for effectiveness. On the second path, we revise the leadership practice with the intention of securing the desired results.

If we deploy leadership practices by design, we will become what we want to be, what we know we can be: leaders who play a dynamic and vital role in each child's life. We will not only have a school in which there is order, discipline, and learning, but it will be a school that brings out the best qualities in both the teacher and student, that allows for individual growth and differences. We will have created lasting meaningful improvements in learning; thus, we will have sustainable leadership. How do we develop leadership practices by design?

Figure 4.1   New Practice Cycle

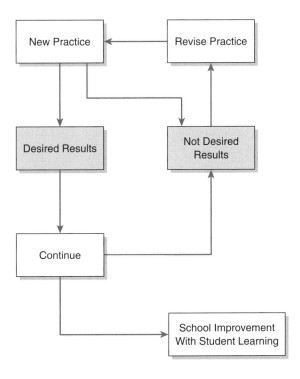

A FRAMEWORK FOR SYSTEMIC LEADERSHIP ENHANCEMENT

Maximizing Leadership Impact

The Distributed Leadership Improvement Framework (Figure 4.2) serves as an outline and a structure, but more so, as a framework for attaining a sustained Leadership Practice aspect. It shapes how we think about and frame investigations of our leadership practice. The framework serves as the systemic diagnostic, design, new practice creation and monitoring tool, intended to maximize the lived leadership practices within your organization. The framework itself is a tool used to mediate leaders' practices for creating effective sustained leadership so as to create a school that lives within the Leadership Practice aspect. In doing so, leaders will have an impact across numerous leadership and organizational factors (see Table 4.1). The framework sets the stage for ensuring that our leadership practices are having a lasting impact on student learning.

As a *diagnostic* device, the framework presses us to investigate the leadership practices in direct relationship to classroom practice, including routines, tools, and structures in the lived reality, as well as in the formal structure of our school. As a *design* device, the framework encourages us to make data-driven decisions with measurable outcomes. As a *new practice* device, the framework challenges us to take action and monitor the results. As a *result-driven* device, the framework creates opportunities to reflect on new practices prior to formal analysis. Most important, the tool provides an ongoing systemic thinking and processing, professional learning, leadership practice framework called the *Infinity Cycle*. Most notably, the framework provides the model for leadership inquiry within this Distributed Leadership Toolbox.

Problem-Solving Tool

Research has supported the effectiveness of using clearly defined methods to determine school improvement needs and to develop and evaluate implementation strategies. The Distributed Leadership Improvement Framework is similar in its intentional efforts to help leaders problem solve. However, within this framework the practice of leadership is the central focus. At its core, the Distributed Leadership Improvement Framework requires answering four critical, interrelated questions:

1. Do our leadership practices meet the needs of their intended purposes?

2. How do I (we) know?

Figure 4.2 The Distributed Leadership Improvement Framework

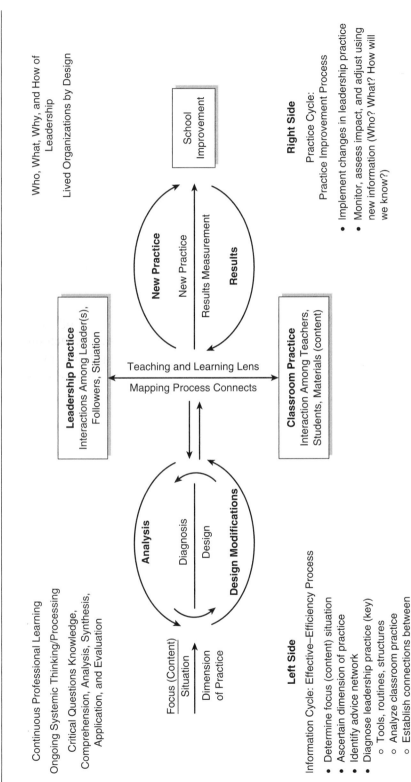

Source: Created by McBeth & Wheeles (2005.) Revised by McBeth in 2007.

3. What am I (are we) going to do about it?

4. Did the implemented practice enhance and change teachers' classroom practice?

This thinking process can be applied to a single leadership routine as well as to systems of practices. This method of thinking is easily inlayed within many other school improvement models; in fact, the framework identifies school improvement as the intended outcome. The essential difference is that leadership practice is the underlying factor that contributes to the success of this improvement model, an often overlooked component in other improvement models.

Content: Ready, Set, Go

As a starting point within the framework, we must solicit input regarding the instructional concerns, problems, gaps, or weaknesses of

Table 4.1 Maximizing Leadership Impact

Leadership Aspect	=	Leadership practice aspect
Leadership Type	=	Cohesive maturity
Awareness of Leadership Impact on Student Performance	=	Focused leadership
Essential Leadership Question	=	Who, what, why, and *how*
School Improvement	=	Infinity of practice
Improvement From a Leadership Practice Perspective	=	Analysis; design; *new practice*; monitor results
Organizational Culture	=	Community of practice
Professional Development Criteria	=	Content, context, and *process*
Leadership Communication	=	Dialogue
Instructional Focus	=	Teaching and learning are the *Central focus*
Structure	=	Situational: Leadership practice is paramount
School Decision Making	=	Wisdom of all stakeholders for each child
Leader Decision Making	=	Inspires followers to lead

the school. In other words, what is the topic of our efforts? These do not need to be fully supported by data at this point. Data that can support viewpoints at any given time are great, but the dialogue is a key necessity. Wellman and Lipton (2004), in their book *Data-Driven Dialogue*, define *dialogue* as a process of listening and speaking to understand each other's ideas, assumptions, beliefs, and values. As you go through the framework, you will be asking yourself, or team members, critical questions such as: "How do I (we) know?" It is at this point that some evidence needs to be offered. At times more data will need to be collected or created to allow the team to diagnose various practice impacts on teacher classroom practices, and ultimately student learning.

To begin to explore leadership practices from a distributed perspective, we need to find a focus (see Figure 4.3). As identified in the last paragraph, we need to start our efforts with our most challenging academic issues. Once we have an academic issue, we can narrow it to a focused dimensional practice (see Figure 4.4). This dimension of practice will make the essential connects between the leadership practice and classroom practice. Chapter 5, Section A, has a tool to help you or your leadership teams get started in identifying dimensions of practice.

Three Exploratory Process Cycles Leading to School Improvement

The framework is made up of three cycles: the Information Cycle, the Practice Cycle, and the Infinity Cycle. The Information and Practice Cycles are divided by a two-directional arrow, "Mapping Process Connects" and "Teaching and Learning Lens" (see Figure 4.5). The intent of this connection between leadership practice and classroom practice is to draw our attention continually to their relationship. Without the reminder of their presence, we might fall back on analyzing leadership practices with very little or no direct relationship to classroom practice. If we are to view leadership from a distributed perspective, we must maintain our attention on classroom and leadership practice at the same time. This connection serves as the heart of the framework. We should always tie our diagnosis, design, new practice, and data results to these two practice perspectives. In doing so, we ensure that we are keeping instruction and learning as our central focus.

Information Cycle: Effective–Efficiency Process

Value. The *Information Cycle* is the moral fiber of the framework and is intended to be the diagnosis and design cycle. It lays the foundation for practices to be deployed by design. The leadership practices that are deployed by design as a result of the Information Cycle drive the Practice

Figure 4.3   Finding a Focus

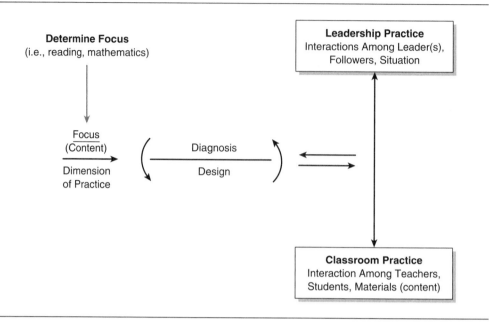

Figure 4.4   Narrowing the Focus to a Style Dimensional Practice

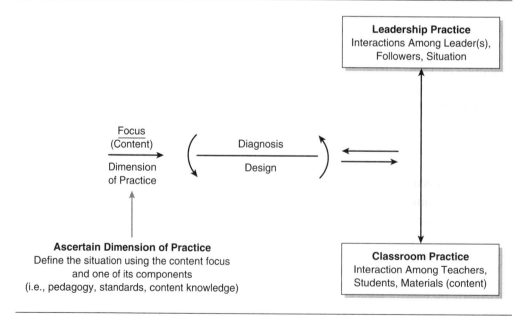

Figure 4.5   The Division Between the Information and Practice Cycles

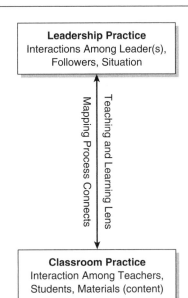

Cycle. Chapter 5 will explore the tools that you can use to diagnose and design your leadership practices.

The Information Cycle is extremely valuable to determine if our present practices are fulfilling their intended purposes. To prevent teams from jumping to a new practice without true intentions, the Information Cycle is divided into three core phases: focus, which we explored above, and diagnosis and design (see Figure 4.6). The Information Cycle enables you or members of your leadership team to share information, analyze practices, and develop new practices with intentional outcomes that can be measured for results. The Information Cycle encourages team members, even reluctant ones, to share beliefs and knowledge related to the deployed leadership practices that are within the school. By exposing these often unconscious practices, you are able to have meaningful and mindful dialogue about your leadership practices. You are able to investigate whether the practices are enhancing and changing classroom practices. In addition, you are able to determine whether the practices are directly or indirectly enhancing student performance.

Caution. Diagnosis, prior to design, is critical for leaders or leadership teams because it allows them to share understandings, see new possibilities,

Figure 4.6   The Diagnosis and Design Portion of the Information Cycle

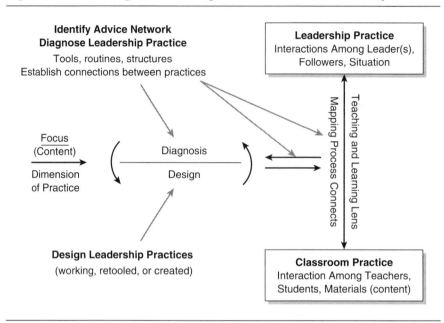

frame issues, and define solutions. Although design is important, *diagnostic* work is equally vital. School leaders are notorious for jumping directly to design and often layer practice upon practice. At times, new design might be a conscious decision, but often the old practices remain as part of an unconscious safety net. In other words, on the surface, it appears that change has happened, but under the surface, the old practices still exist. The emergence of leadership practice dialogue through diagnosis capacitates teams to work differently with genuine intention, purpose, and by design. Old practices are kept if they work; others are redeveloped, whereas others are thrown out completely.

Facilitative Help. As you and your leadership team begin inquiries into the Information Cycle, Chapter 5 will serve as a facilitative guide. The chapter is divided into seven sections labeled A thru G, empowering your team to move successfully throughout the Information Cycle: focus to diagnosis, diagnosis to design, and design to preparation for new practice.

Practice Cycle: Practice Improvement Process

The Practice Cycle is extremely valuable as it sets the scene for plan development proportionate with new practice. It facilitates a means for measuring the impact of the practices pertinent to *school improvement* (enhancing and changing classroom practices or enhancing and changing student learning performance). The Practice Cycle is divided into two core phases: new practice and results measurement (see Figure 4.7).

Value. The Practice Cycle provides the opportunity for leaders to develop strategies, routines, and tools to implement the new practice. The designed leadership practices can then be honed over time by using a set of reflective tools and routines. The Practice Cycle creates the lived reality of practice within the school. It ensures that leadership practices are deployed and that they secure the desired results. If the desired results are not brought to fruition, then the practice is reworked until success is obtained.

Caution. Practitioners in a hurry for quick returns will often overlook the power of planning for implementation. Implementation without design will drag school leaders down a cultural path of continual flux. Leadership practiced subconsciously will drive leaders to a sustained Leader Superhero aspect, or worse, to the No Noticeable Leadership aspect. A designed leadership practice that is not monitored for results may result in no substantial enhancements of teachers' classroom practices, or worse yet, a negative influence leading to a state of disadvantageous status quo.

Facilitative Help. As you and your leadership team begin preparation for the Practice Cycle, Chapter 6 will serve as a facilitative guide. The chapter

Figure 4.7   The Practice Cycle

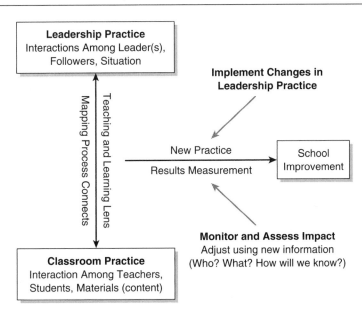

is divided into three sections, enabling your team to move successfully throughout the Practice Cycle.

Infinity of Practice Cycle: The Perpetual Phase of Improvement

A true measurement of a school's effort to cultivate a successful professional community could be how often, and in what context, they revisit their practices. When leadership teams within a school are functioning within the Leadership Practice aspect, they have a confidence in their own capacities and with the capacities of others, and contain an infinitude of problem-solving solutions. They have a combined wisdom to put each student first and foremost in their decision-making processes. This eternal problem-solving and decision-making teaching and learning mentality creates a never-ending practice cycle of school improvement. I refer to this unbounded perpetual sequencing as the *Infinity of Practice Cycle* (see Figure 4.8).

The Infinity of Practice Cycle starts where the Practice Cycle ends, with results measurements. As teams gather their data within the Practice Cycle, they will need to analyze that data to determine the practice's effectiveness in enhancing and changing classroom practice. Upon the *analysis* of these data, the team will need to determine if the designed leadership practice needs to remain in practice or needs *design modifications* (see Figure 4.1). Teams routinely functioning within the Leadership Practice aspect create a culture that enables *breakthrough routines* to be styled within existing or new practices. Upon modification, or even if remaining the same, the designed *new practice* then needs to be deployed. The new practice is monitored for desired or undesired *results*.

The cycle continues in a never-ending Infinity of Practice. The Infinity Cycle resembles a figure eight placed on its side. As we trace this path on the outskirts of the Information and Practice Cycles, we find that we don't find a finish line. We just keep circling, and we go on for eternity through the Infinity Cycle. At the junction of the two loops, we find ourselves crossing the Mapping Process Connects, which in turn creates what I refer to as the *Teaching and Learning Lens.* Teams continue to cycle through the improvement phases with premeditated effort to enhance classroom practice, which in turn enhances student learning for each child.

Value. Ultimately, a cycle develops within the bounded dimension of practice, leading to a search for alternative guiding data sources. A team functioning within the Leadership Practice aspect takes this cycle trip often, which then creates an environment conducive to replication. The team creates a culture in which the Infinity of Practice Cycle itself becomes routine.

Figure 4.8 The Infinity of Practice Cycle

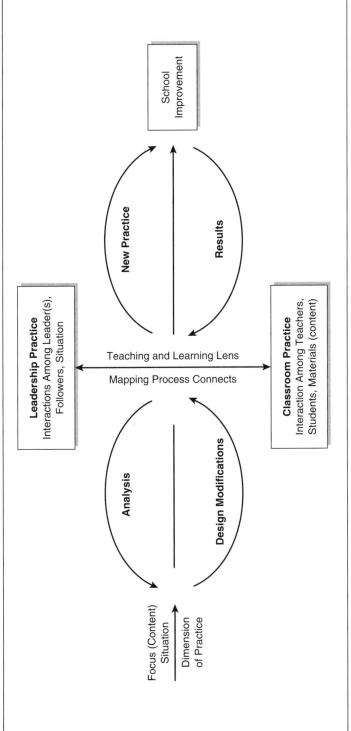

Source: Created by McBeth & Wheeles (2005.) Revised by McBeth in 2007.

As student needs arise, new problems emerge, leading to a need to engage the team in the Information Cycle, which in turn leads to new decisions and Infinity of Practice exploration and growth. As more and more teachers meet the needs of their students within a dimension of practice, leadership teams then start to look more closely at other measures. Dimensions of practice are identified, and they begin to strengthen their expectations for all learners across multiple contents and dimensions.

Each time you or a team uses the Distributed Leadership Improvement Framework to guide and facilitate your designed leadership practice, you increase your confidence, trust, and success in working with practices that enhance teacher classroom practices. Like the mouse in the maze at the beginning of this chapter, leaders and leadership teams that use the framework will find their way through a maze that continues to change on a daily basis. The mouse desired food and created a systems-thinking framework to cycle through each time he faced a new passageway in the maze. The mouse found comfort within his maze world. Our comfort food at the end of the maze is the reality of meeting the needs of our students' learning. As leaders and leadership teams learn to use the Distributed Leadership Improvement Framework, new possibilities for cultivating communities of practice emerge, and richer forms of professional practice surface.

Facilitative Help. Any of the tools in Chapters 5 and 6 can be used during the Infinity Cycle. Chapter 7 is devoted to the framework evaluation, which is encapsulated in the following question: What tools did we as a team use that we want to use again the next time we investigate a Dimension of Practice? Chapter 7 explores the collaborative successes and struggles of the team as they use a number of different Information and Practice Cycle tools. Teams look at the impact of the practices and distill a formula for improving their routine and tools and to apply this knowledge to future leadership practice reviews. This process of self-evaluation will breathe life into the Infinity Cycle.

CONCLUSION

The tools within the Distributed Leadership Toolbox are meant to be a starting point for your leadership practice diagnosis and design rather than as a paint-by-numbers approach. I have outlined a framework for school improvement of leadership practice that has the potential to enhance and change your practice if you follow the framework as designed. For many of you, this will be your first time to take a distributed perspective on leadership, and the framework will serve well as a systematic, step-by-step guide to your school improvement efforts. As you become more proficient in your practices of thinking about leadership from a distributed perspective, the framework might become a free-flowing guide.

The tools within this book were developed under the premise of the distributed leadership perspective, and the tools are intended to engage you and leadership teams in the diagnosis, design, and practice of leadership in direct relationship to classroom practice. It is critical that you not lose sight of the foundation of the distributed leadership perspective. Chapters 1 through 3 were devoted to teaching you about this leadership perspective.

Use the first three chapters routinely to reflect upon your practice of the framework and the tools within this book. The chapters create a distributed leadership foundation that is imperative and unique to this fundamental work.

You are encouraged to adapt, change, or create any new tool that might help your team during any of the cycles or phases of the framework. Caution should be heeded if you decide to create your own tools or chose to revise the tools I have provided. It is essential that you not lose your focus on the interactions of leaders, followers, and their situations as they are spread across time. Often when efforts are made to create different tools, school leaders get caught up in the concept of leadership actions, not the leadership interaction and practice. Leadership *practice* is systemically more complex than leadership *acts;* it expands the mental model of distributed leadership, and leadership in general. It probes for the connections between **leadership practice and classroom practice.** Besides the *who, what,* and *why* questions, the **how** question now can be answered by using the Leadership Practice aspect.

Information Cycle

Effective–Efficiency Process

> *If we are together nothing is impossible. If we are divided all will fail.*
>
> —Winston Churchill

Certainly the times have changed and will continue to change along with society. School leaders owe it to themselves, their teachers, and their students to constantly investigate new avenues and approaches to all aspects of educational life. To the everlasting credit of our profession, many educators have done just that. Indeed, a majority of educators realize the need for new, effective methods of teaching and learning. Yet we continue to fall short in changing our practices.

Chapter 5 is broken into seven sections, labeled A through G. Within this chapter you are given the opportunity to explore the lived reality of your leadership practices and an opportunity to put practices in place by design. You will be escorted through the Information Cycle in preparation for the Practice Cycle. A wide array of diagnostic tools, each with stories, examples, facilitator instructions, and rationales, is explored. As mentioned in previous chapters, you may select any single tool, or all the tools, to use in any order you wish. Not all tools are appropriate for every situation.

> *If you don't know where you're going, you might end up somewhere else.*
>
> —Yogi Berra

SECTION A: DIMENSION OF PRACTICE

TOOL: A Vertical Leadership Component Map

Introduction: Determine Focus (Content) or Situation

One way that we can ensure we are diagnosing leadership practices that are directly linked to classroom practice is to narrow our focus to an academic content. This may include, but not be limited to, mathematics, reading, science, social studies, and so forth. The examples within this book mostly relate to mathematics and language arts in all their divisions. This is due to the unprecedented attention that schools are giving to these two content areas in the past five years, mainly due to federally mandated policy.

Subject content can serve as a common factor between classroom practices and leadership practices, thus creating a common dimension of practice as referenced in the earlier chapters. Extreme caution must be taken if you choose to bypass content as a focus. School leaders without this focus find themselves falling back on the traditional methods of reviewing the school's structures and not the lived reality of practice. As mentioned in the previous chapters, at the very core of distributed leadership is the situation. Content must be part of that situation if we are to map leadership practice to classroom practice. The situation is given focus by its content; after all, math is different from science, and music is different from literacy. Determining the content focus is the first and an eminently important step in the journey to school improvement through the use of the Distributed Leadership Improvement Framework.

Ascertain Dimension of Practice

To think about the content area "reading" can be problematic; it is just such a broad topic. When traveling in Italy years ago, I swapped travel stories with Steve, a gentleman from Tasmania. During the exchange he told me he did not need to return to the United States because he had already been there. Long story, made short, he spent two weeks in Los Angeles. I would refer to his travel to Los Angeles as a focused trip and not all-encompassing of the USA. Steve's suggestion of visiting the USA can be compared to school improvement and general conversations about reading. Both topics can cover amplitudes of addition contexts. I refer to this content breadth of covering everything at once as *umbrella issues*. We must learn to focus our attention from the umbrella issues (see Figure 5.A.1).

To determine the impact of our leadership practices, we must narrow the focus within the content. We must ascertain a *dimension of practice* that is reasonable and measurable. One way to do that is to delineate the

Figure 5.A.1   Umbrella Issues

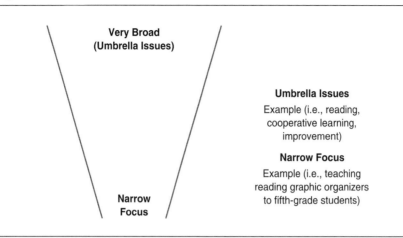

differences in the components of the content, such as pedagogy, components, standards, engagement, or even content knowledge itself. Again, we are trying to define the situation that gives shape to the leader and follower interactions. Reading pedagogy is different from reading comprehension. Even though the pedagogical strategies may be used to bring the comprehension component to life, they could also be used in teaching reading phonemic awareness. By ascertaining the dimension of practice, you are able to have a common denominator to diagnose your leadership practices and your teachers' classroom practices. Figure 5.A.2 represents the *Practice System of Thinking Model*, a diagram that acknowledges the umbrella issues in connection to a dimension of practice in symbiotic relationship to leadership practice and classroom practice.

Purpose: Vertical Leadership Inventory

The Vertical Leadership Component Map tool has at least two useful applications. First, it can be used to guide your way through creating a *leadership inventory*. This can be done from a narrow focus, which identifies the content area, dimension of practice, and so forth, or from a broad focus such as reading or math (Example 5.A.1). Second, it identifies a starting point for diagnosis of leadership practice.

Figure 5.A.2   The Practice System of Thinking Model

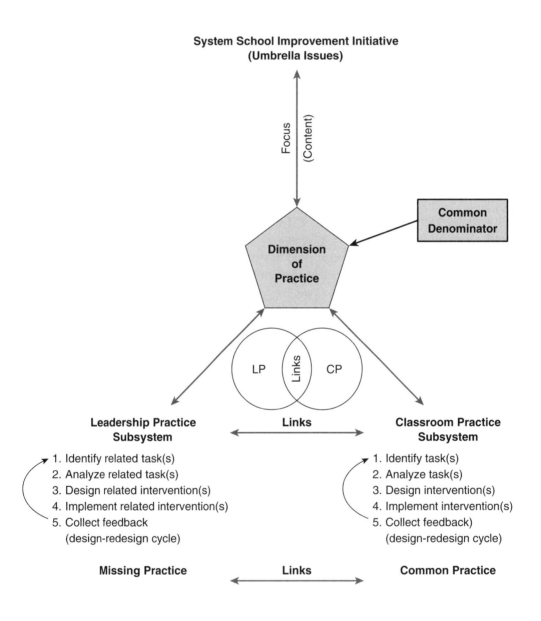

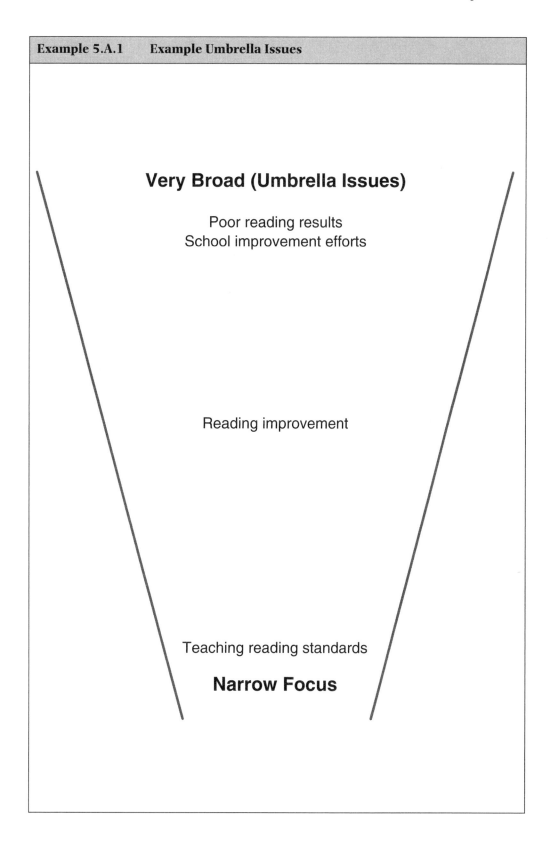

Example 5.A.1   Example Umbrella Issues

Very Broad (Umbrella Issues)

Poor reading results
School improvement efforts

Reading improvement

Teaching reading standards

Narrow Focus

Case Study 1: Where to Start? (Listen for the Clues)

An elementary principal called me on the phone one day asking for my help with a classroom situation. She mentioned that the issue was really in her reading classrooms. Teachers just weren't on target with the use of graphic organizers in the fifth-grade classrooms. She wanted teachers to be using them more often than they were—after all, the strategy was emphasized in their building improvement plan.

Wow! I thought to myself. This was a perfect opportunity to address leadership practice with this principal. She has given me a clue base that has identified a narrowly focused dimension of practice. Can you identify the clues this principal has given? Use Template 5.A.1, "A Vertical Leadership Component Map," to answer the question. I have identified five to six essential components. How many can you identify?

Template 5.A.1	
A Vertical Leadership Component Map	
Umbrella issues	
Focus area (content) • *Reading* • Writing • Mathematics • Science • Social Studies • Other academic areas as needed • Grade level	
Dimension of practice • Content • Standards • Pedagogy • Components • Engagement • Social/Behavioral	
Leadership practice • *Routines* • Tools • Leaders and followers • Interactions • Functions	
Classroom practice	
Routine Microanalysis	

The Clues

Example 5.A.2 identifies the clues discovered during this brief conversation with the elementary principal. The first clue she gave was the content focus area (reading). Second, she identified the grade level. Third, she identified teachers using graphic organizers as the classroom practice she wanted to enhance and change. Fourth, she mentioned a leadership tool (the building improvement plan). Finally, she said, she was looking for a leadership routine to ensure teachers were using the graphic organizers. This was ascertained by her statement of wanting the teachers to do more with the graphic organizers, and by asking for help. This is enough information to fill in some essential data on the Vertical Leadership Component Map. By recognizing the clues, the principal and I were able to focus our conversation on the dimension of practice "Teaching reading graphic organizers to fifth-grade students." As a result, we were able to focus our attention, which enabled us to diagnose the lived leadership practices. In turn, the principal was able to design, with purpose, meaningful classroom and leadership practices to enhance students' ability to use graphic organizers.

Example 5.A.2	
A Vertical Leadership Component Map (Case Study 1)	
Umbrella issues	• Reading
Focus area (content) • *Reading* • Writing • Mathematics • Science • Social Studies • Other academic areas as needed • Grade level	• Reading • Fifth grade
Dimension of practice • Content • Standards • *Pedagogy* • Components • Engagement • Social/Behavioral	• Teaching reading graphic organizers
Leadership practice • *Routines* • *Tools* • Leaders and followers • Interactions • Functions	• Wants a routine to support teachers' efforts in teaching graphic organizers. • Building improvement plan
Classroom practice	• Using graphic organizers
Routine microanalysis	

Philosophy: Narrow the Focus

Example 5.A.2 has a few important components to start with, but at times, teams start their conversation with a very broad perspective (umbrella issues). There is really never a typical map. That is why we must learn to identify the clues. In the previous example, I did not need the map to facilitate the brief conversation. However, I did complete the tool later and gave it to the principal as a means of focusing her attention on the identified clues. In any case, the process requires a need to narrow the focus, and in doing so, you need to complete the entire map.

Case Study 2: Step by Step

A nine-member leadership team, made up of staff from Pleasanton Middle School and their feeder school Pleasanton Elementary, were having a difficult time narrowing their thinking to a manageable dimension of practice. In this situation, they were trying to find a common focus area that both schools could diagnose. As a facilitator, I literally walked them through the process from umbrella issues, to focus, to a dimension of practice, to leadership practices, and finally to microanalysis (see Example 5.A.3). The Vertical Leadership Component Map tool was used to facilitate the process. It served as a launching point for the team to delve into their improvement issues. Upon finding a common umbrella issue, I used critical questions (see *Critical Questions* within the resource section) to help the team narrow their focus. The narrow focus then became our dimension of practice, which we explored in more depth during the diagnosis phase of the improvement framework.

Example 5.A.3	
Vertical Leadership Component Map Tool **(Pleasant Middle School Example)**	
Umbrella issues	Poor assessment results • *Reading scores are not where we would like them.* • Maintaining mathematics while working to close the gap in other areas. School improvement efforts • *Teachers buy into the building improvement plan.* • *Professional learning communities.*
Focus area (content) • Reading • Writing • Mathematics • Science • Social Studies • Other academic areas as needed • Grade level	*Reading improvement*
Dimension of practice • Content • Standards • Pedagogy • Components • Engagement • Knowledge of learner • Social and behavioral	Teaching reading content *Teaching reading standards* Teaching reading methodologies (pedagogy) Teaching reading components Engaging students in authentic learning
Leadership practice • Routines • Tools • Leaders and followers • Interactions • Functions	*Standards in practice* *Quarterly assessment* *Walkthroughs* *Building improvement planning* *Two-week highlights* *(See Identified Leadership Practices Chart)*
Classroom practice	
Routine microanalysis	*(See "Routine Microanalysis" tool)*

A VERTICAL LEADERSHIP COMPONENT MAP

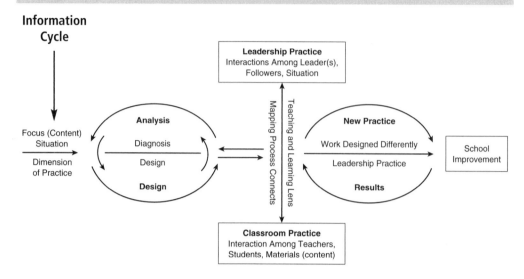

Purpose of Tool:

Gives guidance to creating a leadership inventory. This can be done from a narrow focus, which identifies the content area, dimension of practice, and so forth, or from a broad focus such as reading or math. Identifies a starting point for a diagnosis of leadership practice.

Facilitator Help:

1. Review ground rules for brainstorming. (see Resources Brainstorming Protocols)

2. Choose a recorder, using whatever strategy you prefer.

3. Describe a round-robin process in which each participant will take a turn in sequential order contributing ideas and thoughts to the topic at hand. One person at a time contributes a thought or passes to the next person around the table. The note-taker will take his turn as part of the team rotation. A member who passes one turn may contribute during the next cycle.

4. Ensure that all contributions are recorded on a chart. Note-takers sometimes filter thoughts and ideas; it is your role to facilitate what is recorded and to ensure nonjudgmental quality brainstorming.

5. Use critical questions to drive depth into the brainstorming.

6. After each brainstorm, shift the thinking of the team to categorizing their ideas. Use the categories for discussion purposes, for further exploration in the next step of the template outline.

7. Use the Vertical Leadership Template tool as an outline for your brainstorming.

8. *Note:* Retain all the flip-chart notes. Teams often refer to the notes for guidance when working on the next steps.

Tips:	**Resources:**
Set a minimum target for number of ideas to be generated. Keep time short to maximize attention, focus, and creative instincts. Create a structure for inclusion of all participants.	• One master template. • Flip-chart paper and markers. • *Note:* It is also useful to have the directions and template electronically displayed.
Variations and Applications:	**Sample Critical Questions:**

• Use a single prompt for brainstorming. As the facilitator, drive the process by continuing to ask critical questions. Work from knowledge to comprehension and on to analysis. Once complete, channel the team's thinking to fill in as many steps in the template as possible. The team then can clarify and add to the steps as needed. *Note:* You are facilitating the response, not leading persuasive argument.
• Same as above, except as a facilitator, you place the contributions of the steps in the template as you hear them and then ask the team for accuracy and clarity.
	Knowledge Questions
	   – What are the pressing issues your (our) school is facing?
	   – Which content area will serve as a good starting point?
	   – What tasks (leadership practice) are used to support . . . ?
	   – What in particular are you addressing in this content area?
	
	Comprehension Questions
	   – Which one is the most pressing?
	   – How do you know?
	
	Analysis Questions
	   – How do you know?
	   – What is the purpose (or purposes) of the practice?
	   – What evidence supports . . .?
	   – How do you know these practices support this?

Template: Page 238

A VERTICAL LEADERSHIP COMPONENT MAP

Instructions:

1. Answer the following questions:
   - What are the student learning issues facing your school that need additional attention?
   - What content areas need to be given priority or need to be explored?
   - What dimension of the content is of concern or needs to be addressed?
   - What leadership practices (i.e., routines, tools, functions, or interactions) are presently being used to address your answers to the above questions?
   - What classroom practices are presently being used to address the above questions?
   - What subtask (routine microtask) gives support to your identified leadership practices?
2. Fill in the template with your responses as they seem fit.
3. Skip steps if you don't have responses.
4. Share your responses with team members to condense your and their insight into a single template.
5. Prioritize and categorize individual responses into a team response.
6. Narrow the focus to a single dimension of practice (i.e., teaching reading graphic organizers to fifth-grade students).

Example:

Vertical Leadership Component Map Tool	
Umbrella issues	Poor assessment results • *Reading scores are not where we would like them.* • *Maintaining mathematics while working to close the gap in other areas.* School improvement efforts • *Teachers buy into the building improvement plan.* • *Professional learning communities.*
Focus area (content) • Reading • Writing • Mathematics • Science • Social studies • Other academic areas as needed	*Reading improvement*
Dimension of practice • Content • Standards • Pedagogy • Components • Engagement • Social or behavioral	Teaching reading content *Teaching reading standards* Teaching reading methodologies (pedagogy) Teaching reading components Engaging students in authentic learning
Leadership practice • Routines • Tools • Leaders and followers • Interactions • Functions	*Standards in practice* *Quarterly assessment* *Walkthroughs* *Building improvement planning* *Two-week highlights*
Dimension of Practice: Teaching reading standards in the classroom	

SECTION B: IDENTIFY ADVICE NETWORK

> . . . [S]chool leaders should harness the power of the networks that they already have by listening to their key members—which is the greatest leadership technique of all.
>
> —Doug Reeves (2006c, p. 35)

TOOL: Advice Network Map

Introduction: Who Talks to Whom?

Doug Reeves (2006a) asked a group of Kansas school leaders recently whom would they ask for help if they had a hardware question about their computer. Whom would they ask if it was a software question? Would the people identified be one and the same or different people? In other words, would you go to the same person for help on how to cook a steak as you would someone who replaces the battery in your car? These two examples have clearly different skill sets and knowledge acquisitions.

We can ask the same type of questions regarding who talks to whom about instruction. Do teachers go to the same people for mathematics content knowledge as they do for reading content knowledge? For that matter, do they go to the same person for reading content as they do for reading instructional practices? By seeking advice from another person who in turn may seek advice from someone else, we begin to create what we can refer to as an *advice network*. An advice network is a set of people that connect with each other professionally on a regular basis within a dimension of practice.

Purpose: Network Maps Determine Influence

The purpose of networking maps, or surveys, is essentially to determine who the influential formal and informal leaders are within a dimension of practice. Identified advice networks give powerful insight into the dimension of practice you or your team is working on. In some cases, you might identify a person who is an informal leader who is getting a great deal of attention from followers. This leads the team through a discovery process of why followers are going to this person for advice.

Understanding, identifying, and deploying networks for positive results is the central challenge of leaders who seek to transform the status quo.

—Doug Reeves (2006c, p. 37)

In addition, the team might begin to ask how this person is practicing their leadership. Although it is a crude and vague instrument, the Advice

Network Map is a useful tool to launch interaction discussions. From a distributed perspective, the focus needs to be on the interdependencies of the leaders and followers (Spillane, 2004a).

Although actions are important, the shift to interactions needs to occur. Barabasi (2003) says real networks are self-organized independent actions that lead to spectacular emergent behaviors. Network maps are a fact and not a positive or negative fixation. Formal and informal leaders leverage, redesign, and influence networks. Leadership practices that influence networks are situational, meaning that leadership practices within various academic contents require a different leader or leadership approach.

> Teachers do not always identify the individuals who help in the performance of leadership routines or who have formal responsibility for a particular leadership function as influential leaders when it comes to their classroom work.
>
> —Spillane (2006a, p. 47)

It is important to keep in mind that the advice network changes each time you look at a different dimension of practice. It will change depending on content, routine, tools, structures, and other factors. Leaders' interactions are sometimes similar when crossing over to various dimensions of practice, but at the same time, there are variations in them as well. Some leaders focus on pedagogical strategies, whereas other leaders focus on setting direction (see also the section "Shaping of Leadership Functions Form").

Case Study: Influence, Not Position, May Determine Identified Leaders

In 2005, at the Kansas Exemplary Educators Network (KEEN) conference, Larry Wheeles, the Kansas Academy for Leadership in Technology Director, and I were doing a presentation titled "The Distributed Leadership Perspective's Impact on Classroom Practice." We asked the 100-plus exemplary educators, "Who do you perceive as the instructional leaders in your building?" What do you think was their response to this question? The overall response we heard was instructional coaches and peer teachers were the instructional leaders within their buildings. Another distributed leadership study that supports this informal data is one made of more than 100 elementary comprehensive school reform schools (Camburn, Rowan, & Taylor, 2003). Camburn and colleagues estimated that the responsibility of leadership functions were typically distributed across three to seven formally designated leadership positions per elementary school. Support coaches made up a large portion of these formal leaders.

> The majority of employees take their cues from a trusted colleague rather than from the boss, the employee manual, or a silver-tongued trainer.
>
> —Doug Reeves (2006c, p. 33)

"Do you perceive the principal as the instructional leader?" we asked the KEEN participants. They responded, "Yes," but not as much, or at least not in the same light, as the others they identified (McBeth & Wheeles, 2005b). Spillane and colleagues' (Spillane, Hallett, & Diamond, 2003) work with the Distributed Leadership Study further supports this. Only 8.3% of the teachers cited position alone when determining influential leaders of their classroom practices. Some people who perform leadership routines do not hold formal positions of leadership yet were influential on the teachers' classroom practices (Firestone, 1989; Reeves, 2006a; Spillane, 2006a).

Theory: Capital Influence

Spillane, Hallett, and Diamond (2003) identify four different forms of capital influencing teachers' classroom practices: human, social, cultural, and economic. They used these four forms of capital when questioning teachers during their Distributed Leadership Study done in the Chicago public school system. There were some interesting discoveries in the teachers' perceptions of their building principals and peer teachers. This data further supports the KEEN conference informal data.

The four forms of capital are:

- *Human capital* involves a person's knowledge, skills, and expertise.
- *Cultural capital* refers to a person's way of being and doing, interactive styles that are valued in particular contexts.
- *Social capital* refers to a person's social networks or connections, but also concerns the prevalence of norms such as trust, collaboration, and a sense of obligation among individuals in an organization.
- *Economic capital* includes money and other material resources, including books, curricular materials, and computers, among other things.

(Spillane, 2006a; Spillane, Hallett, & Diamond, 2003)

Teachers in the Distributed Leadership Study identified cultural capital (70.2%) as the form they associated with their building administrators. On the other hand, teachers identified other teachers within a mix of human (45%), social (50%), and cultural (59.5%) capital that were influential upon their classroom practices (Spillane, Hallett, & Diamond 2003).

These forms of capital can give valuable insight into the question, "What makes each of the people you have identified leaders?"

Interaction Patterns

The nature of the interactions among leaders and followers differs, depending on the subject (Spillane, Diamond, & Jita, 2003). The one key phrase we heard from the 100-plus KEEN participants was that the people they perceived as leaders depended on the subject area and grade level (also see *A Side-by-Side Content Comparison*). In large part, the academic content determines the number of people who perform a leadership routine. Research points to the fact that leadership practice interactions differ greatly between literacy and mathematics. In Figures 5.B.1 and 5.B.2, you can see sample graphics of the leader-follower interaction differences between mathematics (5.B.1) and reading (5.B.2) within a middle school. Notice the difference in the quantity of people who interact with each other as leaders and followers in the two charts. In addition, draw your attention to the two building principals, Janice K. and ZZ T. The associate principal, ZZ T., is formally in charge of attendance and discipline. What are the roles of the principals in these content maps? Lynn Z. is the literacy coach, and Karen J. is the math coordinator. What are their roles within these content maps? As you look over the charts, a number of questions may surface. If so, then you can see the power of network mapping. Network mapping enables you to see the lived interactions within your school around a particular dimension of practice such as reading content. The map generates questions that might otherwise be overlooked associated with the present leadership practices. Let us take a closer look at the interaction patterns within two content areas, literacy and mathematics.

Interaction Patterns: Literacy. Spillane and colleagues (Spillane, Diamond, & Jita, 2003) point out that building administrators often participate in routines within literacy-related dimensions of practice. Dimensions of practice associated with literacy have a balance between formal and informal leaders in their interactions with followers. Therefore, teachers play a much more essential role as leaders within literacy. Teachers within the school perceive those with formal coaching positions as valuable instructional leaders (Camburn et al., 2003).

Interaction Patterns: Mathematics. Building administrators participate less frequently in routines within mathematics-related dimensions of practice, yet formally, designated leaders play the roles of mathematics leaders. Unlike the teachers' involvement within literacy, teachers infrequently engage in leadership within mathematics. In addition, teachers

Figure 5.B.1   Math Content Networking Map

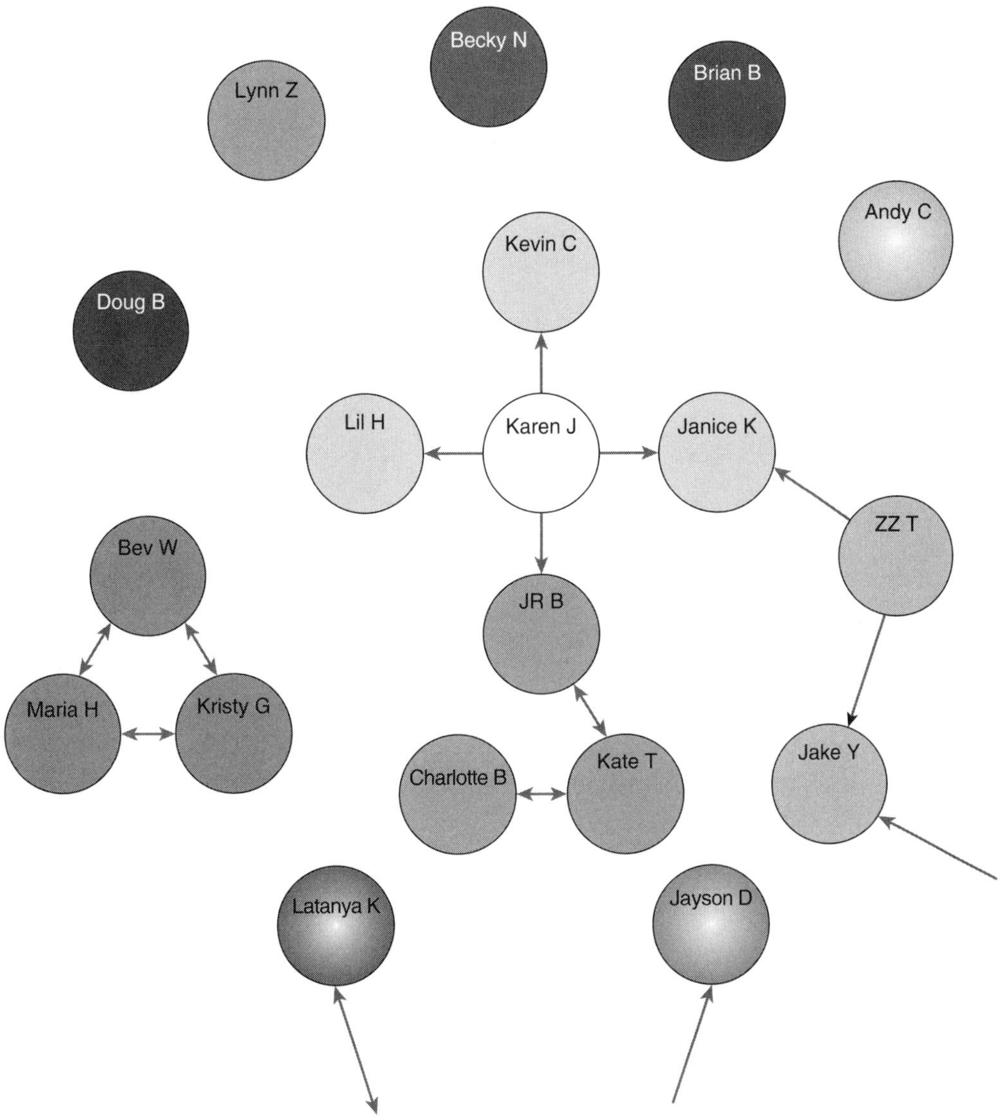

Source: McBeth & Wheeles (2005a).

often pursue external resources as legitimate sources of knowledge and ideas for instruction (Spillane, Diamond, & Jita, 2003).

Philosophy: Reading a Network Map

As we look over the network maps, we might see isolated *nodes* of contact (see Chart 5.B.1). Within this dimension of practice, these educators

Figure 5.B.2   Reading Content Networking Map

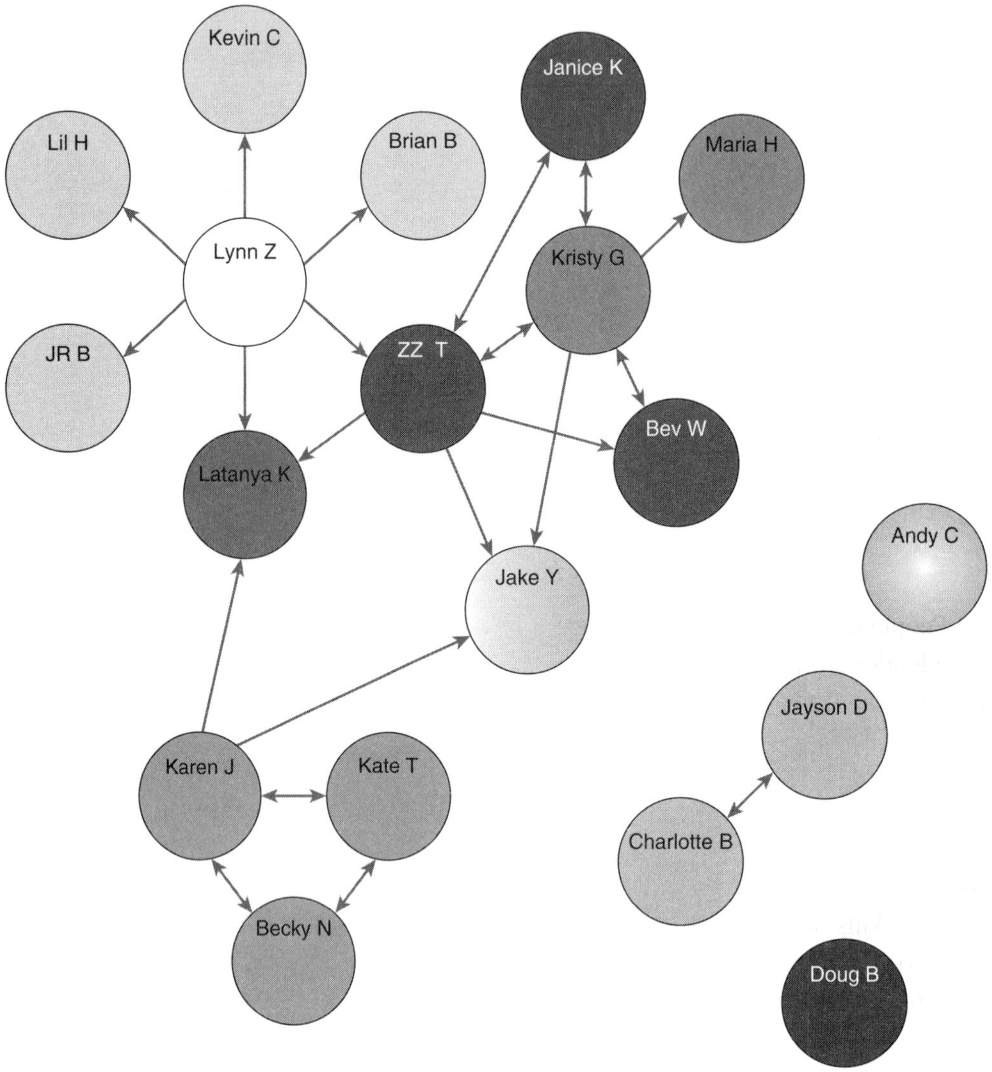

Source: McBeth & Wheeles (2005a).

are not making connection with other staff for some reason or another. There might be a logical explanation for some, but for others the team might want to explore the rationale for the isolation. We can see an example of an isolated node (Andy C.) in Figures 5.B.1 and 5.B.2

A map may also uncover *hubs*, which is a node with multiple connections to it. An example would be Kristy G. in Figure 5.B.2. A node might exhibit the characteristics of a *superhub*. An example of a super-hub would be Lynn Z. in Figure 5.B.2. A superhub is a node to which an exceptionally large number of other nodes and hubs are connected. Schools with systemic maturity and functioning within the Leadership Practice aspect have superhubs. However, on a rare occasion, super-hubs are within schools that function within another leadership aspect.

Chart 5.B.1 Network Theory (Barabasi, 2003)

- **Node:** Any single point of contact in a network.
- **Hub:** A node with multiple connections to it.
- **Superhub:** A node to which an exceptionally large number of other nodes and hubs are connected. Far-reaching direct and indirect impact.

People who represent a superhub are extremely valuable because they are a leader connected in such a way that they have a huge influence on most of the other hubs and nodes, even when separated by one or more nodes (Barabasi, 2003). In other words, they are able to influence the organization directly and indirectly, even when there is a degree of separation.

Leveraging Your Informal Leaders. Nurture your identified superhub leaders' skills and acknowledge them by giving them more opportunities to learn. Use their skills and knowledge by engaging them in coopera-tive opportunities. Learn from your identified leaders; listen not only to the content they deliver to others but also to how they communicate the message. There is a reason teachers follow these informal leaders. Try to discover their articulate and sometimes subtle methods. Support them and leverage their time so they can assist in the learning of others (see Chart 5.B.2). Doug Reeves (2006a, 2006b) encourages us to provide opportunities for positional advance-ment, but not to ever pressure them out of their classrooms. Great teach-ers are hard to replace, and sometimes we can remove them from the very environment that makes them great.

> School leaders should harness the power of networks by listening to their key members.
>
> —Doug Reeves (2006c, p. 35)

Chart 5.B.2 Leverage Your Superhub Effective Leaders

- Use their skills and knowledge.
- Learn from them.
- Listen to how they communicate.
- Discover their methods of leading.
- Support them.
- Leverage their time to assist others.
- Acknowledge them.
- Offer them advanced training.

Caution: Toxic and Contentious Hubs

Toxic Hubs

Be aware that at times a hub or superhub might be led by toxic leaders. These might be people who are not competent within the dimension of practice for which they are being recognized. They may be leading in contradiction to the school's mission, vision, and goals, purposefully or aimlessly. In other words, they are leading a set of followers down a path that may be counterproductive to the school's mission (Reeves, 2006c).

Contentious Hubs

An isolated node might be cut off from the others because there is a point of contention. This person maybe unwilling to share his or her knowledge or expertise. On another note, a contentious node might be isolated because others try to avoid the person. Fellow staff might try not to serve on the same team, committees, or activities. This could be for a number of reasons, which your team will need to honestly decipher.

Lost Hubs

Isolation from the other staff may create lost nodes or hubs. Sometimes hubs can be identified by vicinity within a school building. A school building may have multiple floors or hallways, which contribute to who talks to whom. High school freshman academies, middle school teaming or elementary looping can be factors associated with lost hubs. Location in a building might not allow for neighborly networks. Mobile buildings have caused isolation of many quality educators.

Sample Survey of CallOway County School

Name: _____

Which of these sources are you most likely to turn to for reading strategies?
(Please rank 1–4)

____ **Instructional Materials**

____ **Internet Resources**

____ **Standards and Curriculum**

____ **People** (Please list)

_____
_____
_____
_____

Please check your predominant assignment.

___ Language arts   ___ Math   ___ Science   ___ Social studies   ___ Other

Which person do you turn to the most?

_____

Why do you choose this person? Check all that apply

Application expertise	Approachability	Content	Knowledge	Proximity	Other (Please explain)
☐	☐	☐	☐	☐	_____
☐	☐	☐	☐	☐	_____
☐	☐	☐	☐	☐	_____
☐	☐	☐	☐	☐	_____
☐	☐	☐	☐	☐	_____

Sample Results of Calloway County School

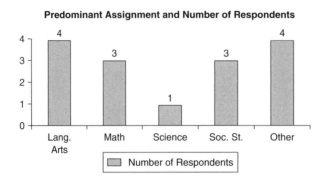

Predominant Assignment and Number of Respondents

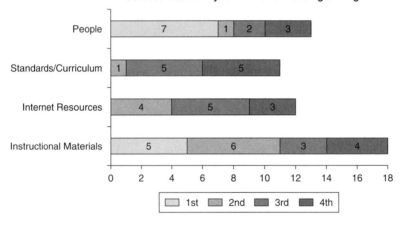

Sources Most Likely to Turn to for Reading Strategies

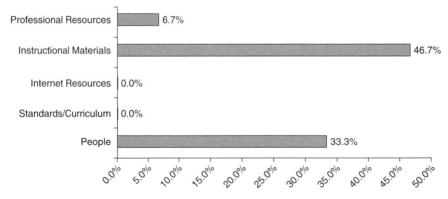

First Choice Percent for "Turn to" Sources

"Turn To" People - Top Selection

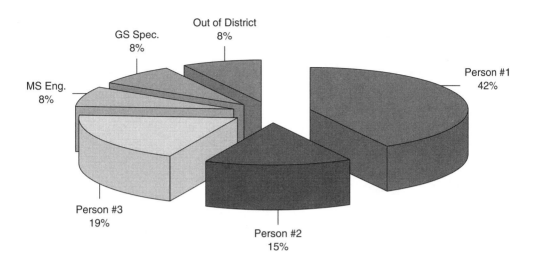

GS Spec.
8%

Out of District
8%

MS Eng.
8%

Person #1
42%

Person #3
19%

Person #2
15%

"Turn To" People - All Selection

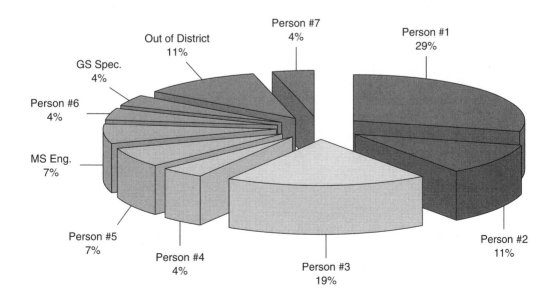

Person #7
4%

Out of District
11%

Person #1
29%

GS Spec.
4%

Person #6
4%

MS Eng.
7%

Person #5
7%

Person #4
4%

Person #3
19%

Person #2
11%

Source: Northwest Kansas, KDLA.

Create Your Own Survey

Creating your own survey is a great idea. In doing so, keep these key questions in mind:

- What is the focus content area (i.e., reading, mathematics, science)?

- What is the dimension of practice (i.e., pedagogy, engagement, content)?

- Where do teachers go for instructional resources (i.e., curriculum, instructional material, test items)?

- Who goes to whom within these dimensions (i.e., Joe [follower] goes to Linda [leader] for reading pedagogy)?

- When you have a work-related challenge, whom do you ask for advice?

- How frequently do they have these interactions?

- Are these formal or informal interactions (i.e., faculty meetings, teacher lounge)?

In addition:

- Use the surveys to map informal conversations around other school improvement issues.

- Consider a Web-based survey by a third party server to guarantee confidentially.

- Use the results of a network map to create a visual chart of some sort. Figures 5.B.1 and 5.B.2 are examples of Web graphics. These are good models for mapping the leader-follower interactions. However, any graphic organizer can work as long as it creates a visual representation of the interactions.

ADVICE NETWORK MAP

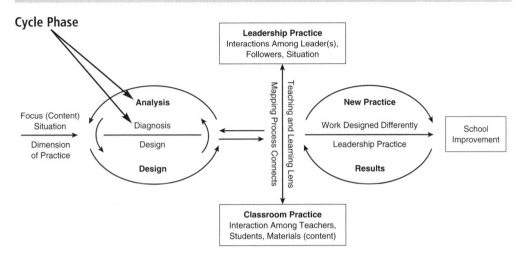

Cycle Phase

Purpose of Tool:

Networking maps help determine who the influential formal and informal leaders are within a dimension of practice. Identified advice networks give powerful insight into the dimension of practice you and your team are working on.

Facilitator Help:

1. Identify the dimension of practice that will be network mapped.

2. Have individuals on the team respond to the four key questions on their own.

3. Explain the function of each column to the group members.

4. In small groups (4 to 6 people), come to a consensus on the answers to the key questions.

5. After a designated amount of time, engage in full-group dialogue. Have each small group share their insights to the team as a whole. Record this on a chart.

6. In the same small groups, have the members respond to the critical questions. Have them again share their insights with the team, and record this information on a chart.

7. Create a flowchart that represents the interactions between leaders and followers.

Note: By using a computerized template, everyone is able to see the responses, and edits.

Tips:	**Resources:**
Keep the Advice Network Map visible and available for team members as you continue through the Information Cycle.	• One template per person • Flip-chart paper and markers • Directions handout
Caution:	**Sample Critical Questions:**

Take caution when identifying leaders and followers. Prior to engaging in this particular tool, identify with whom the list will be shared and if shared, could someone be hurt by its contents? If your answer is yes, take extreme caution.
The intent of this tool is not to harm any individuals or groups. Engage in the use of this tool with individuals or teams who have high levels of trust.
	Knowledge Questions
	   — Who is involved (leaders and followers)?
	   — What do they know?
	
	Comprehension Questions
	   — Why do they follow . . . ?
	
	Analysis Questions
	   — How do you know?
	   — Compared with the goal, is this routine meeting the needs?
	   — What evidence supports . . . ?
	   — How do you know an individual is a leader or a follower in this situation?

Template: Page 243

ADVICE NETWORK MAP

Instructions:

1. Whom do you perceive as the leaders within the identified dimension of practice? Write their names in the space provided.
2. How do you know the people you identified are leaders? Identify the actions they take as leaders and the interactions they have with others routinely within the identified dimension of practice. Place your responses in the space provided.
3. What in particular makes each person a leader (i.e., vicinity to others, expertise, formal positional leader)? Place response in the space provided.
4. Whom does this identified leader lead? Place responses in space provided.
5. Share your results with other team members.
6. Create a flowchart that represents who interacts with whom.

Example:

Advice Network Map			
Dimension of Practice: Math comprehension for fifth grade			
Who are the leaders?	**How do you know the people you identified are leaders?** *Actions and interactions*	**What makes each of the people you identify a leader?** *List more than their personal attributes.*	**Who are the followers for each leader?** *Defined by interactions*
Fred B.	*Facilitates grade-level meetings and focuses on math*	*20 years of teaching math*	*Jim, Jack, Kent, and John*
Jane C.	*I see people talking to her about math comprehension in the teacher workroom.*	*I do not know.* *???*	*Sue, Joan, Linda, Judi, Norma, and Sid*
How were these leaders assigned to their leadership positions? *Fred has been here the longest.*			
How do leaders (teacher-leaders) in your school know what is expected of them? *I don't know?*			
Where did they get their leadership skills? *Fred attended a facilitators' training. Jane appears to be a born leader.*			
What kind of support do your leaders (teacher-leaders) get? *Fred attends a weekly leadership meeting. Jane does not that I know about.*			
How do we make sure the appropriate leaders and followers are engaged in the enhancement and changing of teachers' classroom practices? *We need to focus more training and support on those folks that are leading.*			

Note that this person did not have all the answers, but when shared with other team members, these answers will most likely contribute essential insight leading to a joint expanded version of the template. Also note that the last question's response is very vague, but will frame a discussion when the team addresses bridging the gap between diagnosis and design later in the Improvement Cycle.

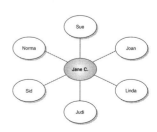

SECTION C: DIAGNOSE PRACTICE: ROUTINE

> *The first responsibility of a leader is to define reality.*
>
> —Max DePree, *The Art of Leadership* (2004)

There was a man named Johan who had a malfunctioning watch, a family heirloom. He asked the man behind the counter, "Why does my watch not work?" The man took the watch, shook it, and then held it up against his ear. He replied to the customer, "I don't know." The customer asked, "Can you repair it?" The man opened the back of the watch and said, "I don't see how the system works, but I can sell you a new watch."

Johan went home and laid out a white cloth on the countertop and began to disassemble the watch. At first, he divided the components of the watch into five distinctive parts. Each part appeared to have its own purpose; turning the hands, maintain pace, and so forth. He used a magnifying glass to explore the intricacies of the microparts that made up each of the five parts. He discovered how the parts functioned and how the microparts interplayed with each other. Upon reassembling the parts, Johan was able to see how each part functioned within the system. He was able to discover why the watch was not working as it was intended.

How many educators would buy the new watch instead of repairing the old one? How many educators would have kept the old malfunctioning watch and not fixed it? Johan would not have made his discovery without understanding the interworkings of the watch. The same is true for leaders. If we do not explore the intricate components of our leadership practices, we will not be able to see why our system is not functioning in the manner we prefer.

There are three tools within the Systems of Practice section. Each tool used in seclusion serves teams fittingly for the exploration of the intricacies of leadership practice. However, the three tools used as a collective will create a more comprehensive picture. In other words, each tool strengthens the next when collectively combined in a systematic manner.

The Identified Leadership Practices tool will create a dialogue about what practices are being deployed within a single dimension of practice—in other words, *an opportunity to look at the parts.* Upon the discovery of the interrelationships of their identified routines, tools, people, and functions, teams tend to have a need to dig deeper into the lived interactions. How does each of these routines play out within the school? The Routine Microanalysis tool enables teams to explore the intricacies of the routines—*an opportunity to see how the micro parts make the bigger parts function.* Once teams have dismantled the dimension of practice, made their discoveries, there is a need to *reassemble the intricate components into some meaningful depiction of effectiveness or ineffectiveness.* The Systems of Practice tool depicts that picture, enabling teams to diagnose their overall leadership practice effectiveness within their identified dimension of practice.

TOOL: Identified Leadership Practices

Introduction: Discovering Leadership Practices

In Section A, within the Vertical Leadership Component Map tool, we identified "teaching reading standards in the classroom" as a dimension of practice. What might be some leadership routines that exist associated with this dimension of practice? What identifies your response as a routine? How does it happen? These are a few of the critical questions asked of the Pleasanton Middle School leadership team.

> *A routine is "a repetitive, recognizable pattern of interdependent actions carried out by multiple actors."*
>
> —Feldman and Pentland (2003, p. 96)

Purpose: Teaching and Learning Focus

Leadership practice anchored within a vision for teaching and learning has a superior opportunity to enhance overall student performance. Therefore, we need to determine whether and how routines connect with teaching and learning. The Identified Leadership Practices tool helps give focus to the leadership routines that give shape to teaching and learning within a particular dimension of practice. The tool assists in organizing the functions that frame the routines and the tools used to mediate the interactions. The identified leaders and followers who are engaged in the interactions help complete the tool.

Case Study: Pleasanton Middle School Discoveries

The Pleasanton Middle School leadership team was able to make a number of practice discoveries by using the Identified Leadership Practices tool (see Example 5.C.1). One in particular was how the middle school principal, Markus Long, had created the "Two-Week Highlights" (see page 115) as a leadership routine and its value to the staff. He created the routine with the intended purpose of

- monitoring instruction and progress,
- developing teachers' knowledge and skills,
- providing encouragement,
- providing recognition and support,
- developing a sense of accountability for performance, and
- sustaining a vision and maintaining high expectations.

Example 5.C.1	Identified Leadership Practices (Pleasanton Middle School)		
Dimension of Practice: Teaching reading standards in the classroom			
Routine	**Functions**	**Tools**	**Leaders and followers**
Walkthrough	*Human Development* – Monitoring instruction and progress – Developing sense of accountability for performance – *Providing encouragement, recognition, and support*	Walkthrough observation instrument (district protocol)	Principal, assistant principal, and instructional coach or teachers
Standards in Practice	*Organizational Development* – Building a culture that de-privatizes classroom practice, supports collaboration among teachers, and maintains high expectations *Human Development* – Developing teachers' knowledge and skill, both individually and collectively	Lesson plan, Standards in Practice worksheet	Instructional coach or teachers
Quarterly Assessment	*Human Development* – Monitoring instruction and progress	Quarterly assessment, data reports	Principal, teachers, and instructional coach
Two-Week Highlights	*Human Development* – Monitoring instruction and progress – Developing teachers' knowledge and skill – Providing encouragement, recognition, and support – Developing sense of accountability for performance *Setting Direction* – Sustaining a *vision* – Maintaining *high expectations*	Two-Week Highlights form	Principal and instructional coach or teachers
Building Improvement Planning	*Setting Direction* – Constructing and maintaining a vision – Getting cooperative commitment for organizational goals	Improvement Plan template	Principal and central office or teachers

Note: Italics = To a lesser extent

The Two-Week Highlights Routine

Markus Long, the principal at Pleasanton Middle School, created this routine out of a necessity to monitor the instructional practices and progress of his teachers; to help to develop their knowledge and skill; to provide encouragement, recognition, and support for their efforts; to create a sense of accountability for performance associated with the school's vision; and to maintain the high expectation of teaching and student learning.

The Two-Week Highlights Worksheet consisted of a series of standard biweekly questions that addressed the teachers' progress with the strategies that were outlined within the School Improvement Plan. In addition, there were a few new questions added each cycle. These questions solicited teacher responses on how they were using the knowledge they gained in the weekly Standards in Practice sessions.

The Two-Week Highlights Worksheet was electronically sent to the teachers every two weeks by the principal. The teachers in turn reflected on their classroom practice over the last two weeks and responded to the questions. They were sent back to the principal, who read them that evening and returned them to the teachers the following day with detailed notes of support and advice.

Each two weeks, the principal would meet with his instructional coach, and together they would lay out a plan of support for the next two weeks for any teacher who appeared to need additional help.

Markus had put the routine in place by design with no input from his staff, and therefore, one discovery the teachers on the team made through the Identified Leadership Practices tool was why this routine existed and how it fit into the dimension of practice system. Nearly all the teachers identified the Two-Week Highlights as the routine that enhanced and changed their classroom practices.

An interesting side note might be the discoveries made at another school (Grant) within the same district. The Two-Week Highlights routine did not exist within the Grant school, and there was not another accountability routine. There was no routine for maintaining high expectations. In turn, the Grant staff was not able to pinpoint a routine that truly enhanced and changed their classroom practices. Upon this discovery, the principal and a team of teachers began the process of creating a routine that would similarly address the functions that gave shape to the Two-Week Highlights. They knew they did not want to replicate the Two-Week Highlights because their situation at their school was much different from that of Pleasanton Middle School.

Another interesting difference in the two schools was the structures that shaped the "standards in practice" routine (see the following sidebar.). Pleasanton Middle School was able to meet once a week to practice this routine, whereas Grant met only once a month. Thus, the Grant staff met maybe 7 to 8 times a year to practice this routine, whereas the Pleasanton Middle School staff was able to meet 28 to 32 times a year.

The Standards in Practice Routine

Teachers bring their assignments and the work done by students from the classroom to a weekly or monthly team meeting. In a six-step facilitated process, teachers discover whether their assignments are rigorously aligned with standards, what instruction their students need to reach standards, and how to change their practice so that all students are successful. The Standards in Practice form is a tool that is used to evaluate the classroom assignments, ensuring that all activities in classrooms parallel the state's standards. The form works by engaging teachers in examining their assignments, as well as in the resulting student work. You can discover more on this from The Education Trust (2006) (http://www2.edtrust.org/EdTrust/SIP+Professional+Development/Standards+in+practice.htm).

To be able to make these discoveries about leadership practices, facilitators need to consider the following key points:

- Ask critical questions often, more than once, and in different ways.
- Vocabularies may differ from person to person even within the same school.
- Be prepared for divergent perspectives on the same practices.
- Clarify how the tools are used. Tool use can vary depending on the participant. Does the tool help in mediating the routine?
- Identify the structure. Does the structure support or limit the effectiveness of the leadership routines?
- Does the leadership practice enhance and change classroom practice?

IDENTIFIED LEADERSHIP PRACTICE

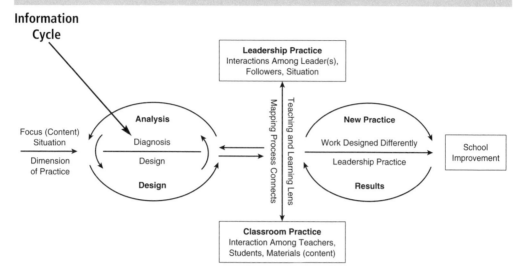

Purpose of Tool:

Helps give focus to the leadership routines that shape teaching and learning within a particular dimension of practice. Organizing the functions that frame the routines and the tools used to mediate interactions. The tool identifies leaders and followers who are engaged in the leadership interactions.

Facilitator Help:

1. In small groups (4 to 6 people), have participants respond on flip-chart paper to the following questions. Be prepared to define routine, function, tools, leader, and followers. Use examples to clarify expectations as needed. Hand out a Leadership Practice Diagnosis Card to each team member (see Resources).
   a. What are the routines for this dimension of practice?
   b. How do you know these are routines?
   c. Who is responsible for the execution of these routines?
   d. Who are the followers? Who are the leaders?
   e. What tools are used to mediate the interactions between the leaders and the followers?
   f. What leadership functions address this routine and tool? (Not the intended function, but the lived functions.)

2. Have each small group share their insights to the team as a whole. Record this on a chart.

3. Combine the responses on one Identified Leadership Practices template.

4. In the same small groups, have the members respond to the critical questions. Have them again share their insights with the team, and record this information on a chart.
   a. What did we discover?
   b. What were the key points that we discussed?
   c. How do these leadership routines connect to teaching and learning?
   d. As a whole, do the routines in the dimension of practice enhance and change classroom practice? How do you know?
   e. What do we *not* know that we would like to know?

Tips:	Resources:
Always give more credence to the dialogue than to filling in the template. Sometimes groups get intent on filling in the blanks and thus sacrifice the true dialogue needed to gain mutual understanding that will assist in the later stages of design.	• One template per person • Flip-chart paper and markers • Directions handout and Leadership Practice Diagnosis Card • *Note:* It is also useful to have the directions and template electronically displayed.
Alternative Use:	**Critical Questions:**
Use the tool when teams jump to design without diagnosis. Use the tool to prevent unnecessary overlap, replication, or functional misdirection.	• What are we doing (routines)? • Who is involved (leaders and followers)? • What is the purpose (function)?

Templates: Pages 244–245

IDENTIFIED LEADERSHIP PRACTICE

Instructions:

1. Select a dimension of practice.
2. Reflect on the following questions:
   a. What are the routines for this dimension of practice?
   b. How do I know these are routines?
   c. Who is responsible for the execution of these routines?
   d. Who are the followers? Who are the leaders?
   e. What tools are used to mediate the interactions between leaders and followers?
   f. What leadership functions addresses this routine and tool? (Not the intended function, but the lived functions.)
3. Write your responses to each reflection in their corresponding columns (routines, functions, tools, and leaders and followers). Use additional templates as needed.
4. Reflect on the following questions:
   a. What did I discover (celebrate or concern)?
   b. I was surprised with . . .
   c. What were some of the key points I would want to share with others?
   d. How do these leadership routines connect to teaching and learning?
   e. As a whole, do the routines in the dimension of practice enhance and change classroom practice? How do I know?
   f. What do I *not* know that I would like to know?

Example:

Identified Leadership Practices			
Dimension of Practice: Student engagement			
Routine	**Functions**	**Tools**	**Leaders and Followers**
Instructional Practice Inventory (IPI)	*Human Development* – Monitoring progress	IPI IPI Data Profile Progress Graphs	Outside certified IPI observer Principal and all staff
Four professional development days	*Human Development* – Developing teachers' knowledge *Organizational Development* – Procuring and distributing resources	Multiple handouts by trainers	Various visiting trainers
Building Improvement Planning	*Setting Direction* – Constructing vision – Getting cooperative commitment for organizational goals	Building Improvement Plan	Principal and building improvement team Followers?

What did I discover upon reflection of this dimension of practice (celebrate or concern)?

Very little to *celebrate,* but we did address all three functions. *Concerns:* We hardly addressed the three functions adequately. Data shows a decrease in student performance gains on IPI data. *Concern:* I wonder if the professional development days need further support in the classroom. As a teacher, when we review the IPI data graphs, I am not sure what to do with the data. The routine does not change my classroom practice. I wonder if staff could share what is working in their classrooms and what is not.

Notes:

TOOL: Routine Microanalysis Chart

Introduction: Routine Microanalysis as a Diagnostic Tool

"Okay, aren't we getting just a little too detailed here? After all, we have identified the routines." This was a statement made by a Pleasanton central office administrator when working with the "teaching reading standards in the classroom" dimension of practice mentioned earlier.

From a distributed perspective, exploring leadership practice is not an easy task. Teams and individuals on a number of occasions have said this is hard work and creates some difficult discussions. This is in part because we have rarely had professional conversations about leadership practice; however, if we are to get to the root causes of our practices, positive or negative, it is essential that we explore the depths of the conscious and, more important, the unconscious leadership practices.

In science, we often use a microscope to view what we cannot see with the naked eye. The small microscopic parts make up a larger organism. We can say the same about our leadership practices within our schools. Sometimes we cannot see what is right in front of our eyes because it is too microscopic. If we intend for our leadership practices to positively influence teachers' classroom practices, we need to use a microscope to inspect the micro bits that make up the larger organism (routines).

> *You can't **expect** what you don't **inspect**.*
>
> —Peter Senge and colleagues (1994)

Purpose: Day-to-Day Work

The Routine Microanalysis tool can serve as a diagnostic tool for assessing leadership in schools so that it takes us directly to leadership practice—the day-to-day work of leading a school. Spillane (2004b) refers to this as the "lived leadership practices." As a diagnostic device, the distributed perspective, beginning with the Leader-Plus aspect, presses us to investigate the *leadership routines* in the lived reality of schools. Peter Gronn's (2002a) view of distributed leadership holds that structures and the routine interactions are essential as a paired partnership when working within a distributed perspective. With this implication, we must explore the depths of the interactions within a routine. These smaller interactions are referenced here as *microtasks*. Therefore, a microtask is a subtask that, with other subtasks, defines a larger task or routine.

Theory: Sequenced and Coordinated Microtask

Routines involve a number of interdependent, sequenced components, illustrating how leadership practices consciously stretch over coordinated microtasks (Spillane, 2006a). Each microtask depends on resources generated from a prior microtask. Multiple interdependent microtasks, arranged sequentially, are critical to the performance of the leadership routine (Figure 5.C.1).

Philosophy: Understanding the Interactions

Keep in mind that more routines or microtasks do not ensure enhanced and changed teacher practices. The quality of the interactions within the microtask enhances and changes teaching practices. It is only when we analyze the collective microtasks that we can see how the routine takes shape. This can sometimes be challenging for the reason that often the microtasks distribute over several different leaders (Spillane et al., 2001).

The Routine Microanalysis Chart is a tool to organize a team's thinking in analysis of a routine right down to the interaction that shapes the routine. The dialogue is very essential at this point. Filling in the blanks should be only a third of the efforts associated with this tool. The interactions discussion must get to the very essence of the purpose and impact of each microtask, each person's role, and each tool that mediates the interaction.

Figure 5.C.1   Microtask Interdependence to Routines

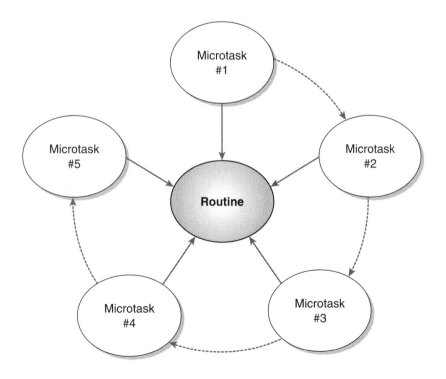

Case Study: Pleasant Middle School Microtask

Let us look at two of Pleasanton Middle School's routines (Examples 5.C.2 and 5.C.3), which were identified earlier within the dimension of practice "teaching reading standards in the classroom." There is one noticeable similarity between the two Routine Microanalysis Charts; all the identified leaders are formal leaders (principal and instructional coach). There is, however, one exception: In the Standards in Practice routine, teachers took the lead in the lesson plan analysis. Markus, as you may recall from the Leadership Impact Survey Case Study in Chapter 3, had moved his team to the Leader-Plus aspect via the Leader Superhero aspect. He did so by practicing routines such as Standards in Practice. By doing so, Markus was able to set the stage for de-privatizing classroom

Example 5.C.2 Routine Microanalysis Chart		
Routine: Standards in Practice		
Dimension of Practice: Teaching reading standards in the classroom		
Microtask	**People**	**Tools**
Invite teacher.	Instructional coach	
Schedule meeting time.	Instructional coach	Schedule
Distribute Standards in Practice form.	Instructional coach	Standards in Practice form
Analyze lesson plan. This is done as a whole faculty. A teacher presents the lesson and there is a question-and-answer session. Teachers talking about the teachers practices in association with standards being taught in the classroom. Instructional coach maintains the focus.	Teachers and instructional coach	Lesson plan, Standards in Practice form
Written analyses of the dialogue from the session are created.	Instructional coach	Standards in Practice form
Distribute analyses to all staff including principal.	Instructional coach	Standards in Practice form
Monitor application.	Principal and instructional coach	Two-Week Highlights, lesson plan

Example 5.C.3	Routine Microanalysis Chart	

Routine: The Two-Week Highlights

Dimension of Practice: Teaching reading standards in the classroom

Microtask	People	Tools
Principal receives the Standards of Practice forms from the weekly meetings.	Instructional coach	Standards in Practice form
Add the standards in practice learning to the Two-Week Highlights questions.	Principal	Two-Week Highlights form (Some questions are always on the form and related to the building improvement plan.)
Send out the highlights form electronically every two weeks.	Principal	Two-Week Highlights form and e-mail
Teachers reflect on classroom practice and respond to the questions. Form returned to principal signed.		Two-Week Highlights form
Principal reviews all forms and writes critiques back to teachers on their practices. Done in one night at home.	Principal	
Principal and instructional coach meet the next morning. Instructional coach assigned to teachers who appeared to need help as a result of the principal's review of the highlights.	Principal and instructional coach	Critiqued Two-Week Highlights
Highlights returned to teachers		
One-on-one follow-up with teachers in need of assistance.	Principal and instructional coach	

practice by establishing time for the teachers to dialogue about each other's classroom practice.

It is also important to note that the instructional coach offered direct instructional support, thus the instructional coach led the human development function of the routines. The principal, on the other hand, led the microtask associated with the Setting Direction function. A quick check back to Example 5.C.1 lets us see the connection between the identified functions and their deployment within the microtasks here.

Another valuable insight discovered here is how the two routines, when broken down into microtasks, depict a point of overlap, as if in partnership with each other. The Standards in Practice routine's final step is to monitor the application of the Standards in Practice lessons.

ROUTINE MICROANALYSIS CHART

Information Cycle

```
                              Leadership Practice
                          Interactions Among Leader(s),
                               Followers, Situation

                          Analysis              New Practice
Focus (Content)
   Situation              Diagnosis      Work Designed Differently      School
                                                                     Improvement
Dimension                 Design             Leadership Practice
of Practice
                          Design                  Results

                             Classroom Practice
                          Interaction Among Teachers,
                          Students, Materials (content)
```

(vertical labels: Mapping Process Connects / Teaching and Learning Lens)

Purpose of Tool:

The chart serves as a diagnostic tool for assessing the lived interactions of the day-to-day leadership microtask. The tool allows us the opportunity to explore the depths of the interactions within a routine. Therefore, it defines the larger leadership task or routine.

Facilitator Help:

1. Supply each member of the team with several Routine Microanalysis templates.

2. Divide the team up into groups of three to four people. Have each group analyze a routine. *Note:* Each group should work on the same routine.

3. After each analysis, have the groups share as a whole. Come to a consensus on the list of microtasks, tools, and people. Track them on flip-chart paper or projected computer images.

4. Be prepared for the team to identify more than one person within the same routine and even the same microtask. Identify how the multiple leaders are coperforming the leadership practice. A more in-depth analysis can be done by the team in this area by using Multiple Leaders Practice Diagnosis tool.

5. Ask these critical questions to determine what the team's next steps will be. Use the Microanalysis Chart Reflection tool as a mediating device.
   a. What has become clear to you as a result of your reflection upon this activity?
   b. What needs to happen with each of the routines (i.e., keep, enhance, create new)?
   c. What needs to happen with each of the microtasks (i.e., keep, enhance, create new)?

6. Be prepared with additional tools to keep the team's diagnosis interactions going. The team may want to jump to reshaping the practice. This urge needs to be curbed until your diagnosis is completed. Ultimately, you want to put effective and efficient practices in place by design, but not before it's time.

Tips:	Resources:
Be prepared to ask critical questions to deepen participants' thinking each time they identify a component (microtask) that brings life to the routine. Keep the list of critical questions on hand to use as a tool to bring the team members to a higher order of thinking.	• Several templates per person • Additional tool templates (as needed) • Flip-chart paper and markers • Directions handout
Next Steps:	**Sample Critical Questions:**

Team diagnosing dimension of practice –
    Tool: Systems of Practice
Team identifies need for change –
    Tool: Practice Gap Summary
    Tool: Forecasting Leadership Initiatives
      Grid
Team needs to identify new solutions –
    Tool: Alternative Solutions
      Applied Chart
Team discovers multiple leaders doing different task –
    Tool: Multiple Leaders Practice
      Diagnosis
	• What is the purpose of . . . ?
	• Is this . . . essential for the overall success of the routine?
	• Are the right people involved?
	• Is there a . . . that is missing?
	• How do we know this is making a difference?

Template: Page 246

ROUTINE MICROANALYSIS CHART

Instructions:

1. Select a leadership routine, a dimension of practice, or both.
2. Systematically list all interdependent and sequenced components of your identified practice, illustrating how the practices are carried out. These are quick and to-the-point statements (i.e., notify teacher of rotations, 3-minute laser talks).
3. List the corresponding leaders in the people column (i.e., Principal, John Doe). *Optional:* Some teams have identified the intended recipient of the interaction, when applicable. For example, the microtask identifies a *3-minute laser talk.* The leader identified is the *principal.* The identified follower is a *teacher.*
4. Identify the tools used to either manage the microtask or used to create the interactions between the leaders and followers.
5. Repeat steps 1 through 4 for each routine if you are diagnosing the effectiveness of a dimension of practice.
6. Reflect on the completed chart(s). *Optional:* Use the Microanalysis Chart Reflection tool.

Example:

Routine Microanalysis Chart		
Routine: Walkthrough		
Dimension of Practice: Teaching reading standards in the classroom		
Microtask	**People**	**Tools**
Monitoring rotation list	Principal	Rotation list
Schedule walkthrough	Principal	Written form letter
Notify teachers	Principal	
Do walkthrough (goals-focused)	Principal or instructional coach	District walkthrough observation form
Analyze classroom practices		District walkthrough observation form
Share in writing walkthrough observation	Instructional coach	District walkthrough observation form
Schedule meeting with teacher	Instructional coach	
Coaching session with teacher on observation	Instructional coach	Walkthrough observation form
Post meeting notes	Instructional coach or principal	Walkthrough coaching data form

Notes:

TOOL: Systems of Practice

Introduction: Teachers Use a System of Practice, so Why Not Leaders?

Does a geography teacher teach about maps without ever using a map? Does a geography teacher teach students without creating some sort of interactive reflection or assessment to ensure learning is in fact happening? The answer to these questions would, of course, be "no." Teachers deploy a series of classroom practices associated with the students' stages of social and academic development. The teacher uses strategies according to the goals, mission, and desired learning outcomes of the school, as well as tactics that maintain student engagement, order, and a culture of high expectations. Considering the intricate system of routines and tools of teaching and learning from this perspective gives a holistic view of a teacher's practices. A *system of practice* is a representation of how routines and tools mediate the interaction between teacher and student in the instructional practice of the school (Halverson, 2003, 2005b). Similarly understood are the interactions between leaders and followers.

Purpose: Dimension of Practice in Relationship

The Systems of Practice Interactions tool helps us define a network of leadership routines, tools, and structures that clarify a single dimension of practice that influences the practice of followers. It creates a visual representation of the lived interactions of leaders and followers. In turn, we are able to diagnose the leadership aspect and culture that exist in association with a single dimension of practice. This tool serves to reveal powerfully the reality of teams' leadership practices. It also adds to our ability to determine whether the practices, used individually or together, are adequately addressing the situation. One common discovery is how, if at all, the routine effectively addresses the *organizational development function,* particularly the de-privatization of classroom practice.

Theory: Creating Systems

In schools, the practice of teachers and students is composed of their involvement in the system of teaching and learning. Whereas researchers have paid considerable attention to the nature of the system of practice in schools from an instructional perspective (Ball & Cohen, 1996; McLaughlin & Talbert, 1993), school leaders, formal or informal, stand in a different relation than do teachers to this instructional system of practice. Not unlike the need for a classroom teaching system of practice, so there is a need for a leadership system of practice.

Leaders typically do *not* engage directly with students, but they do interact with teachers who do. Halverson (2005b) brings light to the system of practice framework by suggesting that leaders use tools and routines to establish structures that facilitate the closure of professional networks among teachers, which in turn builds a professional community. A system of practice, therefore, clearly encompasses the Leadership Practice aspect of leader-follower interactions and suggests that the Leader-Plus aspect maximizes the creation of a professional community (Halverson, 2005a; Spillane, 2006a).

Halverson (2005b) suggests that a handful of routines, structures, and tools that shape the school as a whole makes up a system of practice, thus creating a professional community. This is good, but it is awkward when thinking about leadership practices within the scope of various content and dimensions (i.e., situation). Ogawa and Bossert (1995) refer to a system of practice as the structural constraint through which leadership, teaching, and learning "flow" in a given school context. In other words, the situation frames the interactions of practice and, in our case, it is a dimension of practice. I have defined a system of practice as a network of leadership routines, tools, and structures that resides within a single dimension of practice that influences the practice of followers. Although not in conflict with Halverson's use of systems of practice, this I define slightly differently to meet the context of the Dimension of Practice concept outlined within this toolbox.

Philosophy: The Importance of Addressing All Three Leadership Functions

As mentioned in Chapter 3, school leaders must consciously consider how and when they are addressing the three leadership functions (setting direction, human development, and organizational development). A single leadership routine often will not suffice to enhance and change a teacher's classroom practice. This is in large part due to the fact that a single routine rarely addresses all three essential leadership functions. When two or more leadership practices are purposefully pooled together to address a single dimension of practice, a system of practice is created. Systems of practices, therefore, need structures, routines, and tools that address all three leadership functions.

Case Study: Five Interrelated Routines

Pleasanton Middle School engaged in five leadership routines within the dimension of practice "teaching reading standards in the classroom."

1. Building Improvement Plan
2. Standards in Practice

3. Two-Week Highlights

4. Walkthroughs

5. Quarterly Assessment

Pleasanton Middle School used these five routines in an attempt to enhance teachers' abilities to teach reading standards within their class-rooms. The five routines clearly approached their modes of interactions very differently. We reviewed two of the five routines within the Routine Microanalysis tool. Each routine created a unique interaction between leaders and followers. When combined together, all these routines and interactions created an effective system of practice.

To remove one of these routines from the system would make the system ineffective. This system of practice worked well for them. Some people might even say Pleasant Middle School modeled a professional learning community. I would challenge this to say they were a profes-sional learning community when it came to teaching reading stan-dards in the classroom, and if we look at the Leadership Impact Survey example in Chapter 3, we notice that they were in the early stages of the Leader-Plus aspect.

Building Improvement Plan. Example 5.C.4 represents the building improvement plan. The interactions that take place in this routine stretch across the entire school year. There are two key phases of the plan: the front-loading phase (setting direction) and the implementation phase (human development).

Phase One: In phase one, the central office handed down a building improvement plan template to the building principal to be completed and submitted for review. In Example 5.C.4, you can see an arrow represent-ing the pushdown of the improvement template and a return arrow for submission. The arrow stays open-ended, because upon review, the cen-tral office may request amendments to the plan to ensure it stays within district goals and expectations.

The building principal then brought all his teachers together and they reviewed the school's data and together fabricated an improvement plan to address the deficiencies. The single arrow between the instructional leaders and the teachers represents this. A single arrow represents the principal asking the staff as a whole to work on the plan. The arrows between teachers represent their horizontal communication as they reviewed the school's data. Notice that the arrow emblematizes organiza-tional interactions. They did not break down the data and begin to talk about strategies in each other's classrooms.

Example 5.C.4   Building Improvement Plan

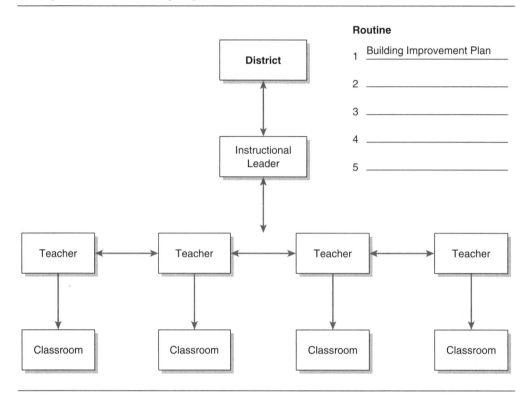

Phase Two: This phase addresses the implementation of the plan. The arrows from the district represent an expectation of implementation of the plan; the arrow from the instructional leader represents expectations for teachers to implement the plan. The building principal often reminded staff of the plan's goals and objectives during faculty meetings. The arrows from teachers to the classroom represent a "hope and prayer" that the teachers implemented what was in the plan. Notice that there is not a return arrow, which might represent data that would verify that the teachers had implemented the plan.

The "hope and prayer" mentality of improvement planning is a common practice. If it's in the plan, therefore, "it is." If we would rely on this improvement plan as our sole leadership routine and leadership interactive tool, we would never know if the plan is working. We would not be able to monitor it to see if it truly is enhancing and changing classroom practices. Neither phase did anything to de-privatize classroom practices. Furthermore, neither phase of this routine did anything to develop teachers' knowledge and skills. Schools that stop here often score in the "No Noticeable Leadership" section of the Leadership Impact Survey. If we are to address all of the leadership functions and to create some resemblance of a professional learning community, then additional routines will need to be added.

Standards in Practice. The Standards in Practice routine (Example 5.C.5) was a district-adopted initiative. The district trained the formal leaders of each building. As I mentioned earlier in the chapter, Markus Long adopted the initiative in a manner that de-privatized classroom practices, with the purpose of developing teachers' knowledge and skills, both individually and collectively.

The arrow between the district and the instructional leader emblematizes the expectation for implementation of the routine. Notice that there is no return arrow; the district did not have a routine that created follow-up support for building leaders.

The arrows between the instructional leader and the teachers represent the weekly Standards in Practice meetings held by faculty. You may want to look back at the microtask example (Example 5.C.2) to see how this routine was broken down.

Example 5.C.5   Standards in Practice

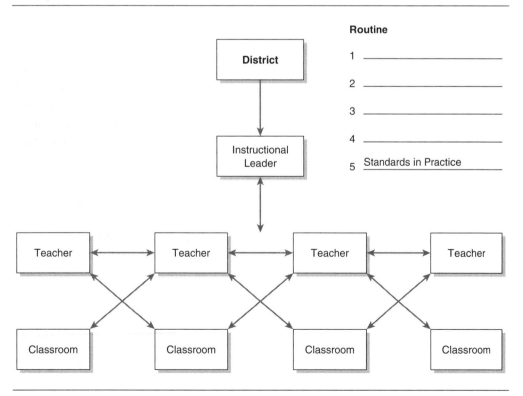

Note the arrows crossing from teachers to classrooms of other teachers, and horizontally from teacher to teacher. The interactions created within these weekly meetings encouraged teachers to talk about classroom practice in general—*organizational talk*—but it also created an atmosphere in which teachers talked about each other's classroom practices, thus de-privatizing classroom practices and addressing the *organizational development* function. Thus, the interactive dialogue that took place during this routine helped to remove the walls of isolated classrooms. Note that there are no arrows from the teacher to their own classroom. A culture in which teachers talk about the other teachers' classroom practices does not guarantee that teachers will return to their classrooms with enhanced and changed practices.

More times than not, when I share Example 5.C.5 with a group of educators, they will claim that this is a professional learning community. I challenge you to think beyond the mere fact of teachers talking about instruction. When teachers take action upon their interaction experience, a professional community is formed. Halverson (2003) further supports this by stating that a professional community results from the intentional coordination of social interaction among teachers through a design of structures in situations of practice. To move the Pleasanton Middle School teachers beyond their complacence of community, we had to ask a few critical questions. How do you know this routine is enhancing and changing classroom practice? The question got a response, but with limited measurement of implementation. In asking this critical question, we challenge our teams to look at additional routines that do monitor implementation. In addition, dialogue is encouraged among the teams to determine any lack of leadership routines, the presence of which effectively ensures success of the Dimension of Practice.

Two-Week Highlights. The Two-Week Highlights routine (Example 5.C.6) was designed to address monitoring of classroom practices as well as to help develop teachers' knowledge and skills individually. Through the deployment of this routine, the principal was able to monitor the instructional practice of his teachers. In particular, he was able to ascertain whether the Standards in Practice routine was enhancing and changing the teachers' classroom practice, while at the same time creating a sense of high expectation of application of the Standards in Practice routine.

Note that the arrows from the instructional leader create an interaction with each teacher one on one. Also note that each arrow is two-directional, meaning that input and feedback is taking place. The arrows between the teachers and classrooms are two-directional, meaning that

Example 5.C.6   Two-Week Highlights

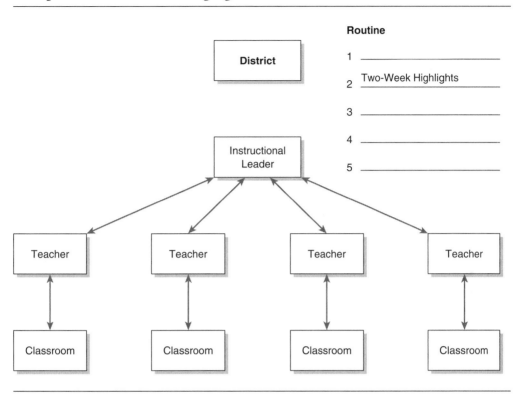

the teachers are deploying a practice and reflecting on its effectiveness within the context of their classrooms. This routine clearly adds a new dimension to the system of leadership routines. It is the first routine we have reviewed that creates a one-on-one monitoring of classroom practice and the development of teacher skills.

Walkthrough Practice. The Walkthrough routine (Example 5.C.7) was used to monitor the teachers' efforts in incorporating the strategies that were outlined in the improvement plan. The walkthrough routine was a district expectation communicated to building leaders. To monitor principal compliance of implementation, the district administrators requested copies of the walkthrough observation sheets. I asked a central office administrator, "What happens with the sheets upon arrival at the district office?" The administrator could not explain what happens to the observation sheets upon receipt to the office and also could not answer the question, "How do you know if this practice of collecting the observation sheets enhances and changes your building instructional leaders' practices?" The "practice" walls of the central office are thick, high, and very

Example 5.C.7   Walkthrough Routine

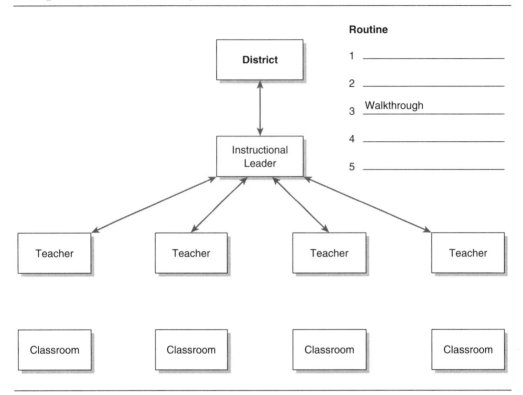

tough to penetrate. However, we need to be aware of how these central office practices and policies give shape to the building leadership practices. Therefore, sometimes district practices need to be analyzed in relationship to that of the building's practices.

Quarterly Assessment. The Quarterly Assessment routine (Example 5.C.8) allowed building leaders to monitor the students' attainment of reading. They were able to do so for each individual classroom. Although not directly reported to the instructional leaders, the data were informally reported from the classroom through the assessment result, a measure that determined whether or not the students were mastering the reading standards that were taught during that quarter. A dotted line from the classroom to the instructional leader documented the quarterly assessment interaction.

The teachers used the assessment as direct feedback from their classrooms to monitor their own progress. Note that there are not any arrows

Example 5.C.8   The Quarterly Assessment

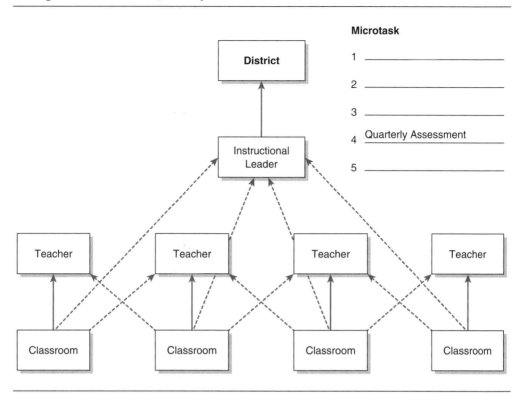

representing interactions between the instructional leaders and the teachers. This was determined a shortfall within the routine, and this insight led to its redesign. As it stood, the practice did not enhance classroom practice in any formal manner. The dotted lines between teachers and other teachers' classrooms represented an informal meeting of teachers that took place outside of a formal, designed interaction. Teachers claimed they talked about their scores with each other, but only to teachers they trusted as part of their reading social network.

The Systems of Practice. The Systems of Practice Interaction tool allows us to look at each routine in isolation, and in doing so we can ask our critical questions for each one of them. Is this routine enhancing and changing classroom practices, and if so, how do we know? In some cases, we will say, "No, it doesn't enhance classroom practice," but when combined or layered within the system of practice, we might say, "Yes, it does enhance classroom practice."

Example 5.C.9   The Quarterly Assessment

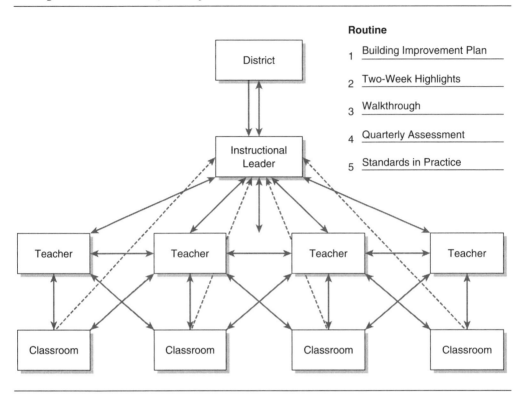

In Example 5.C.9, we can see all five routines stacked up on each other like a series of overhead transparencies. Examine the combination of interactions represented within this layer of practices called a system of practice. Do you see directional arrows going in multiple directions? Are there areas where directional arrows are missing?

The directional arrows represent a solid series of professional interactions between leaders and followers in association with a dimension of practice. In reviewing this figure, we can see the school is functioning within the Leader-Plus aspect. However, we might not be able to say the same if we were to look at another dimension of practice such as teaching of mathematics standards in the classroom.

Let us keep in mind that rarely does a single routine address the three essential leadership functions. On the other hand, 50 routines, as in the

Baker example in Chapter 1, do not effectively address the dimension of practice and can drain our leadership capacity.

> *I personally would never take a team through the Systems of Practice tool if they had identified 50 practices. Once the team had thrown out a number of the routines, I might use the tool to visualize the interactions we have maintained and then ask the very same questions I would have in a traditional approach. Another approach might be to use the tool to narrow down the essential practices. Begin by mapping out routines and tools that address each function, analyze and add as needed. Upon creating an effective system, discard all other routines and tools.*

SYSTEMS OF PRACTICE INTERACTIONS TOOL

Information Cycle

Purpose of Tool:

Helps us define a network of leadership routines, tools, and structures that give classification to a single dimension of practice that influences the practice of followers. The lived interactions of leaders and followers are visually displayed, enabling teams to do a deeper diagnosis of a dimension of practice. It adds value to a team's ability to determine if the practices deployed individually or together are adequately addressing the situation.

Facilitator Help:

1. Prior to facilitating the use of this tool, it is vital that you read the Systems of Practice tool description.

2. Explain and model the process for identifying interactions on the Systems of Practice Diagram templates. Have a visual display of prior diagnoses available as you model. Have team members reflect on the identified dimension of practice they are going to explore. Supply the participants with the following materials.
   • Systems of Practice Interactions instruction page
   • Labeled (with identified routines) or Systems of Practice Diagram blank templates
   • Additional data source handouts (i.e., Identified Leadership Practices, Routine Microanalysis, Multiple Leaders Practice Diagnosis)
   • A different-colored marker for each identified routine

3. Direct small groups of 3 to 5 people to chart the interactions associated with their identified routines, beginning with whatever routine they prefer, and working through one at a time. Have participants draw, using arrows, their perceived interactions on their blank Systems of Practice Diagram templates.
   Option 1: Divide out the routines one or two to each team (time-saver).

   Option 2: Have each team do all and build consensus at the end.

4. After a designated time, have groups share their results to the group as a whole, highlighting their rationale for their arrow selection. Have groups chart their routine interaction arrows on a master Systems of Practice Diagram so the whole team can visualize the interactions of each corresponding routine. Each team in turn contributes to the master chart.

   Option 1: Have teams transfer their maps to an overhead laminate template (preferred) and when sharing, each sheet is layered onto the next, creating a master.

   Option 2: Draw the map onto a master using markers and a flip chart.

5. Facilitate the team's reflective dialogue through a set of **critical questions.**

Tips:	Resources:
Use this tool after you have spent time discussing the intricacies of the dimension of practice. Monitor teams while they create charts to insure they are following the protocol. In particular, be sure interactive arrows represent repetitive behavior identified in the analysis of microtasks (Routine Microanalysis Chart). Participants will sometimes want to escape routine interactions behavior by making statements like "one time the principal."	Flip charts (optional) Systems of Practice templates Chart markers or overhead markers Overhead laminate sheets (optional) Systems of Practice templates (Participants X [number of routines/2] = number of copies) Instructional page
Caution:	**Critical Questions:**
The Powerful Insight that one acquires from the systems of practice tool should not be underappreciated. The *visual* representation is essential for the overall success of this tool. Statistically, 80% of people in our society need to see and manipulate visual and tangible displays (Kolbe, 2004a).	• Does the system of practice enhance and change classroom practice? How do we know? • What connections can we make between professional learning communities and our charted system of practice? • Is the system of practice meeting its intended purpose? Is there another way? • If we were to remove (or add) a routine, would the system be less or more effective? • What might be missing that could enhance our system of practice? • How could we enhance any of the routines in order to better support the system of practice? • What do we know? • What are our new goals?

Template: Page 249

SYSTEMS OF PRACTICE INTERACTIONS TOOL

Instructions:

1. Chart the interactions for each routine within your identified dimension of practice.
2. Place a different routine on each tool template. Use directional arrows to represent the lived interaction (i.e., use arrows to represent policy, tools, routines, communication, and leadership function). Use a different-colored marker for each routine.

   • One-way directional arrow: Represents one-direction interaction between leaders and followers (i.e., principal directive, written policy, set and get professional development).

   • Two-way directional arrow: Represents two-way interactive exchange between leaders and followers (i.e., walkthrough followed by one-on-one follow-up with teacher, leader expectation for lesson plan design or instructional coach reviews plans followed by leader or coach response to classroom teacher).

   • One-on-one arrow: Represents interaction between a leader and followers (i.e., teacher and classrooms, instruction leader, and teachers).

   • Whole-group arrow: Represents interaction directed at a group as a whole (i.e., one arrow from instructional leader to all teachers, expectation from instructional leader that all teachers will implement improvement plan).

   • Dotted arrow: Represents informal routine interactions (i.e., teacher workroom discussions), indirect interactions (i.e., classroom data to instructional leaders), less-frequent interactions (i.e., routine student data analysis, but not routinely scheduled).

   ▬ ▬ ▬ ▬ ▬ ▬ ▬ ▬ ▬ ▬ ▬ ▬ ▬ ➤

3. Using the various-colored markers, chart all the routines onto a single master copy of the template. The interactive arrows may overlap or layer on top of each other; this is ok.
4. Reflect on the following critical questions:
   • Does the system of practice enhance and change classroom practice? How do we know?
   • What connections can I make between professional learning communities and my charted system of practice?
   • Is the system of practice meeting its intended purpose? Is there another way?
   • If I were to remove (or add) a routine, would the system be less or more effective?
   • What might be missing that could enhance our system of practice?
   • How could I enhance any of the routines in order to better support the system of practice?
   • What do I know?
   • What are my new goals?

Example

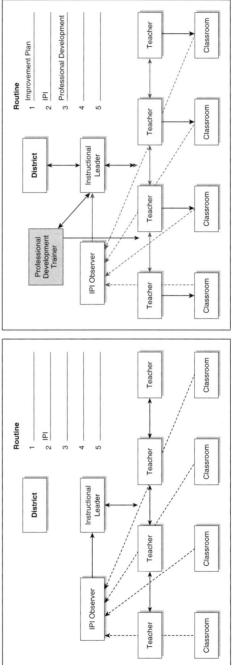

Notes:

SECTION D: DIAGNOSE
PRACTICE: PEOPLE AND DIRECTION

TOOL: Multiple Leaders Practice Diagnosis

Introduction: Multiple Leaders

Systems of practices are rarely if ever deployed by a single leader. Rather, they are made up of two or more formal and informal leaders (Halverson, 2003; Spillane et al., 2001). Even in the superhero environment of Pleasanton Middle School, we still see more than one individual involved within the practice of leadership: Markus Long practiced these routines in relationship to other building leaders. In many ways, leadership is a stage performance with multiple dancers working in rhythm, but not always in tempo. In schools, leadership practice is stretched across multiple leaders. Therefore, it is essential to ensure that the leaders with a positive influence are the ones leading, and leading by design.

> *Leaders lay down the basic melody line and encourage individual "band members" to improvise the theme.*
>
> —Bradley Portin (2004, p. 16)

Purpose: Analyses of Multiple Leaders

People, whether identified as leaders or followers, are central to any analysis of leadership practice. The challenge is to determine how leadership stretches over two or more leaders and how they function in relationship to each other. The Multiple Leaders Practice Diagnosis tool enables us to determine how the collective practices of multiple leaders influence routines and systems of practices. This tool brings clarity to how these leaders coperform their leadership routines, which in turn enables the team to analyze the norms of the leadership functions as a collective. It permits the team to think about how they might design coleadership to ensure an effective system of practice.

Theory: Diagnosing Interactions
Among Leaders in a Coperformance of Practice

Is there more than one way to coperform leadership practices? In diagnosing interactions among leaders in the *coperformance* of leadership practice, Spillane and his colleagues (Spillane, Diamond, & Jita, 2003; Spillane, Diamond, Sherer, & Coldren, 2004) have identified three types of distribution: collaborated, collective, and coordinated.

Coperformance of Leadership Practice

- *Collaborated distribution* characterizes leadership practice that stretches over the work of two or more leaders who work together in place and time to execute the same leadership routine, such as facilitating a faculty meeting. The copractice in this situation is similar to that in basketball, in which players must interact with one another, passing to teammates when they stop dribbling and working to set one another up to shoot.

- *Collective distribution* characterizes practice that stretches over the work of two or more leaders who enact a leadership routine by working separately but interdependently. The interdependencies are akin to those in baseball, in which players at bat perform alone, but their actions in interaction with that of the pitcher collectively produce the practice.

- *Coordinated distribution* refers to leadership routines that involve activities that have to be performed in a particular sequence. The interdependency in this situation is similar to that in a relay race in track; the coperformance of the relay race depends on a particular ordered sequence.

Source: Spillane, 2006a; Spillane, Diamond, & Jita, 2003; Spillane, Diamond, Sherer, & Coldren, 2004

Case Study: Pleasanton in Coperformance

Although the instructional coach leads the majority of the Standards in Practice microtasks, the principal sets and maintains the expectation (see Example 5.D.1). A collective distribution partnership is essential as one person plays off the other by design. As mentioned earlier, the instructional coach was more involved in the human development end of the relationship, and the principal was more the direction setter. There is a unique trust here between the two leaders because they needed each other to perform their microtasks without fail. Markus knew and expected that the instructional coach would give him the minutes from each Standard in Practice meeting, enabling him to develop questions for his Two-Week Highlights routine. Teachers did not question the process because it was routine and influential in enhancing their classroom practice. Teachers perceive there is a

Coperformance

- *Collaborated distribution:* Tasks completed at the same time and in the same place.
- *Collective distribution:* Tasks completed separately, but interdependently.
- *Coordinated distribution:* Tasks completed sequentially.

unified front within the direction of the building goals. Teachers share their classroom practice during the Standards in Practice routine as other

Example 5.D.1   Multiple Leaders Practice Diagnosis

Leadership Dimension: Teaching Reading Standards

Routine	Functions	Leaders Followers	Leadership Distribution	Practice Description
Walkthrough	*Human Development* – Monitoring instruction and progress – Developing sense of accountability for performance *– Providing encouragement, recognition, support*	Principal, assistant principal, coaches or Teachers	(Collaborated) Collective Coordinated	The identified leaders do the walkthroughs at the same time and collaboratively analyze the observations made. Appears to meet the purpose of the routine.
Standards in Practice	*Organizational Development* – Building a culture that de-privatizes classroom practice, supports collaboration among teachers, and maintains high expectations *Human Development* – Developing teachers' knowledge and skill, both individually and collectively	Coaches or teachers	Collaborated (Collective) Coordinated	Instructional coach does most of the microtask. The principal monitors its application to the classroom. He also maintains high expectation for learning within this routine. One person plays off the other and all trust that the microtask will consistently take place. Teachers do not question the process, because it is routine. Teachers perceive there is a unified front within the direction of the building goals. Teachers share their classroom practice as other teachers freely ask questions associated with student learning. There is a high level of trust and learning.

teachers freely ask questions associated with student learning. There is a high level of trust and learning.

In the walkthrough process, the principal, assistant principal, and instructional coach worked in a collaborative distribution. The formal leaders accomplished this by doing their observation walkthrough and analyzing their observations together at the same time, giving the practice strength in its effectiveness for "leader-shared understanding."

MULTIPLE LEADERS PRACTICE DIAGNOSIS

Information Cycle

Leadership Practice
Interactions Among Leader(s), Followers, Situation

Focus (Content)
Situation

Dimension
of Practice

Analysis
Diagnosis
Design
Design

Mapping Process Connects

Teaching and Learning Lens

New Practice
Work Designed Differently
Leadership Practice
Results

School
Improvement

Classroom Practice
Interaction Among Teachers,
Students, Materials (content)

Purpose of Tool:

To determine how leadership stretches over two or more leaders, and how they function in relationship to each other. It enables you to determine how the collective practices of multiple leaders influence routines and systems of practices. To bring clarity to how these leaders coperform their leadership routines, this in turn enables the team to analyze the norms of the leadership functions as a collective. It encourages teams to create an effective system of practices with coleadership by design.

Facilitator Help:

1. Be prepared to define routine, function, tools, leader, and followers. Hand out the Leadership Practice Diagnosis Card sheet located in the Reproducible Resource section.

2. In small groups (4 to 6 people), have participants respond on flip-chart paper to the following questions; use examples to clarify expectations as needed.
   a. What are the routines for this dimension of practice?
   b. How do you know these are routines?
   c. Who is responsible for the execution of these routines?
   d. Who are the followers? Based on the intended interactions, who are the leaders?
   e. What are the tools being used to mediate the interactions between the leaders and the followers?
   f. What leadership functions are we addressing with these routines and tools? (Not the intended function, but the lived functions.)
   g. Is there more than one leader involved in each routine? If so, how are they working together in coperformance (Collaborated, Collective, Coordinated)?

3. Have each small group share their insights with the team as a whole. Record this on a chart.

4. Combine the responses on the Multiple Leaders Practice Diagnosis template.

5. In the same small groups, have the members respond to the critical questions. Have them again share their insights with the team, and record this information on a chart. *Note:* By using a computerized template, everyone is able to see the responses and edits.
   a. What did we discover?
   b. What were the key points that we discussed?
   c. How do these leadership routines connect to teaching and learning?
   d. As a whole, do the routines in the dimension of practice enhance and change teacher's classroom practice? How do we know they do or do not?
   e. What do we *not* know that we would like to know?

Tips:	Resources:
This template can be front-loaded with the routine, functions, and leaders and followers data if your team has already used the Identified Leadership Practice tool. Depending on your outcome objectives, this tool may replace the Identified Leadership Practice tool. Be aware this template does not identify tools.	Leadership Practice Diagnosis Card (1 per person) Flip-chart paper Markers Master copy of Multiple Leaders Practice Diagnosis
Variations:	**Caution:**
Use this template in lieu of the Identified Leadership Practice tool. Use the practice description section as a means to capture the use of the tools used to mediate the practices.	This particular template has many spaces for writing. Place time limitations on participants filling in the blanks. More time must be devoted to the dialogue portion of the activity than filling in the blanks. However, the master copy will serve as a historical reminder and benchmark for future diagnosis and design.

Template: Page 250

MULTIPLE LEADERS PRACTICE DIAGNOSIS

Instructions:
1. Select a dimension of practice.
2. Reflect on the following questions:
   a. What are the routines for this dimension of practice?
   b. How do I know these are routines?
   c. Who is responsible for the execution of these routines?
   d. Who are the followers? Based on the intended interactions, who are the leaders?
   e. What leadership functions are we addressing with these routines and tools? (Not the intended function, but the lived functions.)
   f. Is there more than one leader involved in each routine? If so, how are they working together in coperformance (Collaborated, Collective, Coordinated)?
3. Write your responses to each reflection in their corresponding columns. Use additional templates as needed.
4. Reflect on the following questions:
   a. What did I discover?
   b. What were the key points?
   c. How do these leadership routines connect to teaching and learning?
   d. As a whole, do the routines in the dimension of practice enhance and change my classroom practice or that of others? How do I know they do or do not?
   e. What do I not know what I would like to know?

Example:

Multiple Leaders Practice Diagnosis				
Leadership Dimension: Mathematics Student Engagement				
Routine	**Functions**	**Leaders Followers**	**Leadership Distribution**	**Practice Description**
Walkthrough	*Human Development* − Monitoring instruction and progress − Providing encouragement, recognition, and support	Principal and teachers	**Collaborated** **Collective** **Coordinated**	The principal does the walkthroughs in isolation. Appears to meet the purpose of the routine.
Late-arrive common time	*Setting Direction* − Selling and sustaining the vision − Maintains high expectations − Gets commitment to goals *Organizational Development* − Building a culture that de-privatizes classroom practice, supports collaboration among teachers, and maintains high expectations	Principal and Michelle and teachers	(**Collaborated**) **Collective** **Coordinated**	The principal is big on vision setting and he also maintains high expectation for learning within this routine. He relies on Michelle a lot to share about the engagement activities she does with the students. I do not believe it is by design. I do respect her expertise; however, she is the only one he calls on to share. Teachers share their classroom practice with other teachers informally outside of the designed meeting.

TOOL: Directional Intentions of Leadership Practices

Introduction: Which Way Are We Going?

As mentioned in the preceding tool, a focus on coperformance of leadership routines can demonstrate how leaders work together to accomplish the same objective. However, sometimes a leader can be pushing or pulling in an opposite direction from other leaders. This pushing and pulling of leadership practices comes about for a number of reasons: from difference in communication styles to traditional conflicts in thinking.

Purpose: The Discoveries

The Directional Intentions tools help teams create visuals of the present leadership practices within your school in direct connection with one or more dimensions of practice. The Directional Intentions tools are beneficial for teams when they have unexpected discoveries while using other leadership practice diagnosis tools. For example, a team may discover multiple practices and microtasks with multiple leaders while using the Identified Leadership Practice tool and the Routine Microanalysis Chart. The team would want to create a visual representation of the practices with the use of a Parallel Merger tool. In doing so, the teams create a visual flowchart of their schools' leadership practices. This in turn can create a powerful learning dialogue for the team on the value and worth of each practice. The opposing leadership practice tool will bring to light conflicting practices and their underlying causes. The Advice Network Map may also create questions associated with multiple leaders with multiple practices. For example, teams may discover two unconnected superhubs. Teams could use the opposing leadership practice tools to pinpoint each

---

Underlying Causes for Opposing Leadership Practices

- Consensus efforts have not been made to gain cooperative commitment to organizational goals
- Traditional thinking is challenged by innovation
- Leaders are uncertain about their role responsibility
- Differences in communication styles
- Different perspectives on what leadership aspect the schools need
- Conflicts in unequal distribution of power among staff
- Disagreement on agenda or priorities for the school
- Different data justifications

superhub's directional intention. The competing and common dimensions of practice charts could also bring some clarity to the superhubs' intentions and routines.

Case Study: Hunter Versus Carol

Hunter, a new high school principal (hired from outside the district), initiated a new routine to address the Human Development leadership function. The routine monitored instructional pedagogical practices and created a sense of accountability and acknowledgment. He did this through a teacher-and-student recognition activity called "Caught Doing the Right Thing" (see below). Hunter, as part of his standard Walkthrough observations, carried a digital camera instead of a pen and paper. He looked for students who were engaged in the instructional lessons designed by the teacher. When he spotted a student doing the right thing, he would snap a shot of him or her. When Hunter observed an outstanding, student-engaging teaching practice, he would do the same.

Carol, the new assistant principal and a promoted tenured teacher, created her own routine. In her routine, she promoted traditional standardized instruction by dropping "praise notes" into teachers' mailboxes when she observed such classroom-worthy practices. The praise notes recognized teachers for keeping an orderly classroom using lectures, question-and-answer sessions, and instructional seatwork.

Caught Doing the Right Thing!

The principal, as part of his standard Walkthrough observations, carries a digital camera instead of a pen and paper. He looks for students who are engaged in the instructional lessons designed by the teacher. When he spots a student doing the right thing, he snaps a shot of him or her. When he observes an outstanding teaching practice, he does the same. When he first started this practice, he took pictures of students who were not publicly recognized for their academics or extracurricular activities.

The principal takes the photos, types in a statement of what the student or teacher was doing right, and prints out three copies. One photo he displays on a bulletin board in the hall labeled "Caught Doing the Right Thing." Another photo he signs and sends home in the mail to the student's parent. He shares another copy with the local news media, which publishes them weekly. The photos of the teachers are mailed home to spouses, children, or even to parents. One teacher's parents said they hung their photo on the refrigerator door.

Some teachers resisted Hunter's efforts and collaboratively engaged in their own aligned alliances with the assistant principal, Carol. The positional leaders, principal and assistant principal, were pulling in opposing directions, and they were aware of one another's actions (see Figure 5.D.1).

Section Reflection

Take a moment and reflect upon the following questions: What do you think might be some of the underlying causes for the discourse between Hunter and Carol?

How might this discourse be addressed if a leadership team was given a diagram similar to Figure 5.D.1.?

The principal swayed some teachers, while the assistant principal swayed others, thus creating conflicting interactive leadership practices. So, is this an example of distributed leadership? The answer would be yes. Most of us would agree, however, that it is not the desired perspective we are looking for, but it does exist. Figure 5.D.1 shows two leadership routines practiced by two different leaders headed in two different directions. In this case, these walkthrough practices are opposing each other and, in fact, they divided the teaching staff. This would represent an undesirable representation of leadership practices within a school. That is why we must diagnose the present practice that exists within our organizations. We then must take appropriate steps to reroutine and retool ourselves when we discover leadership practices headed in opposite directions. Do you know if all of your leadership practices head in the same direction?

Figure 5.D.1   Opposing Leadership Practices

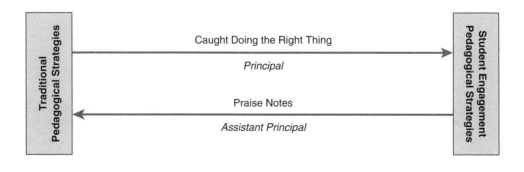

Case Study: Pleasanton Direction

In Figure 5.D.2, Pleasanton Middle School has five routines functioning in collaboration for the common purpose of addressing "teaching reading standards in the classroom." The Parallel Merger Diagram is used to represent copractices all headed in the same direction.

At the top of the diagram is the identified dimension of practice. Represented at the bottom of the diagram are all five leadership routines. The arrows represent the directional purpose of the practice. In this case, all the arrows are merging toward the identified dimension of practice. Therefore, this case represents a desirable system of leadership practices.

Sequential Practices Dimension of Practice. This example also shows a set of microtasks that clearly define the routine Standards in Practice. By listing all the microtasks in this manner for each routine, teams can identify a systematic, ordered deployment for each of the microtasks. Does

Figure 5.D.2   Copractices Functioning in Collaboration

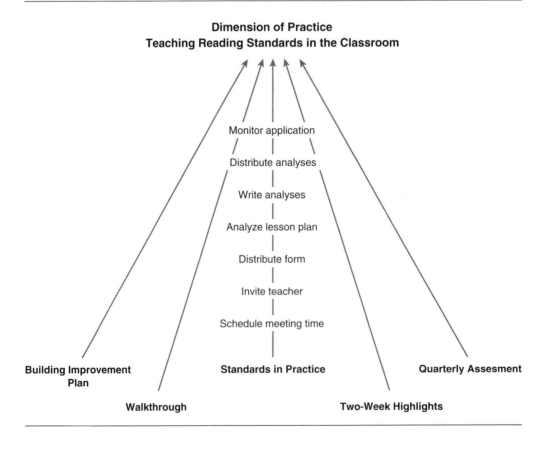

the microtask "Principal receives the Standards in Practice forms from the weekly meetings" within the Two-Weeks Highlights come before or after the "Analysis of the lesson plans" within the Standards in Practice routine? By understanding the sequencing of the microtask, leaders by design create timelines and notifications tables to ensure a successful functioning system of practice. The tool also identifies single, or even multiple, microtasks that are missing that may prevent a parallel merger.

To use the Parallel Merger Diagram to map out all the microtasks associated within each routine within a dimension of practice, we can ask the following questions:

- What routine happens prior to the next or needs to happen?
- In what sequential order do the microtasks happen or do they need to happen?
- Do any of the routines or microtasks happen simultaneously?

Competing Dimensions of Practice. In the Hunter Versus Carol case study, there were two competing dimensions of practice that, in turn, pulled the staff in divergent directions. This can be detrimental to the overall mission of the school. At times, people may be very aware of the divergent directions, and at others, they may not. In either case, a Competing Dimensions of Practice Diagram could be a helpful tool as we diagnose our present practices. When there is awareness of divergent practices, the tool may create meaningful dialogue to transform the present practice so that the efforts of the leaders in the building are better aligned. In a case in which there is not an evident awareness, the tool determines if there are two competing dimensions of practice. At times, various leaders are not aware of the subtle differences their practices have in determining the direction a teacher will take in the classroom. Figure 5.D.3 will serve as a model for two competing dimensions of practice.

As we study Figure 5.D.3, we can see there are two different dimensions of practice, each with five routines. The "Teachers using higher-order pedagogical strategies in math to engage student learning" dimension on the left is the one that Hunter supports. The circles and ovals represent the routines that support this dimension. The assistant principal, Carol, supports the "Teachers using traditional pedagogical strategies in math to maintain student order" dimension on the right. The squares or rectangles represent these routines.

In this case, the two dimensions of practice do not support each other and, in fact, leave teachers confused about their classroom practice. Some teachers choose to align their practices in the traditional ways of teaching,

Figure 5.D.3 Two Competing Dimensions of Practice

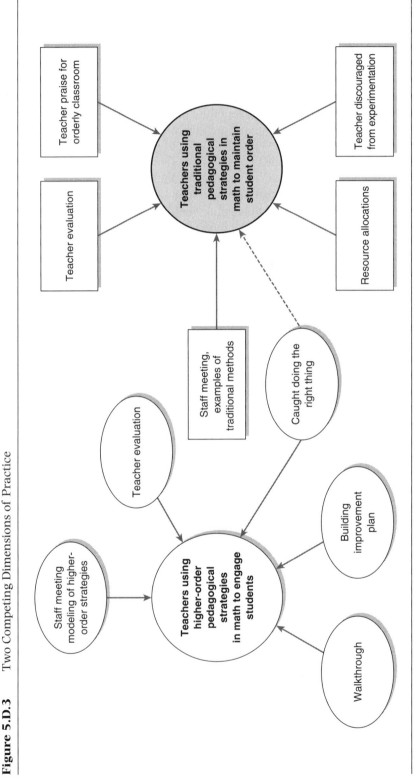

whereas others align their practices with higher-order teaching strategies. The staff hears loud and clear Hunter's vocal expectations, yet the divergent lived practices of the two formal leaders shove the school in dissimilar directions. A serious dialogue will need to take place to determine the direction the school should head. One of the two dimensions of practice needs to be revised or removed. The principal most likely would agree that teachers should maintain student order; however, he might not agree with the traditional classroom instructional pedagogy used to do so. Therefore, there needs to be a middle ground to fashion results. In order for teachers to better sense their instructional expectations, the two formal leaders must reduce wasted energy.

Common Dimensions of Practice. There are times when two or more dimensions of practice merge and actually support each other. In Figure 5.D.4, the two dimensions of practice have two very distinctive practices and different content focuses. Cooperative learning, however, is a common link between the two dimensions of practice.

As we look at Figure 5.D.4, we can see there are two different dimensions of practice, each with multiple routines. The "Teachers using cooperative learning strategies in **math**" dimension has two routines that are strictly associated with math. The "Teachers using cooperative learning strategies in **language arts**" dimension has several routines that address language arts. Arrows represent directionally which of the dimensions the routine is decisively supporting.

The biweekly district math meeting routines did have impact on the teachers' language arts practices directly. However, the language arts routines that disbursed among several of the building leaders were much more prevalent and timely. Although the dimensions were addressing two different content areas, they had cooperative learning as a common ground; therefore, the teachers were able to make some connections. The teachers stated that the leadership support they received in language arts also enhanced their practices in mathematics. The common routines such as grade-level meetings, walkthroughs, and school improvement planning played an essential role in making the connections between the support teachers were receiving in mathematics and language arts. These two dimensions of practice merge and support each other, in spite of having two very distinctive practices and content focuses.

Figure 5.D.4   Supporting Dimensions of Practice

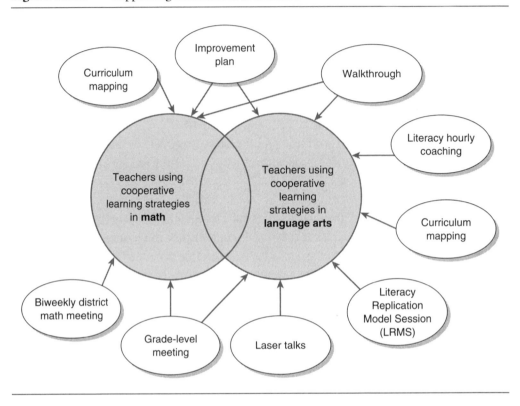

DIRECTIONAL INTENTIONS

**Information
Cycle**

Purpose of Tool:

The purpose of the Directional Intentions tools is to create discussion among team members to determine if there is a need for a corrective path as a result of misaligned leadership efforts. The Directional Intentions tools are beneficial for teams to use when they have unexpected discoveries while using other leadership practice diagnosis tools. The Directional Intentions tools help teams create charts of these leaders' practices, both collaborative and oppositional, which lead to critical analysis of their effectiveness. This in turn can create a powerful learning dialogue for the team on the value and worth of each practice.

Facilitator Help:

1. Identify a situation or concern for which the group will be generating a chart.

2. Generate the possible causes for the concern using critical questions.

3. Choose a charting tool from the insight gained from the critical questions.
   • *Opposing Leadership Practices:* when two or more leaders are leading followers in opposing directions.
   • *Parallel Merger Diagram:* Use when there is a question as to each routine's directional intention. Use this tool when determining the sequential value of each routine and microtask in relationship to the dimension of practice.
   • *Competing Dimensions of Practice:* Use when there appear to be two or more competing dimensions of practice or two or more theoretical philosophies within a building.

- *Common Dimensions of Practice:* Use when two or more dimensions of practices merge and actually support each other. Use this chart when two dimensions of practice have two very distinctive, different practices and different content focuses yet have a common link between them.

4. Have participants divide into small groups to construct a chart based on insight from the critical questions or from previous tools.
   Option 1: Hand out copies of various chart templates for examples, but have the teams create their own on flip-chart paper. Use sticky notes to write each routine and dimensions of practice on. Members can manipulate them in several ways prior to using markers to draw connections.

   Option 2: Have teams use the templates to create their visual charts.

5. Groups then record their concerns and celebrations on a Reflection Worksheet.
   See Templates in the "Reproducible Blank Templates" section of this book.
   Opposing Leadership Practices
   Parallel Merger Diagram
   Competing Dimensions of Practice
   Common Dimensions of Practice

Templates: Pages 268–270

DIRECTIONAL INTENTIONS

The purpose of the Directional Intentions tools is to determine if there is a need for a corrective path as a result of misaligned leadership efforts. The Directional Intentions tools help you create charts of these leaders' practices, both collaborative and oppositional, which enable critical analysis of the leadership effort's effectiveness.

Instructions:

1. Identify a situation or concern for which you will be generating a chart.
2. Construct a chart based on insight from previous tools.

   Option 1: Create your own chart on flip-chart paper. Use sticky notes to write each routine and dimensions of practice on. Manipulate them in several ways to create a chart that represents the people in coperformance, the dimensions of practice, and the leadership routines. Use a marker to draw connections between various components.

   Option 2: Use the provided templates to create a visual chart.

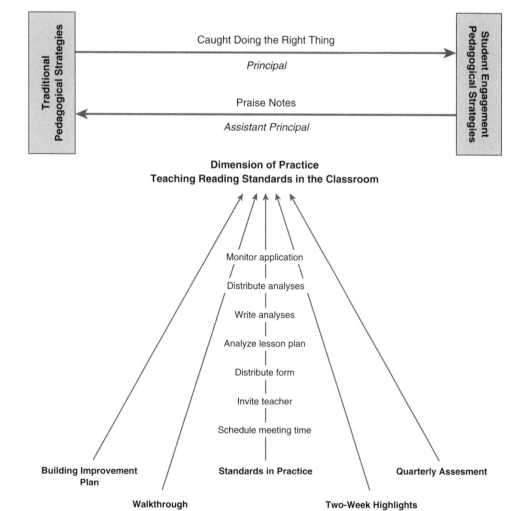

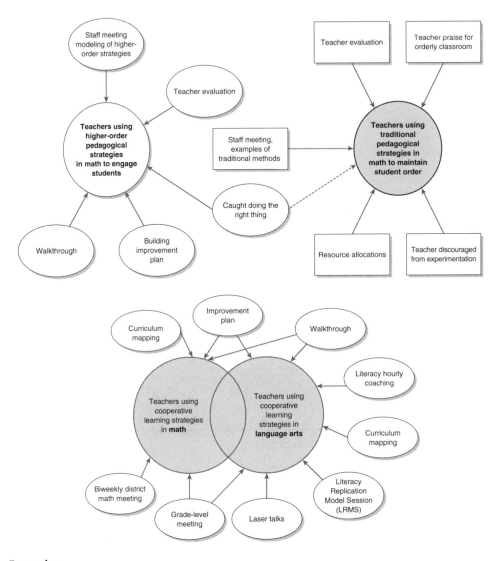

Examples:

- *Opposing Leadership Practices:* When two or more leaders are leading followers in opposing directions.

- *Parallel Merger Diagram:* Use when there is a question as to each routine's directional intention. Use this tool when determining the sequential value of each routine and microtask in relationship to the dimension of practice.

- *Competing Dimensions of Practice:* Use when there appears to be two or more competing dimensions of practice or two or more theoretical philosophies within a building.

- *Common Dimensions of Practice:* Use when two or more dimensions of practices merge and actually support each other. Use this chart when two dimensions of practice have two very distinctively different practices and different content focuses, yet have a common link between them.

TOOL: Shaping of Leadership Functions Form

Introduction: Surface-Level Functions Are Not Sufficient

Frequently leaders in schools can be stretched extremely thin and, as a result, often confront their practices with a mediocre vigor. The mediocre approach is a result of unconscious acts. It just happens, due to the influences of the circumstance and complexity of the educational system. At times, leadership methodologies barely probe below the surface of the water. In some cases, this may be sufficient to enhance classroom practices, and at other times, it does not get to the depth of support needed to cause systemic meaningful enhancements and changes to classroom practices. Thus, the practice really has not addressed the purpose for its very existence in the first place. The three leadership functions identified in Chapter 3 give purpose to effective practices.

Purpose: Measuring Up

The use of the "Shaping of Leadership Functions Form" (see Template 5.D.1) can be a tool to measure the degree to which a function is being addressed within a particular routine or dimension of practice. In addition, the Shaping of Leadership Functions Form is a good tool to identify functions that address leadership by default or by design.

Theory: Default Practice Discovery

Have you ever acted alone or collectively with someone else to step in to fill the void in an area in which leadership was lacking? If you have not, surely you have seen countless others who do so. Often this happens because you or another individual see a particular leadership function falling through the cracks, or you believe the functions need to be kicked up a notch for the betterment of the school's success. These folks do not need to be formal leaders; in fact, they may be informal leaders (i.e., classroom teacher, specialist, and parent). Spillane (2004a, 2006a) refers to this unprompted leadership gap practice as "practice by default." This means that there has not been a grand design to have leadership distributed, even though it is anyway. Leadership practices by default, although addressing leadership function gaps, can be problematic. Let us look at an example in which this might be an issue.

> *I am a leader by default, only because nature does not allow a vacuum.*
>
> —Bishop Desmond Tutu

Template 5.D.1   Shaping of Leadership Functions Form

Dimension of Practice:						
Leadership Routine:						
Directions: Record your responses in the columns of the Shaping of Leadership Functions Form. Use the five-point scale from **Continually (A)** to **Rarely/Never (D)** to describe how regularly the following statements apply to your school leadership routines. Select **(E)** if you do not have sufficient information to respond to the statement.	Continually	Frequently	Sometimes	Rarely/Never	Insufficient Information	**Who is this leader?** Identify the leader(s) that fulfill these functions during the implementation of the routines. Are they formal (F) or informal leaders (N)?
Setting Direction						
Leaders sell and sustain the school's vision and mission during this routine	A	B	C	D	E	
Getting cooperative commitment for the goals	A	B	C	D	E	
Maintain high expectations	A	B	C	D	E	
Human Development						
Monitor instructional progress	A	B	C	D	E	
Monitor instructional progress	A	B	C	D	E	
Develop teachers' content knowledge	A	B	C	D	E	
Develop teachers' pedagogical skills	A	B	C	D	E	
Provide encouragement, recognition, and support	A	B	C	D	E	
Create a sense of accountability for performances	A	B	C	D	E	
Organizational Development						
Adapt and modify tools as needed to improve instructional improvement	A	B	C	D	E	
Support and maintain high expectations of collaboration among teachers	A	B	C	D	E	
Procure resources for teachers	A	B	C	D	E	
Distribute resources to teachers	A	B	C	D	E	
Handle disturbances that interrupt teaching practices	A	B	C	D	E	
Create and maintain an orderly work environment	A	B	C	D	E	

Case Study 1: Contradictive Communication

Jane, an assistant principal at Jackson Heights High School, steps up by default when it comes to effectively communicating with the teachers. This course of action is unknown to Anton, the principal. The message Jane is communicating contradicts Anton's message. In this situation, the two principals are addressing the same function without coordination between themselves. It does not take a rocket scientist to see the potential fallout in this situation. The two principals need to create a coperformance arrangement by design in order for it to become a very powerful practice.

Case Study 2: No Noticeable Leadership

Chapter 3 introduced you to the Western School. As you may recall, the Western leadership team had to take responsibility for the leadership functions and routines in order to make up for the leadership gap created by the resignation of two formal leaders who had not been effective prior to this point in time. In this case, it was a much-needed move in the right direction, and because of their awareness and knowledge about distributed leadership, they were able to create some recognizable leadership (Leader Superhero).

Distribution of Leadership by Design. Leadership decisions made by design can influence the distribution of responsibility for leaders and followers in the performance of leadership functions and routines in schools. This can happen in one of two ways. First, it can happen by creating formally designated leadership positions or by reframing existing positions. In doing so, it can shape the distribution of leadership among formal leaders and teachers. Second, leaders can influence this distribution of leadership by creating structures and routines that enable the distribution of responsibility for leadership and teacher development. If done by design, and the leader's skills are honed, these distributions will be able to effectively enhance and change classroom practice. They will do this with purpose and meaning through their contributions to the three leadership functions.

SHAPING OF LEADERSHIP FUNCTIONS FORM

Information Cycle

Purpose of Tool:

Use this tool to measure the degree to which a leadership function addresses a particular routine or dimension of practice. In addition, the form identifies the functions addressed by default and by design.

Facilitator Help:

1. Have the team members read the introductions to this tool. Have them dialogue the different perspectives of leadership functions.

2. Identify a routine, tools, or dimension of practice to do a leadership function analysis. If you identify a single routine, you will need to repeat the process for all routines within the system of practice.

3. Give each team member a form to complete (they should complete only the response columns). Perception of frequency may vary for each individual based on time exposed to the routine, leader or follower role, and relationship and affective motivation.

4. Record the team's responses on a master Shaping of Leadership Functions Form. Use a highlighter to mark the score with the majority of responses.

5. Have the team address the essential questions provided at the bottom of the form. What do the team's responses reveal? What functions do the identified practices address, either by design or by default? How do you know?

6. Upon exhausting all the critical questions, discuss the next steps and actions that need to take place.

Tips:	**Resources:**
All three leadership functions should be sufficiently addressed within a dimension of practice. A single routine may address one or more functions. Rarely, if ever, does a routine address adequately all three functions.	• One blank template per participant • Highlighters • *Note:* It is also useful to have the directions and template electronically displayed.
Next Steps:	**Critical Questions:**
• Practice gap summary • After implementation of new practice, retake the tool to measure growth.	• Are we sufficiently addressing the three leadership functions needed to enhance and change classroom practices? • If the functions are not sufficiently enhancing classroom practices, are there adjustments that need to happen within the leadership practices? • Are there other leaders who could support the intensity of the leadership functions? • Who are the leaders, and are they formal or informal leaders? • What can the formal and informal leaders do to maximally enhance the routine?

Templates: Pages 253–254

SHAPING OF LEADERSHIP FUNCTIONS FORM

Instructions:

1. Select a dimension of practice and/or leadership routine.
2. Reflect on the interactions that take place between leaders and followers during this routine.
   - Who are the leaders?
   - What function do they address and how often?
3. Read the leadership function descriptions provided.
4. Record your responses in the columns provided. Use the five-point scale from **Continually (A)** to **Rarely/Never (D)** to describe how regularly the statements apply to your identified routine. Select **(E)** if you do not have sufficient information to respond to the statement.
5. Identify the leader(s) that fulfill these functions during the implementation of the routines. Are they formal (F) or informal leaders (N)? Write your response in the space provided.
6. Reflect upon the six questions that follow the scoring diagram.
7. Share your responses with fellow team members.

Example:

Shaping of Leadership Functions Form						
Dimension of Practice: Mathematics student engagement						
Leadership Routine: Late-arrival common time						
Directions: Record your responses in the columns of the Shaping of Leadership Functions Form. Use the five-point scale from **Continually (A)** to **Rarely/Never (D)** to describe how regularly the following statements apply to your school leadership routines. Select **(E)** if you do not have sufficient information to respond to the statement.	Continually	Frequently	Sometimes	Rarely/Never	Insufficient Information	**Who is this leader?** Identify the leader(s) that fulfill these functions during the implementation of the routines. Are they formal (F) or informal leaders (N)?
Setting Direction						
Leaders sell and sustain the school's vision and mission during this routine	Ⓐ	B	C	D	E	*Jim Black, Principal (F)*
Getting cooperative commitment for the goals	A	Ⓑ	C	D	E	*Sue Getaboard, Curriculum Coordinator (F)*
Maintain high expectations	Ⓐ	B	C	D	E	*Jim Black*
Human Development						
Monitor instructional progress	A	B	C	Ⓓ	E	*Jim Black*

Which of the three functions is this routine or dimension of practice addressing?

The Setting Direction function received higher scores than the other two. The lowest subscore was Human Development: Developing teachers' knowledge. Lowest function: Organizational Development.

How do the functions address the intended purposes of the routine or dimension of practice, and/or how do they not?

We know what is expected, but we have not received the support needed to implement the expectation. The routine's purpose is for professional development and collaborative time. We do not appear to do either.

Notes:

SECTION E: DIAGNOSIS: PRACTICE AND CONTENT

TOOL: Practice-to-Practice

Introduction: Classroom Practice or Leadership Practice?

Earlier in Chapter 3, in the section about the One-Function Wonder, you were introduced to Tim Quick. I shared a success story about an afterschool program his staff had started at the school called "Attention." He referred to the afterschool program as a leadership practice. As you may recall, I became somewhat perplexed on how this truly represented leadership practice.

Purpose: Connecting Practices With Practices

The Practice-to-Practice tool is used to mediate a conversation to a point of discovery of a dimension of practice. Often conversations with educators or educational leadership teams start from a single point of reference, such as organizational structure. This tool enables you to facilitate that conversation to a focused "practice" conversation. The practices can then be broken down into classroom practices and leadership practices. In addition, conversations with educational leaders often can center on a philosophy of leadership, such as "principals should monitor instruction." This tool captures the functions that the leadership practice is intentionally or inadvertently addressing. It also creates a visual representation of classroom practices, leadership practices, and a situation.

Case Study: Tim Quick—Attention

To better understand this case study, let's look at how the afterschool program came about and how it was being managed once it was in place. Tim Quick, the principal, was talking to a student one day after school, and during the conversation Mr. Quick ascertained that the student was not doing as well in his classes as he should be, and he also noticed that the student was not taking any work home with him. The next day he discovered that the student wasn't doing well because he wasn't getting his work done. Mr. Quick, deeming this as unacceptable, began his odyssey of what he calls the "Zero-Tolerance Policy." The expectation of the policy was that students will hand in all work, no student will fail, and students will receive assistance on their homework. He announced this to his staff immediately and asked them to figure out a way to ensure that the zero-tolerance policy would be fulfilled. The staff soon came back to Mr. Quick with their suggestion. They wanted to have "Attention" after school for any student still in need of help with their homework.

Attention

The Attention program was designed as an afterschool replacement for detention for students who were behind on their schoolwork. Not all that different from tutoring, but with a direct intention of ensuring that all students were passing their core classes and all students were getting their homework done. Attention therefore became the focus for student learning.

Upon completing his story about how the afterschool "Attention" came about, our conversation shifted to leadership practice. I asked Tim how he thought this was a leadership practice. It appeared we were talking about a classroom practice, perhaps a structure, not a leadership practice. He told me it was a routine to have the "Attention" every day and that he had laid out the Zero-Tolerance Policy. He commented on the value of having his teachers take the lead on addressing the issues. When asked about what subject content he was targeting, Tim replied, "Every core content that students were not completing." He rattled off some statistical data about the success of the program, and I left our meeting somewhat frustrated that I hadn't taken him to the next level of looking at his leadership practice. During the ride home, I reflected on the conversation, and I asked myself the following questions:

- What tool could I have used to mediate our conversation?
- How do we know if this is a leadership practice or a classroom practice?
- If this truly was a classroom practice, then how could we map this classroom practice called "Attention" back to a leadership routine, tool, or even back to a leadership dimension?

Philosophy: Backward Mapping Practices

Truth be told, I fell into the trap of sequential thinking: One model fits all situations, which people sell educators all the time. Second, the principal got trapped in traditional thinking about leadership. I wanted the principal to give me umbrella issues (see Figure 5.A.1 on page 87) so I could facilitate the dialogue down to a leadership dimension. He instead had started with a single classroom routine, or perhaps only a structure. This forced us to try to map a "structure" back to a leadership dimension. Why shouldn't I have seen this from the beginning? After all, we always want to map leadership practice to classroom practices. The Practice-to-Practice tool was created as a reflection of this conversation. As stated in Chapter 5, Section A, a dimension of practice is the conduit that links leadership practices to classroom practices (see Figure 5.A.2 on page 88). The concept is similar to a classroom practice used by master teachers called backward mapping. Teachers use the maps for cause and effect. If this happened, then what would have had to happen prior to that?

The Discovery From a Distributed Perspective. During a follow-up visit with Tim, we began to think about the intentions of his actions and interactions around the "Attention" program (see Example 5.E.1). We agreed that the afterschool program "Attention" was a structure. Second, we agreed that the support teachers were giving students was an extension of the classroom, and therefore was a classroom practice. The tool enabled Tim to identify the leadership functions he had been targeting in his interaction with teachers. He had clearly been selling and sustaining a vision that he and his staff had agreed on at the beginning of the year as part of their professional learning community efforts. He had asked his teachers to modify their standard operating system to support instructional improvement. He did so with questions like this one: "What are we going to do for students who didn't learn it?" Another discovery was that no attention had been given to the Human Development leadership function. The principal saw this as an area he needed to address and set a course to put a new leadership practice in place by design.

Example 5.E.1	Practice-to-Practice: Horizontal			
Classroom Practice	**Leadership Practice**	**Function**	**Structure**	**Comments: Intentions for the practices, purpose, larger picture**
Attention	The continual insistence on a zero-tolerance policy of failure to complete work. Verbalized in faculty meeting.	Setting Direction • Constructing and selling a *vision*. • Getting cooperative commitment for organizational *goals*. • Setting *high expectations*.	Afterschool support for students who have not completed their schoolwork. Led by a teacher.	This was a recently created practice designed by the teachers in response to the principal's insistence of a zero-tolerance policy. Data to support the new practice was minimal.
Dimension of Practice: Student engagement				

PRACTICE-TO-PRACTICE

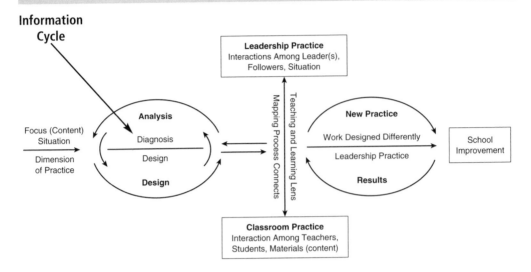

Purpose of Tool:

The Practice-to-Practice tool helps to mediate a conversation to a point of a dimension of practice discovery. This tool enables you to facilitate a conversation to a focused practice. This tool helps identify the functions that your leadership practices intentionally or unintentionally address. The tool creates a visual representation.

Facilitator Help:

1. Hand out a copy of the instruction and blank template to each participant (chose one of two versions: vertical or horizontal).

2. Model the process by facilitating an example using the supplied critical question. Choose a well-known topic for the team. Fill in only what you know. The important discovery will be when you discover the dimension of practice. Use critical questions to facilitate the discovery.

3. Use the tool to create the dialogue of discovery.

4. Instruct the participants to get with a partner, in small groups, or in a large group to acquire the information and fill in the blanks. Use the questions to generate thinking.

Tips:	Critical Questions
There are two versions of the same tool. One has a vertical look, and the other horizontal. Both are useful, but you may find one works better for one-on-one conversations, and the other may work better in a team setting.	*Classroom Practice:* • What is the classroom routine? • Why does it exist? • What tool(s) help mediate the interactions between the teacher and the students? • What content area(s) does this routine target? • What leadership support exists if any?
Resources: • Blank templates • Instructions • *Note:* It is also useful to have the directions and template electronically displayed.	*Leadership Practice:* • What is the leadership routine? • Why does it exist? • What tool(s) help mediate the interactions between the leader(s) and followers? • What content area(s) does this routine target? • To what classroom routine does this routine give support to? *Structures:* • What structure(s) exist? • What structures exist that support one or both of the above practices? *Functions:* • What leadership functions have you identified?

Templates: Pages 251–252

PRACTICE-TO-PRACTICE

Instructions:

1. Take a moment to reflect on the component (i.e., classroom practice, leadership practice, structures, function, dimension of practice, or others) you have identified as an issue.
2. Read the critical questions and begin to fill in the missing pieces. It is not essential to answer each question sequentially. Continue to complete each component of the tool.
3. Answer the following questions:
   - Do I have a better understanding of the differences in each component?
   - What did you discover about your issue?
   - With this discovery, what is my next step?
   - What do I need to change?
   - What do I need to keep?

Example:

Practice-to-Practice: Vertical
Critical Questions
Classroom Practice: • What is the classroom routine? • Why does it exist? • What tool(s) help mediate the interactions between the teacher and the students? • What content area(s) does this routine target? • What leadership support exists if any?
Leadership Practice: • What is the leadership routine? • Why does it exist? • What tool(s) help mediate the interactions between the leader(s) and followers? • What content area(s) does this routine target? • To what classroom routine does this leadership routine give support?
Structures: • What structure(s) exist? • What structures exist that support one or both of the above practices?
Function: • What leadership functions have you identified?

Practice-to-Practice: Horizontal				
Classroom Practice	**Leadership Practice**	**Function**	**Structure**	**Comments: Intentions, practices, purpose, and big picture**
Dimension of Practice:				

Notes:

TOOL: Side-by-Side Content Comparison

Introduction: It Depends on the Subject

Have you ever noticed that the content results in schools vary? Students may do well in math, but not in reading? Why is that? The distribution of leadership among formal leaders and teachers does largely depend on the subject matter.

As part of Spillane and colleagues' (Spillane, Diamond, & Jita, 2003) research with distributed leadership in the Chicago school system, they discovered some essential differences in how teachers talked about math and reading instruction. In an elementary school where the same teachers taught reading and mathematics, the teachers held significantly different conversations.

The distribution of leadership among formal leaders and teachers depends on the subject matter. Two to five leaders, depending on the routine and the school, usually performed leadership routines for language arts. In contrast, two or three leaders carried out leadership routines for mathematics, whereas only one or two leaders took responsibility for leadership routines for science (Spillane, Diamond, & Jita, 2003). In addition, building principals were discovered to be more likely to engage in leadership practices associated with language arts then they would in math, and even more so in math than in science (Spillane, 2006b).

Purpose: Differences and Similarities

A side-by-side comparison of content practices can give us great insight into the differences and similarities associated with various content areas. This comparison can help create meaningful dialogue across multiple content areas. Some replication could potentially be done with routines and tools. More than likely, the content will drive the retooling and development of new or revised routines to meet the contents needs.

SIDE-BY-SIDE CONTENT COMPARISON

Information Cycle

Leadership Practice
Interactions Among Leader(s),
Followers, Situation

Analysis
Focus (Content)
Situation
Diagnosis

Dimension
of Practice
Design

Design

Mapping Process Connects

Teaching and Learning Lens

New Practice
Work Designed Differently

Leadership Practice

Results

School
Improvement

Classroom Practice
Interaction Among Teachers,
Students, Materials (content)

Purpose of Tool:

The Side-by-Side Content Comparison tool gives insight into the differences and similarities associated with various content areas. Use this tool to mediate meaningful dialogue across multiple content areas with your staff.

Facilitator Help:

1. Select the content areas to compare (i.e., reading, mathematics, science, social studies).

2. As a team, write the names of the formal leaders in your school on a flip chart labeled "Leaders of" and the content area (i.e., principals, department heads, grade team chair).

3. Have each team member write on his or her own paper who they believe are leaders within the identified content area.
   a. A leader can be anyone that provides direction or support regarding a specific topic.
   b. Consider who you would consult for input regarding literacy at your school.
   c. This may differ for different participants.

4. Provide markers to all participants so anyone can add a name. Have members write their identified leaders' names on the flip chart with the other formal leaders. The names can be printed anywhere on the page.

5. Now repeat the process for the other content area(s) your team has identified for comparison.

6. Think about where and how interactions take place between the identified leader and the followers.

    a. Why were these people chosen as the leaders?

    b. Who are the followers?

    c. What do the followers do to shape the practice of the leaders? This reflection can often help in identifying the routines in the next step. Place team responses in the routine column.

    d. Have other team representatives ask clarifying questions.

7. Add your final list of leaders to the Side-by-Side Content Comparison electronic version of the chart.

8. Have members pair up and discuss the similarities and differences. Have the pairs share their findings of the differences and similarities in terms of who the leaders are. Record the findings on the Side-by-Side Content Comparison electronic version of the chart.

9. Have each team member write on his or her own paper what might be some leadership routines that exist within each content area. Have them share with a partner and then with the team as a whole. Record the responses on a flip chart labeled for each content and leadership routine.

    a. Have the team agree on what is a leadership routine.

    b. How do you know these are routines?

10. Add your final list of routines to the Side-by-Side Content Comparison electronic version of the chart.

11. Have each member answer the essential questions on their own Side-by-Side Content Comparison form.

12. Have members share and record the agreed-on statements.

Tips:	**Resources:**
Clarify the difference between structures and routines.	• Blank templates for each participant
A routine is a repetitive, recognizable pattern of interdependent actions carried out by multiple actors.	• Markers
	• Flip-chart paper
A structure is a component, property, or relation.	• *Note:* It is also useful to have the directions and template electronically displayed.

Next Steps:

- Look at other tools such as Identified Leadership Practice and Routine Microanalysis Chart.
- Use the directional tools to determine the leadership practice connections between the two contents.

Template: Page 255

SIDE-BY-SIDE CONTENT COMPARISON

Instructions:

1. Select the content areas to do a comparison (i.e., reading, mathematics, science, social studies).
2. Take a moment and reflect on who you think the content leaders are in the content areas identified.
   a. A leader can be anyone that provides direction or support regarding a specific topic.
   b. A leader can be a formal leader, such as a principal, or an informal leader, such as a peer teacher.
   c. Consider who you would consult for input regarding *literacy* at your school.
3. Repeat the process for the other content area(s) you have identified for comparison.
4. Think about where and how interactions take place between the identified leader and the followers.
   a. Why did I choose these people as the leaders?
   b. Who are the followers?
   c. What do the followers do to shape the practice of the leaders? This reflection can often help in identifying the routines in the next step.
5. What are the similarities and differences between people involved in the content areas?
6. Have members reflect on their own: What might be some leadership routines that exist within each content area?
   a. Have the team agree on what is a leadership routine.
   b. How do you know these are routines?
7. Answer the essential questions.
8. Identify next steps.

Example:

Side-by-Side Content Comparison				
	Reading	**Math**	**Similarities**	**Differences**
Who are the leaders?	*Fred and Sara* *Principal Instructional coach*	*Mary and Sara*	*Sara*	*Fred and Mary Formal leaders not involved in math*
Leadership routines	*IC* weekly lesson plan review; IC lesson observation and reflective dialogue; Principal walkthrough; Fred: weekly resource updates. Sara?*	*Mary shares knowledge about standards at faculty meetings. Sara?*	Sara influences my practice, appears to be in informal ways.	*Focused support for reading. Very limited or no focused support in math*
Essential Side-by-Side Content Comparison Questions				

How do you know these people are leaders?

Because they influence what I do. I do things differently after my interactions with them. For example, after IC's last visit, I changed the way I model my pronunciations of new words to students.

*IC = Instructional Coach

Notes:

SECTION F: BRIDGING THE GAP BETWEEN DIAGNOSIS AND DESIGN

Change with less pain involves knowing what already exists in the system that can be revised, as well as knowing how you can redeploy and recombine existing elements in the system into new configurations.

—Michael Fullan, Peter Hill, and Carmel Crevola,
Breakthrough (2006, p. 14)

The Home Design Show Concept

I watch all the home design shows on TV—it helps my imagination go wild. There are a few of the shows that really stand out as great examples of a point I would like to make about jumping straight to designing new practices. The folks on these shows go in, look at the room, and diagnose the house's ailments. They work with the homeowners to create the perfect design, and in doing so, guide the homeowner through the pros and cons of any decision.

Sometimes, the designer has a cool electronic tool that will change the colors of the walls on a mock-up of the room for the homeowner to view. They are able to see the color on the wall long before the paint ever touches the walls. "If you do this, the room will seem larger, or if you do this, it will have a country appearance." In going through this process, the homeowners are given an opportunity to see into the future. The homeowners are able to ask themselves questions like, "Do we want our room to seem larger?" and "Do we want our house to have a country feel to it?"

In a sense, the designer is able to bridge the homeowner's present condition of thinking with the possibilities of the future. In doing so, the designer ensures that the homeowner will be satisfied with the outcome. I would hate to spend a bunch of money and then say to the designer, "Well, it's not quite what I thought it would be. Can we put it all back the way it was before?"

TOOL: Practice Gap Summary

Introduction: In a Fix With Design

All too often, schools jump straight to design from diagnosis. How many times have we as educators jumped to a new design only to fall back on the old ways? As one superintendent told me, if we know we have a problem, we cannot wait to start tomorrow to help fix it. It is a point well taken, but jumping to new designs often leaves us with shoddy workmanship and faulty supplies and equipment. In fact, it is like a remodeling job that falters and changes its appearances repeatedly.

There is a show called "In a Fix." A team of experts comes to the rescue of a lost homeowner who has a house partially remodeled. The homeowner usually claims they just started remodeling and did not know where they were going when they started. I have heard educators repeatedly say, "We just don't know where we are going with this," or "Why didn't someone see this coming?" If we are to make a difference in our leadership practices, then we need to change from being design jumpers. We must put some sort of bridge between diagnosis data and new design. We must slow down for the good of going fast later. By slowing down, we can map out possibilities, both pros and cons, and can see the probabilities of the future.

Purpose: Practice Bridge Summary

There is a huge and important step that must happen between diagnosis and design. I like to refer to this as bridging the gap. Bridging the gap is an opportunity to look at where we are and where we want to go. "What might happen if we choose to go and what might happen if we don't go?"

PRACTICE GAP SUMMARY

**Information
Cycle**

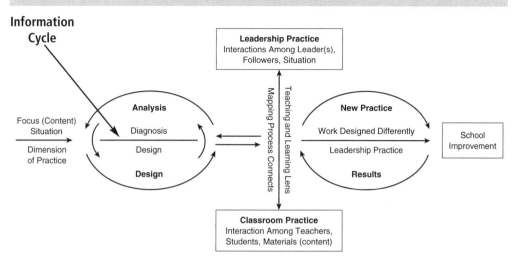

Purpose of Tool:

The Practice Gap Summary is an opportunity to look at where we are and where we want to go. "What might happen if we choose to go and what might happen if we don't go?"

Facilitator Help:

1. Select a leadership routine or a dimension of practice. Teams may start with a single routine and then expand into identifying the dimension of practice that your team will work with in the Practice Gap Summary.

2. What has your team identified as possible gaps in their leadership routines, the tools they are using to mediate interactions, and the structure that places limits on the leadership practices? Place the gleaned gap within the "Identified Gaps" column.

3. Place your team's current routines, tools, and structures in the "Current" column.

4. Place your team's desired routines, tools, and structures in the "Desired" column.

5. Share the template with your team and have each member individually reflect on the pros and cons of the *present* practices.

6. Have each member share his or her reflective thought with the group as a whole. Record all responses and if something is repeated, simply mark it with an * (see Tips).

7. Repeat this process for the *desired* practices.

8. Hand out the Practice Bridge Dialogue Questions

9. Have members in pairs or small groups respond to the questions. Have the groups share with the group as a whole. Record all responses on a flip chart or electronic display.

10. The team must then come to a consensus on present or desired practices. Once consensus has been created, have the teams reflect on next steps. What will they do with this information?

Tips:	**Resources:**
• Front-load present practices if you used other tools to discover them prior to using this tool. • Ask participants to generate reflective ideas to the topic at hand and write them on a sticky note (one idea per card). • Collect all the notes and shuffle them. Have the team begin to sort the notes into categories or groups on the basis of the relationships that they perceive exist between them. • Upon completing the card-sorting, teams should create labels for each category.	• Blank templates for each participant • Practice Gap Summary • Practice Bridge Dialogue Questions • Sticky notes • Flip-chart paper • *Optional:* Have a handout or visual display with the critical questions.
Variations and Applications:	**Sample Critical Questions:**
Use the process outlined in the Tips to assess individual thinking associated with the desired practices. Have members generate alternative options for a desired practice on the sticky notes and then shuffle and sort them.	• What are some patterns you are noticing? • What are some surprises? • What are some generalizations you might make? • How might . . . be impacted if we did . . . ? • Can we improve?

Templates: Pages 257–258

PRACTICE GAP SUMMARY

Instructions:

1. Select a leadership routine or a dimension of practice.
2. What has your team identified as possible gaps in their leadership routines, the tools you are using to mediate interactions, and the structure that places limits on the leadership practices? Place this within the "Identified Gaps" column.
3. Place your team's current routines, tools, and structures in the "Current" column.
4. Place your team's desired routines, tools, and structures in the "Desired" column.
5. Reflect on your present or desired practices. What might be your next steps? What will you do with this information?

Example:

Practice Gap Summary		
Leadership Dimension: Using vocabulary across all contents, Grades 7 and 8		
Identified Gaps	**Current**	**Desired**
Identified Gaps	**Current Routines**	**Desired Routines**
Content teachers talk about classroom management issues and not academic during team time	Talk about student behavior during common time	Plan a common vocabulary selection for the week across multiple content areas
Identified Gaps	**Current Tools**	**Desired Tools**
Nothing in place	Lesson planning books Pacing guides	Team vocabulary tracking form
Identified Gaps	**Current Structure**	**Desired Structure**
Different agenda every week with no academic focus on vocabulary	Teachers submit agenda items.	Every Friday 10 minutes devoted to common vocabulary selection
Practice Bridge Dialogue Questions		
What might be some of the pros and cons of staying with our *present* routine, tool, and/or structure?		
What might be some of the pros and cons of initiating our *desired* routine, tool, or structure?		
Do the pros outweigh the cons on either of the first two questions? If so, would it be better to stay with our present practices, or go with our desired practices? What do you have as evidence to support your response?		

Notes:

TOOL: Forecasting Leadership Initiatives Grid

Introduction: Hesitation Can Lead to the Loss of Great Opportunity

Sometimes, teams hesitate to undertake a major leadership initiative because they fear the potential difficulties and negative repercussions that might ensue from innovative actions. Markus Long, the principal of Pleasanton Middle School, put the Two-Week Highlights into place as a routine, without the guidance of central office and without the initial support of his building staff. If you ask any teacher in that building if that single routine associated with teaching reading standards enhanced or changed their classroom practices, they would unanimously say "yes." If this principal had not scouted out the potential positive rewards and decided to address the skeptics at central office and within his own building, the staff might still be doing the "same old stuff." The positive upward data trend that Pleasanton Middle School has relished over the past few years may not exist if it were not for the Two-Week Highlights routine. The routine effectively addressed the Human Development function, particularly, accountability and monitoring.

Purpose: Forecasting Leadership Initiatives Grid

One way to keep these hesitations and fears in check is to encourage your team to explore all the possible implications of tackling a new leadership practice initiative. The forecasting leadership initiatives grid will encourage your team to think through a variety of consequences that could result from a new leadership practice.

The forecasting leadership initiatives grid has three useful applications. First, it can help your team determine whether the potential payoffs outweigh the potential problems associated with the new initiative. Second, it can guide your team's understanding of the new leadership initiative by anticipating and eliminating potential obstacles. Third, it provides a means of obtaining alignment on the practice's goals, outcomes, and roadblocks well before you undertake the action of the new practice.

Case Study: That Other School (Fear)

As mentioned in the Identified Leadership Practices tool case study, Grant Elementary School within the Pleasanton district did *not* use a routine to monitor the learning and application of their staff within the "teaching reading standards in the classroom" dimension of practice.

Note that the reading data trends at Grant were flat-lined. In other words, their performance data neither grew nor declined for several years, and it remained below the district average.

The principal chose not to adopt the Two-Week Highlights routine and tools out of fear that her staff would perceive her as an authoritarian leader. In addition, she perceived that pursuing a practice like this would take valuable time away from her other instructional responsibilities. She did not know these to be true but, nonetheless, chose *not* to take action, and in turn, missed a valuable interactive learning opportunity with her staff. She was not aware of the unintended consequences of her practices until the team discovered the lived practices and the result of those practices. By not taking action, the principal actually created a state of status quo.

As a result of the leadership practice diagnoses, the leadership team was able to see a potential void. They were aware of the positive results that Pleasanton Middle School was having but knew their situation was distinctively different. The team used the Practice Gap Summary tool to brainstorm a number of new potential routines. Once they completed the list, they used the Forecasting Leadership Initiative Grid to evaluate the impact that the new practice might have on the school and the likelihood that it would happen. Upon scoring their result, the principal was able to give up her fearfulness, and the team decided to pursue a new practice, similar yet very different from that of Pleasanton Middle School's Two-Week Highlights.

Philosophy: Don't Forge Steel—Forge Ahead

Steel is an extremely tough and durable product. If forged thick enough, it will not bend. Sometime as educators, we forge our practices into a solid block of steel because we think it is strong. I argue that we need to create practices that are more like Play-Doh or some other pliable manipulative. Perception and fear create solid steel, a chunk of solid mass that refuses to move. However, if we look into the future and scout out the possibilities, we might see another way to shape our practice.

By forecasting the impact of our practices, leaders ensure that their efforts effectively and efficiently address all three leadership functions. Leaders are able to see if a practice will have a positive or negative impact (see Figure 5.F.1). By forecasting the likelihood of that impact, leaders are able to move away from fear or perception to potential actuality. Bridging the gap is essential to ensure that leaders move to effective leadership practice design. Without a routine or tool like the Forecasting Leadership Initiative Grid, school leaders are likely to forge unintended negative consequences.

Figure 5.F.1   Forecasting the Impact of Practices

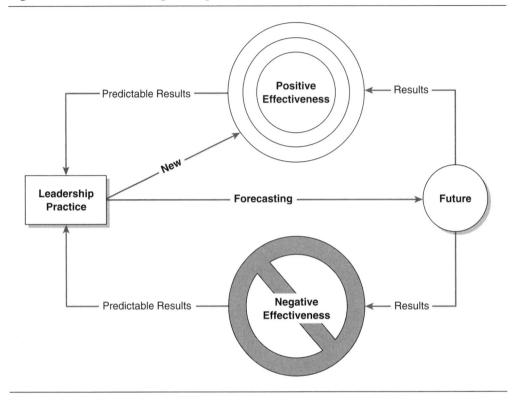

FORECASTING LEADERSHIP INITIATIVES GRID

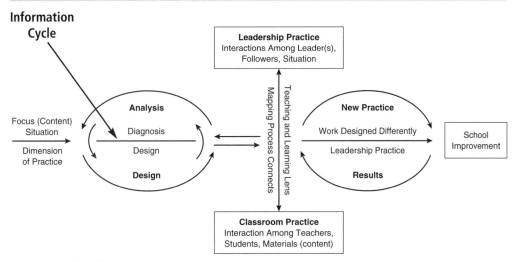

Purpose of Tool:

This tool helps forecast the future to determine whether the potential payoffs outweigh the potential problems with the new initiative and to give guidance in anticipating and eliminating obstacles that might be encountered with new leadership initiatives.

Facilitator Help:

1. Share with the team the new routine, tool, structure, or system of practice that they will be working with. If needed, explain the history of how the new practice came about.

2. Hand out a blank template to each participant and review the four Potential Consequences with them.

3. Review the essential questions that have been provided for each potential consequence. These questions help identify potential positive and negative consequences that could ensue from the implementation of your identified practice.

4. Have team members respond independently first, and then have them share with the whole group. Record the team's conclusions to each question in the "Team Response" column on a flip chart or electronic version of the grid.

5. Use a rating scale of −5 to +5 (−5 is high negative consequences and +5 is high positive consequences) to rate the impact each consequence will have on your school (consider using a fist-to-five method; see below).

6. Use a rating scale of 1 to 5 (1 is unlikely and 5 is very likely) to rate the likelihood that a given consequence could actually occur.

7. Multiply the two rating scales, to arrive at a total score. Note that a given score could be either negative or positive. Record this score in the "Total" column.

8. Select for further discussion and monitoring those consequences with the highest positive total scores and those with the highest negative total scores.

9. Lead a discussion about strategies that could be put in place to reduce negative consequences and strategies that could ensure positive consequences.

TIPS: Fist-to-Five Consensus-Building

- When a group comes to consensus on a matter, it means that everyone in the group can support the decision; they don't all have to think it's the best decision, but they all agree they can live with it. This tool is an easy-to-use way to build consensus among diverse groups.
- Whenever a group is discussing a possible solution or coming to a decision on any matter, Fist-to-Five is a good tool to determine what each person's opinion is at any given time.
- To use this technique, the team leader restates a decision the group may make and asks everyone to show their level of support. Each person responds by showing a fist or a number of fingers that corresponds to their opinion.

Fist: A no vote, a way to block consensus: "I need to talk more on the proposal and require changes for it to pass."

1 Finger: "I still need to discuss certain issues and suggest changes that should be made."

2 Fingers: "I am more comfortable with the proposal but would like to discuss some minor issues."

3 Fingers: "I'm not in total agreement but feel comfortable to let this decision or a proposal pass without further discussion."

4 Fingers: "I think it's a good idea or decision and will work for it."

5 Fingers: "It's a great idea and I will be one of the leaders in implementing it."

If anyone holds up fewer than three fingers, they should be given the opportunity to state their objections and the team should address their concerns. Teams continue the Fist-to-Five process until they achieve consensus of a minimum of three fingers or higher or determine they must move on to the next issue.

Template: Page 259

FORECASTING LEADERSHIP INITIATIVES GRID

Instructions:

To complete the grid, take the following steps:

1. Review the essential questions that have been provided for each potential consequence.
2. Use these questions to identify all potential positive and negative consequences that could ensue from the implementation of your identified practice.
3. Record your response in the "Team Response" column.
4. Use a rating scale of −5 to +5 (−5 is high negative consequences and +5 is high positive consequences) to rate the impact each consequence will have on your school.
5. Use a rating scale of 1 to 5 (1 is unlikely and 5 is very likely) to rate the likelihood that a given consequence could actually occur.
6. Multiply the two rating scales, to arrive at a total score. Note that a given score could be either negative or positive. Record this score in the "Total" column.
7. Select for further discussion and monitoring those consequences with the highest positive total scores and those with the highest negative total scores.

Example:

Forecasting Leadership Initiatives Grid					
New routines, tools, structures, or systems of practice: *Caught doing the right thing*					
Potential Consequences	**Essential Questions**	**Team Response**	**Impact on Leadership Initiative**	**Likelihood**	**Total**
Ripple Effects	How might this practice create additional problems for other practices?	Initially the camera might cause a disruption in class.	−2	4	−8
	How might this practice eliminate other leadership practice gaps in other leadership dimensions?	Has the ability to address all improvement content areas outlined in our improvement plan	5	3	15
Resource Allocation	How might the implementation of this practice require additional resources?	A digital camera will need to be purchased. We will need to find additional funds or we will need to take funds from our supply budget.	−4	4	−16
	Will this practice require additional human resources beyond present capacity? If so, describe it.	Five additional minutes will be needed at the end of every walkthrough to print pictures.	−1	5	−5

Notes:

SECTION G: DESIGN LEADERSHIP PRACTICE MODIFICATIONS

> *Responsibility for innovations' failure is attributed to mismatched goals, priorities, and consultation, between innovators and practitioners.*
>
> —Cohen and Ball (2000, p. 2)

The *design* phase of the Information Cycle serves as a guide to inform our decisions as leaders on not only the actions we can take but also, more important, the interactions between leaders and followers. Design refers to the human endeavor of shaping objects to purposes. The only way leadership practices can become all the things we want them to be is through attention to design. Leaders often feel they do not have time to stop and design. Leadership by design actually can save time and can motivate not only the practitioner but also the recipients (followers) of the practices. Followers know their role and the intended outcomes when leaders practice leadership by design. Leadership practices by design set goals for doing the right thing at the right time in the right situation with the right people, which in turn will promote learning among students. The tools within this section are devoted to helping you find the best leadership practice designs for your given situations.

TOOL: Alternative Solutions Applied Chart

Purpose: Could There Be Alternatives?

The purpose of the Alternative Solutions Applied Chart is to brainstorm alternative solutions to routines and microtasks. The question we must ask ourselves is, "Could there be alternatives to the present practices that might add to the enhancement or changing of classroom practices?" With this technique, your team can attend to a routine, tool, or structure creatively by breaking it down into its microtask and brainstorming alternative solutions. The expectation is for your team to generate multiple solutions to each of the microtasks and, subsequently, choose the greatest impact and probable successful solution for implementation.

Case Study: What—A Different Way?

Carlton school district administrators have an expectation that their entire principal core will regularly do instructional walkthroughs. Walkthroughs were a relatively new practice in the district. In prior years, the teacher contract prohibited such a practice. Upon assuring the teacher's union of its intentions, the district proceeded with their walkthroughs. Not unlike the principal from Grant who feared offending her teachers, Carlton principals were walking on eggshells during their first year of the practice.

Sensing that the walkthrough practice was having a limited impact on classroom practices, the Carlton principal and district assistant superintendent invited me to observe a typical walkthrough in practice. The following example (Example 5.G.1) shows the microtasks that I observed. The principal confirmed these as routine practice.

Example 5.G.1 Routine Microanalysis Chart		
Routine: Walkthrough observations		
Dimension of Practice: ?????		
Microtask	**People**	**Tools**
Monitoring rotation list was shared with staff at the beginning of each semester.	Principal	Rotation List
Reminder letter to staff week before observations.	Principal	E-mail
Do Walkthrough.	Principal	Walkthrough observation card with four observation points (*Note:* none were related to building improvement goals or focus.)
Record observations (in class).	Principal	Walkthrough observation card
Returned to office and sent cards to central office (don't know what happens with them after that, other in file).	Principal	
On **rare** occasions observations would be shared informally with teacher. (*Note:* Often doorway talk)	Principal	

> ## Reflective Question
>
> As you look through Example 5.G.1, do you see anything that would enhance or change teachers' classroom practice? If so, what? If not, what appears to be missing?

I am reluctant to share solutions with leaders and teams, because they often look at the solution list for another school and immediately want to adopt the solutions as their own. To do so goes in the face of what we are trying to learn within the use of these diagnosis and design tools. Every school's situation, leaders, and followers are uniquely different.

—Mark E. McBeth

Upon asking the principal and assistant superintendent the critical question "Could there be alternatives to the present practices?" they responded "NO." The principal and assistant superintendent then used the Practice Gap Summary tool to identify the gaps in the routine and used the Alternative Solutions Applied Chart to brainstorm additional microtasks. To ensure that new perspective microtasks would enhance classroom practices without jeopardizing the tightly wrapped teacher contract, the two chose to forecast the implications of the newly revised routine through the Forecasting Leadership Initiative Grid.

ALTERNATIVE SOLUTIONS APPLIED CHART

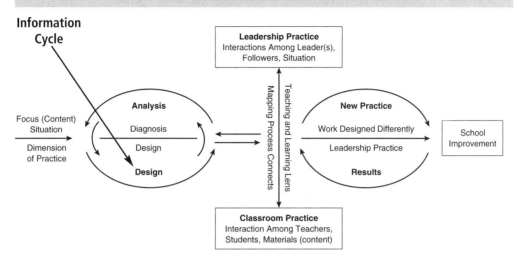

Purpose:

The purpose is to brainstorm alternative solutions to routines or microtasks. Could there be alternatives to the present practices that might add to the enhancement and changing of classroom practices? By generating multiple solutions to the microtasks, you are able to choose new solutions for implementation.

Facilitator Help:

1. Take the results of a routine microanalysis chart and transfer the left column (microtask) to the microtask column on the Alternative Solutions Applied Chart.

2. Have team members, using their own copies of the Alternative Solutions Applied Chart, begin to brainstorm alternative solutions to each of the microtasks. Give them a few minutes to do so. Have individuals then pair up and share their thinking to expand their list. The pair should then combine solutions to make three stronger solutions. You could have quads get together.

3. Have each pair in turn share with the larger group, while someone captures the solution on a laptop projector combination or on a flip chart.

4. Upon listing all possible solutions, have teams of four (no more than five) begin to evaluate the strengths of each solution for each of the microtasks. Have different microtasks for different groups. What solutions will have the largest impact on enhancing or changing classroom practices? Remember, the original microtask might still be the best solution. You may wish to use a scale rating to determine the desirability of each solution according to the overall impact.

Option 1: A scale of 1 to 5 could be used, with 5 being extremely desirable and 1 not so desirable. A 5+ could emphasize that this solution could have a huge impact on the enhancement or change of classroom practices.

Option 2: A scale of A through E could be used, with "A" being extremely feasible that the solution will become a reality and "E" not so much.

5. Have the team highlight the solutions that are desirable and feasible and share with the larger group. Record this on the larger chart.

6. Have the team analyze the new routine as a whole. Will this newly developed routine, if practiced, enhance or change classroom practices? How would you know? How will you measure the impact? What should we do next?

7. Have the team analyze the new routine in how it fits within the systems of practice. How does the new routine influence other routines within the system? Does it have an influence on another dimension, and if so, how?

Tips:

When you are directing a team through the Routine Microanalysis Chart, you may find it helpful to construct a flip chart of the Alternative Solutions Applied Chart. This chart will encourage a team to explore all possible aspects of a routine and provide a quick visual reference for combining separate microtasks into new and unique solutions.

Notes:

Template: Page 260

ALTERNATIVE SOLUTIONS APPLIED CHART

Instructions:

1. Take the results of a Routine Microanalysis Chart and transfer the left column (microtask) to the microtask column on the Alternative Solutions Applied Chart.

2. Begin to brainstorm alternative solutions to each of the microtasks. Write your responses in the spaces provided. One response per column (A–D) for each of the microtasks.

3. Upon listing all possible solutions, begin to evaluate the strengths of each solution for each of the microtasks. What solutions will have the largest impact on enhancing or changing classroom practices? Remember, the original microtask might still be the best solution. You may wish to use a scale rating to determine the desirability of each solution according to the overall impact.

   Option 1: A scale of 1 to 5 could be used, with 5 being extremely desirable and 1 not so desirable. A 5+ could emphasize that this solution could have a huge impact on the enhancement or change of classroom practices.

   Option 2: A scale of A through E could be used, with "A" being extremely feasible that the solution will become a reality and "E" not so much.

4. Highlight the solutions that you have determined as desirable and feasible and share.

5. Analyze the new routine as a whole. Will this newly developed routine, if practiced, enhance or change classroom practices? How would you know? How will you measure the impact? What should you do next?

6. Analyze the new routine within the systems of practice. How does the new routine influence other routines within the system? Does it have an influence on another dimension, and if so, how?

Alternative Solutions Applied Chart (Example)				
Routine: Walkthrough				
Microtask	**Solution A**	**Solution B**	**Solution C**	**Solution D**
Monitoring rotation list	Everyone has the list.	Random with no list.		
Schedule Walkthrough	Not a need to schedule if leaders already know the rotation list.	Don't schedule, just do.		
Notify teachers	Not a need if teachers already know the rotation list.	Don't notify, just show up.	E-mail teachers.	
Do Walkthrough	Have teachers participate in the process.	Do more often.	Revisit class in a timely manner to see if teacher has enhanced practice as a result of prior feedback.	
Share in writing Walkthrough observation	Support with immediate verbal praise.	Change tool to give criticism on how to improve with a timeline.	Don't place Walkthrough sessions in teachers' files.	Share overall observations with entire staff. No names attached.
Schedule meeting with teacher	Do prior to observation.	Share verbally immediately with teacher. Have an aide cover class for 15 minutes.		
Coaching session with teacher on observation	Have a reflective session with teachers about their classroom practices observed that day.	Give advice verbally on how to improve practice.		
Post meeting notes				

Notes:

TOOL: Leadership Function Support Analysis

Purpose: Selecting Leaders for Each Function

To select or identify appropriate leaders for each of the essential leadership functions, use the Leadership Function Support Analysis tool. The tool can be used either for diagnosis of present leaders associated with the various leadership functions or to help in the planning of redesigning the tools or routines within the identified dimension of practice. In addition, the tool helps identify formal and informal leaders for various overlooked functions. What may make your leader identification more difficult is that informal leaders are sometimes hard to identify. The leadership network maps may be of help in a situation in which you do not already know the influential informal leaders.

As you look over the list of leadership functions, you may develop a better understanding of the challenges involved in creating an effective system of practice (see Systems of Practice tools). In a system of practice, you want to address all three functions. As mentioned earlier, it is rare to find a single routine that addresses all three leadership functions; however, if one routine does so, you must ask yourself a couple questions. Is this routine adequate as a stand-alone routine? Are the functions receiving quality attention to sufficiently enhance or change classroom practice?

LEADERSHIP FUNCTION SUPPORT ANALYSIS FORM

Information Cycle

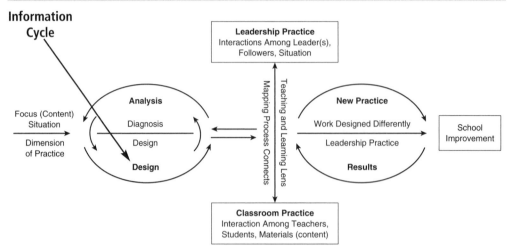

Purpose:

This tool is used to discover the leaders who already are addressing various leadership functions and to identify by design leaders who might be able to lead a particular function.

Facilitator Help:

Diagnosis

1. Identify a dimension of practice for diagnosis.
2. Review with your team the list of leadership functions shown on the chart.
3. Ask the team to suggest leaders who they believe are fulfilling the functions.
4. Your team may identify more than one leader within any given function. They should list all identified leaders. There are four spaces provided; add more if needed.
5. The team may wish to give a weighting score (1–5 scale with 5 being the highest) to the leaders they believe are having the most influence on each function.
6. How do we know these folks are leaders of these functions? This is a critical question we need to ask our groups.

Design

7. Identify a dimension of practice for design.
8. Review with your team the list of leadership functions shown on the chart.
9. Ask the team to suggest leaders who they believe could fulfill the functions.
10. Your team may identify more than one leader within any given function. They should list all identified leaders. There are four spaces provided; add more if needed.
11. The team may wish to give a weighting score (1–5 scale with 5 being the highest) to the leaders who they believe could have the most influence on each function.
12. How will we know or measure that these folks are leaders of these functions? This is a critical question we need to ask our groups.

Template: Page 261

LEADERSHIP FUNCTION SUPPORT ANALYSIS FORM

Dual Purposes:

Use this tool to discover (Diagnosis) the leaders who address the various leadership functions, and use the tool to identify (Design) leaders who might be able to lead a particular function.

Instructions:

To complete this form, take the following steps:

Diagnosis

1. Identify a dimension of practice for diagnosis.

2. Review the list of leadership functions shown on the chart.

3. List leaders who you believe are fulfilling the functions.

4. You may identify more than one leader within any given function; go ahead and list them all. There are four spaces provided; add more if needed.

5. You may wish to give a weighting score (1–5 scale with 5 being the highest) to the leaders you believe are having the most influence on each function.

6. Ask yourself the following question: How do I know these people are leaders of these functions?

Design

7. Identify a dimension of practice for design.

8. Review the list of leadership functions shown on the chart.

9. List potential leaders who you believe could fulfill the functions.

10. You may identify more than one leader within any given function; go ahead and list them all. There are four spaces provided; add more if needed.

11. You may wish to give a weighting score (1–5 scale with 5 being the highest) to the leaders who you believe could have the most influence on each function.

12. Ask yourself the following question: How will I know or measure that these people are leaders of these functions?

Notes:

Practice Cycle

Practice Improvement Process

> *The greatest leader isn't necessarily the one who does the greatest things. The greatest leader is the one who gets the people to do the greatest things.*
>
> —Ronald Reagan

"Work harder" has been the battle cry of most national reform initiatives; but does working hard actually make a difference? Principals are looking for ways to ensure that their schools make adequate yearly progress. Teachers are looking for ways to respond to the increasing demands that all children learn to high degrees. Oops, that is incomparably far from the truth. Most teachers tell me they are trying to find ways to get students to pass state assessments and to ensure that the *school* makes adequate yearly progress.

School leaders both formal and informal are not necessarily looking for practices that enhance student performance, but rather practices that keep them off federal and state improvement lists. Richard Elmore of Harvard University made a similar observation (Elmore, Peterson, & McCarthy, 1996), and he also challenged his readers to rethink that mentality and to address the learning outcomes of each child without the high-stakes measurement. School leaders have driven home the school improvement concept of working harder within a new structure. School leaders rarely measure the impact their working harder has on student performance. After all, how can they? Working harder and using design structures have statistically proven to have failed to create practices that improve learning for all students. Improvement from a leadership practice perspective addresses not only the new design and monitoring of leadership practice, it also addresses the results.

Chapter 6 tools assist leaders as they move from the Information Cycle to the Practice Cycle through a series of new practices and data tools for teams. Each tool comes with its own stories, examples, facilitator instructions, and rationales. Chapter 6 divides the learning into three sections (labeled A through C). The tools give guidance to practitioners as they design and monitor leadership practice that enhances and changes teachers' classroom practice. Only practices put in place by design can be monitored for their effectiveness in enhancing and changing classroom practices. This, in turn, improves student learning.

SECTION A: BRIDGING THE GAP BETWEEN DESIGN AND NEW PRACTICE

> *Effective practice is voluntary and therefore rare.*
>
> —Richard Elmore (2000)

After your team has identified tentative new practices, they must construct a viable action plan together. In my experience, the failure to address leadership practices, in conjunction with poor action planning, is one of the main reasons school improvement efforts fail to produce desired results. Typically, at the end of a team problem-solving session, the meeting room is plastered with flip charts containing generalized descriptions of solutions for classroom problems. Toward the end of the session, with little energy or time remaining, the participants declare victory and congratulate themselves for working hard. Inevitably, someone expresses concern about the lack of clear action planning and someone—or a subgroup within the team—quickly assures this person that the action process is self-explanatory and the subject requires no additional attention.

One of my other favorite scenarios is when someone takes all the charts down and returns to his or her office and types up the notes. This person then tactically manipulates the plan to fit within his or her own image while at the same time promoting the plan as a collaborative effort.

The purpose of bridging the gap is to prevent a well-thought-out plan from becoming nothing more than a plan. A plan without action is nothing more than a piece of paper. The bridge does just what it says: It bridges the gap between design and implementation. It sets the stage for intentional action. From a distributed perspective, we want to be sure that we connect the designed interaction needed for leadership and classroom practice. Metaphorically, as we cross the Mapping Process Connects line, we stop and take a gut check and ask ourselves if our new design truly creates cohesiveness between leadership and classroom practice. Moving from information to practice is like writing the screenplay without a movie or like writing a playbook for the football team without any players to coach. Does our plan address its intended purposes? Without such a gut check, we might become complacent on changing structures and not practices.

TOOL: Intentions Versus Action

Introduction: When Good Intentions Turn to Dust

The "good intentions list": We have all seen them, and some of us even have one of our own. How far can good intentions really get us? I used to tell my wife when I would forget flowers for a special holiday, "Put it on my good intentions list." Well, that verbal vase doesn't hold water for very long. Intention implies little more than what one has in mind to do or bring about (Merriam-Webster Online, n.d.). A quick Google search on good intentions produces site titles such as "Good Intentions, Bad Results," "The Tyranny of Good Intentions," "Good Intentions Are Not Good Enough," and "When Good Intentions Turn to Dust." These titles say more than enough about the deficiencies of good intentions. Kathy Kolbe (2004a) refers to intentions as the bottom of a commitment scale, which implies no current allocation of effort.

> Perhaps the toughest challenge is to remain focused on what teachers and students need most.
>
> —Linda Nathan (2004, p. 82)

Most educators enter the field of teaching with good intentions of helping kids; however, these educators will not meet the needs of their student by merely trying to survive off the good intentions. If good intentions are not good enough, why, then, do we give so much credence to them? When statements by teachers sound something like "I taught them . . . but they still failed the test," the teachers are making a statement of intention. In other words, they are hoping and praying that the students will learn by their intentions alone. In fact, many building improvement plans are similar, full of good intentions. Good intentions do not get us results; however, designed actions do (see Figure 6.A.1). Good intentions often consist of lists of lofty goals and strategies that say we will do training around this or that. Yet, in reality, the team continues to talk in general about the types of theoretical improvements they want to make, while neglecting to constrict themselves to precise actions that help to achieve desired results.

> *If you want a good piece of apple pie, you either have to learn to bake well, or else buy it from someone who can.*
>
> —Author Unknown

Schools that rely too much on good intentions function with limited noticeable results. If plans are defined with theoretical and lofty intentions, practitioners begin to ask, "What was this, and what was that?" In addition, they ask, "How is it (i.e., the plan) going to be done?" Intentions on written plans often lead to lived intentions in practice. In other words, good intentions do not always mirror the daily-lived practices of the school leaders. Teachers, parents, and other educational stakeholders will not accept good intentions without good results. They really do not want to sweep up the dust of good-intentioned leaders.

Figure 6.A.1:   The Dynamic Between Good Intentions and Actions

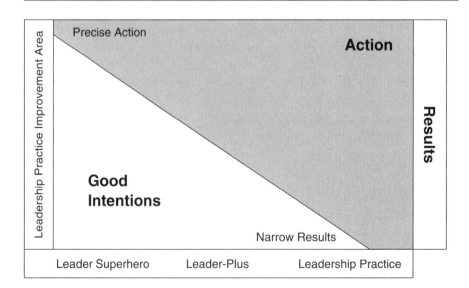

INTENTIONS VERSUS ACTION

Information Cycle

Purpose of Tool:

The purpose of the Intentions Versus Action tool is to help bridge the gap between diagnosis and design. The tool provides teams an opportunity to write down their intended new practices and then shape them into true action statements. By asking critical questions, teams begin to challenge the validity of the new actions, which brings clarity to intentions. The Intentions Versus Action chart can be a tool to give general guidance to your team's efforts to formulate true actions, which are transferable to action plans. Although this step may take some additional time, it will reduce frustrations later on.

Facilitator Help:

Here are a few suggestions for completing the chart:

1. Identify the leadership practice that your team will be implementing. This could include tools, routines, or structures. Place it within the "Leadership Practice Improvement Area" column. Be sure to define it with as much detail as needed for every team member to be able to identify the improvement plan.

2. Write the "good intentions" identified by your team within the "Intentions" column. There may be more than one and that is okay.

3. Team members in small groups (2 to 4) should define the intentions and write them into an action statement.
   - *Explain:* Intentions do not clearly give direction; therefore, teams need to be able to decipher the intentions and convert them to meaningful and purposeful actions.

Option 1: Teams could work on each of the improvement areas one at a time and then the large group comes to a consensus from each of the small groups' work to create one master action.

Option 2: Have each team work on an improvement area and then share with the large group for feedback.

4. Team members must reach consensus on the results they expect from each action.

5. The team needs to write a detailed explanation of the actions that will address the issues in the first column. Give attention to the leadership practice intentions of the plan.

6. Writing a strong action may take some time, so be patient. When you have completed what you feel is a strong action statement, review the following questions: Can you identify what structures, routines, and tools will shape this new action? Can you identify what functions your action will address and by whom? Is there a clear delineation between your intentions and actions? Actions are meaningful and purposeful. If you are able to fill in the questions, then you might have a strong enough action to act upon it.

Tips:	**Sample Critical Questions:**
The plan does not need to be detailed, pretty, or worded with proper grammar; however, the plan needs to be interpretable by those who are going to implement it.	• What is the purpose? • Is there another way to say . . . ? • How could we show . . . ? • What tools . . . ?

Templates: Pages 262–263

INTENTIONS VERSUS ACTION

1. Identify the leadership practice that you will be implementing. This could include tools, routines, or structures. Place it within the "Leadership Practice Improvement Area" column. Be sure to define it with as much detail as needed for others to be able to identify the improvement plan.
2. Write the "good intentions" you identify within the "Intentions" column. There may be more than one and that is okay.
3. Define the intention and write it into an action statement. Intentions do not clearly give direction; therefore, you need to decipher the intentions and convert them to meaningful and purposeful actions.
4. Write a detailed explanation of the actions that will address the issues in the first column. Give attention to the leadership practice interactions of the plan. Writing a strong action may take some time, so be patient. When you have completed what you feel is a strong action statement, review the essential questions.

Example:

Intentions Versus Action		
Leadership Practice Improvement Area	**Intentions**	**Actions**
1. No time has been given to sixth-grade teachers to discuss the comprehension strategies they are using in mathematics.	We will plan on more collaborative time for our sixth-grade middle school staff.	For 6 weeks during the weekly grade-level meetings, we will use the first 15 minutes for teachers to share how they are planning to address math comprehension with their students for that week's lessons. A form will be created prior to the first meeting to assist teachers in having conversations about each other's classroom practices.
2. There appears to be no accountability for sixth-grade teachers to address mathematics comprehension, although it is stated within the building action plan.	The principal will make connections to the plan about the need to discuss math comprehension.	During the grade-level meetings, the principal will be present during the first 15 minutes and will interject expectations and goals associated with the plan as needed. This will not change the role of the instructional coach, who will continue to give suggestions for additional instructional strategies associated with comprehension.

Within these two example actions, can you list what structures, routines, and tools the team has identified?
- **Structure** = *15 minutes of the grade-level meeting.*
- **Tool** = *A form to guide the interactions.*
- **Routine** = *Weekly interaction around mathematics comprehension.*

Can you identify what functions are being addressed and by whom?
- **Setting Direction:** *Principal—during meetings when addressing expectations and goals.*
- **Human Development:** *Instructional coach—contributing to instructional strategies.*
- **Organizational Development:** *Structure—teachers talking to teachers about each other's classroom practice.*

Can you begin to see the difference between intentions and actions? *We are not able to identify the interactions, let alone the intended actions within the intentions.*

SECTION B: NEW PRACTICE—
WORK DESIGNED DIFFERENTLY

> *A vision without action is just a dream. Action without a vision is merely a passing of time. But a vision with action can change the world.*
>
> —Author unknown

If we are to design our work differently, we will need to create a plan to do so. Why? Educational practitioners are notorious for falling back on old habits and old ways of doing things. It becomes essential to create meaningful guiding documents. If we have found deficiencies in our practices in the Information Cycle, why would we want to fall back on these unsuccessful practices again? If we are going to move our schools to a Leadership Practice aspect, then we need to create a roadmap to get there. Plans help us with our destination direction. Who is going on the trip, what are the means for getting there, and how are we going to get there? One promising strategy within the Setting Direction function is for leaders to establish goals on how the staff will create and sustain a professional community. One way to ensure that new proposed practices are actually translated into action is with the New Practice Action-Planning Chart.

TOOL: New Practice Action-Planning Chart

Purpose: Concise and Laser-Focused

The purpose of the New Practice Action-Planning Chart is to create a concise, unambiguous action plan that your team fully supports. The chart helps teams create laserlike plans that simplify the essential components of planning leadership practice to a single template.

Good plans will

- produce desired outcomes.
- create an "Infinity of Practice" or an eternal problem-solving and decision-making, instruction- and learning-driven mentality.
- set directions in particular: Set high expectations; construct, sell, and sustain a vision; and create a cooperative commitment of organizational goals.
- modify standard operating procedure to support instructional improvement.

Good plans

- are written in a collaborative manner with all essential stakeholders at the table.
- are one-page, precise, action-driven implementation charts.
- are written so all stakeholders can comprehend the intended purposes and outcomes.
- assign accountability responsibilities for specific areas.
- establish improvement actions that are doable within a manageable timeline.
- build in a means for evaluation and reflection.

NEW PRACTICE ACTION-PLANNING CHART

Practice Cycle

Purpose of Tool:

The New Practice Action-Planning Chart is used to create a concise, unambiguous action plan that your team will fully support. To help teams create laserlike plans that simplify the essential components of planning leadership practice to a single template.

Facilitator Help:

Here are a few suggestions for completing the chart:

1. Make sure that everyone on your team has input in the completion of the chart.

2. Try not to tackle too many new practices at once. This is particularly true of new practices that include the same identified leader. Focus each action-planning chart around a single dimension of practice and perhaps even around a single routine or tool.

3. Consult your calendars when you are completing the chart. Check for potential conflicts— for example, evaluation dates that fall on weekends, holidays, or days when team members simply will not be able to meet. In addition, check the calendar for start-up dates to be sure they work into the leader's schedule. A missed start-up date could derail the whole effort around the new practice.

4. Save the chart electronically for e-mail distribution to the team and to any other supporter or skeptic that may need to be notified. In addition, the followers of the new practices may need to be notified.

5. *Outcomes:* What specifically will be accomplished as a result of these new practices? Map this directly to classroom practices or at the minimum to the routines and tools associated with the created systems of practices within a dimension of practice.

6. *Evaluation:* How will you know you have met your stated outcomes? What tools might you use to monitor progress? What data can you collect to monitor this practice? Evaluation should be narrowed to the practice identified. Do not settle for more relational data, such as state assessment data.

7. The tools you use to mediate the new practice will be used to shape the interactions among and between the leaders and the followers.

8. Identify whether the tool exists (E), needs to be adopted (A), needs to be revised (R), or needs to be created (C). Describe the steps that will need to take place in the additional information section.

9. Identify any additional information that will support and bring clarity to the new practice. This may include managerial tasks or communication that needs to take place prior to implementing the plan.

Tips:

- The plan should provoke enough insight that leaders understand what is expected, the desired outcomes, what tools they can use, and how they will know they have accomplished what was expected of them.
- The plan should not be superficial, time-consuming, overwhelming, misconceived, or distracting.

Notes:

Template: Page 264

EXAMPLE: NEW PRACTICE ACTION-PLANNING CHART

Dimension of Practice: Teachers using pedagogical strategies for mathematics comprehension

New practice to implement	Leader responsible for action	Intended interactions	Date this practice will begin	Date practice will be reviewed by team	Desired outcome	Evaluation of impact on classroom practice	What tools will be used to mediate these interactions?
During the weekly grade-level meetings, we will use the first 15 minutes for teachers to share how they are going to address math comprehension weekly lessons.	Instructional coach (IC)	Teachers talking to teachers about each other's classroom practice associated with math comprehension	April 3, 2006	May 4, 2006	Teachers will expand their classroom strategies for math comprehension and adjust their lesson plans accordingly to enhance their classroom practice. Students in turn will increase their comprehension scores by 10% of the May quarterly assessment.	Monitoring lesson plans prior to interactive meeting and after the meeting. Teachers hand in both.	A math comprehension form.

Additional information that will support this practice: The IC has always chaired this team meeting and will continue to do so. The IC will collect the weekly lesson plans and document the changes from the pre- and post-grade-level meetings. The instructional coach will outline the microtask needed to fulfill his or her role within this new practice. Mr. Black, the IC, and the principal will create a reflective tool prior to the first meeting to assist teacher conversations.

New practice to implement	Leader responsible for action	Intended interactions	Date this practice will begin	Date practice will be reviewed by team	Desired outcome	Evaluation of impact on classroom practice	What tools will be used to mediate these interactions?
During the grade-level meetings, the principal will be present during the first 15 minutes and will interject expectations and goals associated with the plan as needed. The instructional coach, who will continue to give suggestions for comprehension instructional strategies, will also be present.	Principal and instructional coach (IC)	Principal will interject the expectations and goals outlined within the building improvement plan (math comprehension). The IC will contribute to the instructional strategies by interjecting when strategies might need to be considered for math comprehension.	April 3, 2006	May 4, 2006	Teachers are able to keep the goals and expectations identified in their building improvement plan at the forefront of their efforts and are able to make a connection to the math comprehension strategies they are identifying in the meeting.	A tally log will be collected on the interjections made by both the principal and the IC. Monitoring lesson plans prior to interactive meeting and after the meeting. Teachers will hand in both.	Building improvement plan as needed. Math comprehension strategies as needed.

Additional information that will support this practice: As part of our leadership practice diagnosis we identified that there appeared to be no accountability or support for sixth-grade teachers to address mathematics comprehension, although it is stated within the building improvement plan. This practice will be a collaborative distribution of leadership, and it will be essential that each identified leader will need to honor their identified role. The interactions of the teachers during the meeting will shape the practices of the leaders, so they must be prepared to actively teach and interject when appropriate.

TOOL: Stakeholder Analysis Support Chart

Introduction: It Will Never Work

Repeatedly I hear educators tell me "We can't do that because so-and-so won't support our efforts" or "If we could only get so-and-so to buy into our plan." My response is always, "Do something about it by playing chess." When you play chess, you move the game pieces around strategically. Each move is strategically calculated for loses and gains. Ultimately, a few pieces are left behind, whereas others forge ahead supporting each other in a rhythm of calculated actions and interactions. I use this analogy to set the stage for how leaders can calculate their efforts in an attempt to remove human barriers that might stand in the way of forward progress. At the same time, the chess metaphor can illustrate how leaders can maximize supporters eager for the same progress the leaders seek.

Purpose: Remove Roadblocks

The Stakeholder Analysis Support Chart gives guidance to team members' thinking. This Stakeholder Analysis Support Chart strategically maps out key stakeholders within your school. With a particular leadership practice identified, you use the chart to identify those stakeholders who are supporters or blockers of the proposed practice. Team members can also determine when they might encounter support or skepticism. In addition, they also can try to identify the reasons why a given stakeholder would support or attempt to block their new practice. By using this information, teams can begin proactive action steps to secure support for the practice and attempt to reduce the negative influence of the skeptics.

> *The way you see people is how you treat people. How you treat people is what they become.*
>
> —Goethe

Case Study: Stakeholder Chess Game

Mark was new to his job as Director of Leadership at the university; he reviewed some old records left behind by his predecessors and discovered detailed notes about creating a leadership minor. When Mark approached a past predecessor, a professor on campus, about the leadership minor he replied, "Been there, done that, and had no support . . . too many skeptics on this campus for that to ever fly." Mark asked several questions, but none ended up as important as the following two questions: "Who might be the supporters for the leadership minor, and who might be the skeptics?" His response set the game board to begin Mark's effort to create a leadership minor.

The professor's responses to those two questions laid out a labyrinth of challenges, and for each challenge Mark created a set of moves and countermoves. It was as if it were a chess game, played many times before. Each time a pawn skeptic made its move, a "rook" was put into play, or Mark sent in a "knight" supporter he had coached and who was ready. Sure, Mark hit some turmoil and had a few of his pieces taken from him, but in the end, he set unprecedented history by having a leadership minor passed through the university faculty without a single debated word. This was unheard of at this university, and most universities for that matter. To overlook this essential step of Stakeholder Analysis is like putting your chess king into a corner and never moving it throughout the game: Sooner or later, you are sure to hear "checkmate," and it won't be coming from your own mouth.

STAKEHOLDER ANALYSIS SUPPORT CHART

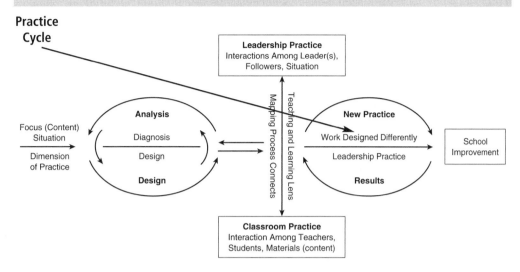

Purpose of Tool:

The Stakeholder Analysis Support Chart strategically maps out key stakeholders within your school system. With a particular leadership practice identified, you identify those stakeholders who are supporters or blockers of the proposed practice. Determines when you might encounter support or skepticism. Teams or individuals take proactive action steps to secure support for the practice and attempt to reduce the negative influence of the skeptics.

Facilitator Help:

Here are a few suggestions for completing the Stakeholder Analysis Support Chart:

1. Select a leadership practice (routine, tool, or structure) to review. This tool is essential when the impact of the practice could potentially reach far beyond a single building or grade level (i.e., district adoption, parent involvement, or use in multiple schools or grade levels).

2. Use a placemat cooperative learning technique to engage all your team members (see Placemat: Reproducible Resources section).
   a. In the center of the chart paper, draw a box about 15 inches high by 10 inches wide. Perfect size is not necessary. Then draw a line down the middle of that box and label one side of the box "Supporters" and the other side "Skeptics."
   b. Using a marker, draw lines from the edge of this box to the edge of the paper and create as many boxes as there are participants (six or fewer people per chart).

c. Each member should write names of potential stakeholders that might be associated with this particular leadership practice in the boxes provided. Each participant will begin this step at the same time. They may wish to identify some stakeholders by name and others by position or representation (i.e., Jack Jones, superintendent, parents). Try to give them guidelines as they attempt to identify stakeholders. Do not attempt to categorize stakeholders at this point.

d. After 3 to 4 minutes, have participants verbally share their response in their group. Once everyone has shared their list, have the team review the stakeholders who they believe are the key stakeholders. In the center of the chart paper, write the top five supporters in the supporter box and the top five skeptics. Do not be surprised to see the same names come up in the supporters and skeptics boxes; it does happen.

3. Each team in turn shares their list. Record them onto the Stakeholders Analysis Support Chart. Display the chart either on a projector or on a flip chart.

4. Have each team determine when, in the course of implementing the new practice, they are likely to encounter the initial signs of support or skepticism from these stakeholders. Have the teams share with the large group and then reach a consensus and record it on the chart.

5. Have teams discuss the reasons for the stakeholders' support or skepticism. Ask them to try to place themselves within the shoes of the stakeholder. If you were in their shoes, why might you be a supporter, or why might you be a skeptic?

6. Identify the actions your team can take to gain support and to limit the skepticism. Record these on the chart.

7. Upon completing the chart, take a few steps back and reflect. Highlight the most important elements of your analysis.

STAKEHOLDER ANALYSIS SUPPORT CHART

Caution:

Take caution when identifying supporters and skeptics. Prior to engaging in the particular tool, you must identify whom the list will be shared with and, if shared, whether someone could be hurt. If your answer is yes, then extreme caution should be taken. These tools are never intended to harm any individual or group. Only individuals or teams who have a high level of trust should engage in this tool.

Hint:

A helpful hint might be to take this analysis with you to the central office and share the finding with your superintendent. Superintendents often are heavily involved in balancing the needs of various stakeholders, and they might be able to contribute support or additional suggestions to the actions your team identified.

Example:

Stakeholder Analysis Support Chart				
Name of New Leadership Practice:				
Type of Stakeholder	**Identify Stakeholders**	**When during implementation will we encounter these stakeholders?**	**Why would they support or resist our new practice?**	**What action can we take to secure support for the new practice?**
Supporters				
Skeptics				

Template: Page 266

SECTION C: LEADERSHIP
PRACTICE DATA AND DATA RESULTS

Up to this point, we have not discussed measuring leadership practices with the intention of discerning their impact on classroom practice and student performance. The next phase of the practice cycle is measuring and monitoring the newly implemented leadership practice in order to specify the intended outcomes. The tools in this section are devoted to this goal. It is important that we secure precise and continuous up-to-date information of the effectiveness of our practices on enhancing and changing classroom practices. We must find ways as leaders to measure our performance outcomes along with the outcomes of classroom practices and student performance.

> *Effective practices never take root in more than a small proportion of classrooms and schools.*
>
> —Tyack and Cuban (1995)

TOOL: Tally Log

Purpose: Measuring Quantifiable Practice

The Tally Log, which counts leadership practices, is not all that different from a teacher evaluation tally system. Use a simple tally log (see Examples 6.C.1 and 6.C.2) if the practice is likely measured by quantifiable events, such as

- how often the curriculum coordinator mentions the relationship of the "standards to pedagogical strategies" in a grade-level meeting,
- how often collaborative leadership takes place between two different identified leaders, and
- how often a tool gets used within a 2-week period.

Pro: Discovering Leadership Practice Patterns

The reason for collecting data is to look for patterns and discover what they reveal about the new practice. In Example 6.C.1, it appears there is something unique about Fridays that creates a significant increase in the use of the Walkthrough tool. In addition, it appears the tool is being used on a fairly routine basis.

Con: What Data Need to Be Collected?

The problem with the Tally Log is that it assumes a consistent volume of practice. For instance, in our tool, the "Walkthrough form" example,

Example 6.C.1		**Tally Mark Monitoring Form**							
Mon. 2	Tues. 3	Wed. 4	Thurs. 5	Fri. 6	Mon. 9	Tues. 10	Wed. 11	Thurs. 12	Fri. 13
//	/		//	////	//	//	/	///	⊬⊬ /

Example 6.C.2	**Leadership Function Monitoring Form**
Routine: Faculty workgroup	**Note:** 50-minute student late-arrival data: Professional development focus
Leaders: Mr. Wise, Principal	

Leadership Functions	**Observation**
Setting Direction	
Leaders sell and sustain the school's vision and mission during this routine	/
Get teachers to buy into the goals	/
Maintain high expectations	///
Human Development	
Monitor instructional progress	
Develop teachers' content knowledge	////
Develop teachers' pedagogical skills	
Provide encouragement, recognition, and support	
Create a sense of accountability for performances	
Organizational Development	
Adapt and modify tools as needed to improve instructional improvement	
Support and maintain high expectations of collaboration among teachers	
Procure resources for teachers	
Distribute resources to teachers	/
Handle disturbances that interrupt teaching practices	
Create and maintain an orderly work environment	

we don't know whether the increased use on Friday is because the leader approaches his or her work differently on that day or because that is the only day available in his or her schedule to do this leadership routine. In addition, a question that someone might ask that is not answered by Tally Logs is, When was the tool not used and could have been used? Is the tool being used for all staff or just a few? One way to account for this uncertainty is to review the information against the backdrop of the total Walkthroughs done by the principal during the week.

TOOL: Data Collection Chart

Purpose: Targeted Measurement

The Data Collection Chart can be completed to identify what the team wants to track to see if the outcomes are met. Although the team retooled the Walkthrough form, they may not only want to know its frequency of use, they may want to know whether it identifies the targeted information during use and whether it changes or enhances teachers' classroom practices. Teams may want to ask themselves what data they need to collect to get them what they want (see Example 6.C.3).

> *What gets measured gets done.*
> —Tom Peters (1986)

Example 6.C.3	Data Collection Chart
Questions we need to ask:	**Possible answers to those questions:**
What dimension of practice are we addressing?	Teachers using engagement activities.
What leadership practice will be monitored or evaluated?	Using the district Walkthrough tool and protocols.
What do we want to accomplish?	Regular use of the Walkthrough tool. – Teachers will enhance and change their student engagement strategies for their students. – Teachers using engagement activities in their classroom practices.
What exactly will we be measuring?	– The consistency of use of the tool with all teachers. – What is the impact on teacher classroom practice? – Does the tool measure the use of engagement activities by teachers?
What do we hope to learn from this information?	– Do the district Walkthrough tool and protocols enhance and change classroom practices associated with student engagement strategies?
Who will collect the evaluation data?	– Consistency data will be collected by the Walkthrough users. – Impact will be measured through the Walkthrough users' repeat visits. (Are teachers enhancing their engagement activities for students on subsequent visits?) – A teacher survey will be used to evaluate teachers' perception of impact and whether the tool measured their engagement activities. – Walkthrough users will evaluate the instrument at the end of the semester on its ability to measure student engagement.
How frequently and over what period of time will information be collected?	– Consistency: daily for a semester by the Walkthrough users. – Impact and measurement: surveys will be pre- and post- for the semester. Impact: Walkthrough users

Template: Page 265

TOOL: Verbal Flow

Purpose: Capture Verbal Flow

The purpose of this tool is to capture the verbal flow of interactions during the deployment of a leadership routine. To capture how leaders and followers talk during a routine

- an observer of the routine records how a leader or multiple leaders respond to followers verbally, and
- an observer draws representations of the interactions to capture verbal flow (see Chart 6.C.1 and Example 6.C.4).

Chart 6.C.1 Verbal Flow Symbols

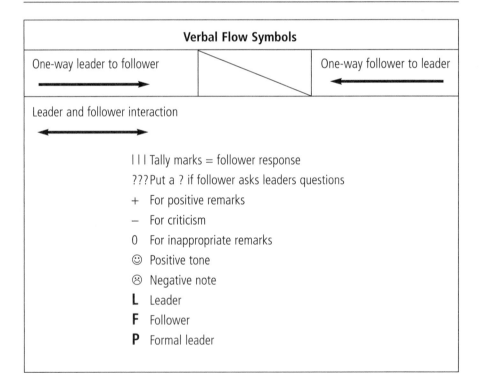

Example 6.C.4   Verbal Flow

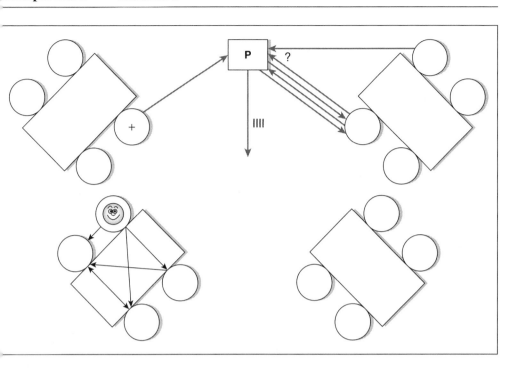

Tools for Reflective Practice

7

> *Non-reflection dooms a group to repeat the same behaviors over and over again, whether they are producing desired results or not.*
>
> —Garmston and Wellman (1999)

Studies of leader-facilitator effectiveness indicate a need for more leaders to develop the skills possessed by those leaders who use processing in their interventions. *Processing* is the all-encompassing term for a set of facilitation techniques (front-loading, debriefing, and feedback) designed to assist people in describing, reflecting on, analyzing, and communicating about experiences (Gass, 1993). Reflective conversations consolidate and extend professional thinking and habits of mind (Lipton & Wellman, 2004). These processing conversations can occur after specific events such as a tool exploration and meetings, or they can occur at intervals scheduled into the meetings. Processing usually involves participants reflecting on patterns of leadership practice and classroom practice. This process is especially useful at transition points in the Distributed Leadership Improvement Framework, when Exploratory Process Cycles switch upon completing a dimension of practice review.

> *Processing is considered an essential element of effective leadership.*
>
> —Phipps and Claxton (1997)

A skilled facilitator will select reflection tools and time their use on the basis of what has emerged during the exploration of a dimension of practice. For example, if a team notes some concerns with focusing on the stage of the Information Cycle, the skilled facilitator will ensure time for processing the experience. Novice teams need to reflect more frequently than teams that have honed their skills over time. The more reflective practices teams engage in, the greater the learning that will occur from experience. In turn, the team will become more focused in its diagnosis and design of leadership practices and will potentially move to a Leadership Practice aspect.

PROCESSING

Processing is a facilitation approach designed to assist learning, awareness, and change. Processing is a tool for facilitating *reflection, dialogue,* and for moving people through and accelerating the change process (Priest & Gass, 1997). Strategies such as front-loading, debriefing, and providing immediate feedback are used to assist individuals in interpreting their participation in activities.

Present research clearly defends the notion that students and adults do not learn, grow, or change without reflecting on their experiences. Research has identified that analysis of our mistakes, failures, or successes is essential for personal growth. In addition, analysis of the impact of our actions and decisions as well as understanding how we can use our new learning lead to more learning and future change. To assure growth, individuals and team members need to be escorted through reflective practices.

PURPOSE

Processing is directed toward helping people transfer or generalize what they have learned in an activity-based experience. Processing involves not only attending to the immediacies of the experience but also relating important aspects of the experience to future issues. That is, what leaders learn today through processing may be applied to the next dimension of practice diagnosis and redesign or the use of a particular tool. The value of our work within the use of the Distributed Leadership Improvement Framework lies in how learning experienced during the activity will serve us, as learners, in the future.

Processing in itself is a process (see the sidebar on page 225). The critical questions (see Resources: Critical Questions) and the reflective tools I have provided are intended to funnel attention from general awareness of one's behavior, feelings, or thoughts to the process of making conscious choices that have been thought through, and then applying these choices to other situations.

Processing the Experience

Processing is best viewed as an activity that is structured to encourage individuals to plan, reflect, describe, analyze, and communicate about experiences. Reflecting on and processing an experience can occur prior to, during, or after the experience. Processing activities can be used to

- help individuals increase their awareness on issues prior to an event or to the entire experience;
- facilitate awareness or promote change while an experience is occurring;
- reflect, analyze, or discuss an experience after it is completed;
- promote integration in participants' lives after the experience is completed.

—Gass (1993)

FORMS OF PROCESSING

Front-Loading

Front-loading is a term used for highlighting, or loading, the learning prior to, or in front of, an activity (Priest & Gass, 1997). In the context of working with school leaders, facilitators set the stage for what is about to occur and identify specific issues to be discussed in debriefing afterwards. By front-loading, the participants have a more purposeful intention during the activity, and the debriefing discussions concentrate on the changes participants experienced. According to Priest and Gass (1997), this type of "prebriefing" that occurs before people participate in an activity can serve five functions:

- review learning and commitments from previous activities;
- review the aims of the activity and what can be learned or gained from the experience;
- encourage reflection on motivations— why the experience may be important to them and how it relates to people's lives;
- anticipate what behaviors will result in success; and, conversely,
- identify what behaviors will hinder success.

> *By loading the learning up front, debriefing simply becomes "direction with reflection," reemphasizing the learning rather than reacting to events.*
>
> —Priest and Gass (1997)

Priest and Gass warn against using extensive front-loading. It can overwhelm participants by giving too much information. Therefore, the technique should be used only occasionally, and only when targeting key points.

Debriefing

Debriefing is a process of guided reflection about the experiences participants had during an activity. Debriefing takes place after the activity has occurred. Debriefing incorporates asking reflective critical questions and actively guiding discussion and analysis of the experience to help people. Debriefing provides order and meaning to the participants' experiences (Priest & Gass, 1997).

When debriefing is used, the facilitator provides participants with feedback, asks them critical (probing) questions, and dialogues with them about their experiences. People who reflect on and interpret their participation in an activity are more likely to assume ownership of their learning experience. However, debriefing is not necessarily useful in all situations.

Feedback

Feedback is a form of supportive communication with participants that is used throughout the Distributed Leadership Framework process. Feedback, intentionally used, is expected to be descriptive (rather than evaluative), specific, well-intended, directed toward change, solicited (rather than imposed), and well timed. Feedback should also involve a follow-up where the sender checks in with the receiver (Priest & Gass, 1997). Facilitators focus on the strengths of participants and direct their supportive comments to reinforcing behaviors the individuals and teams can do something about.

> Feedback involves the leader or other participants providing participants with information about their efforts or accomplishments.
>
> —Priest and Gass (1997)

TOOL: Lessons Learned Questionnaire

Purpose: Lessons Learned

Often teams move from one leadership practice diagnosis to another without processing the tools and courses of action the team used. It is essential that teams review the tools and processes used for the diagnosis to determine what should be repeated, revised, or deleted. The Lessons

Learned Questionnaire can help give some insight to the teams' lessons learned. It is essential to set the stage to ensure that the intentions of this activity are not to assign blame or to find fault with any individual. This tool intentionally focuses on the intended results, not on individuals. Participants reflect on the impact of their practices and distill formulas for improving the routines or tools and to apply acquired knowledge to future leadership practice reviews.

> *The capacity to reflect on action so as to engage in a process of continuous learning is one of the defining characteristics of professional practice.*
>
> —Donald Schön (1983)

LESSONS LEARNED

Purpose of Tool: Use these tools to help others transfer or generalize what they have learned in an activity-based experience. These tools not only attend to the immediacies of the experience but also relate the important aspects of the participants' experience to future issues. There are several debriefing questions that facilitators need to ask of their participants. However, facilitators need to be cautious of overkilling the reflective process. Glean the nuggets, the powerful details, apply them to future experiences, and move on.

Facilitator Help

Here are a few suggestions to think about when leading a Lessons Learned session.

1. Be sure to thank all the participants before and after the session.
2. State the objectives of gathering insight on the present practices, but also how lessons learned can assist with future practices.
3. Ask the participants to select for discussion four to five questions listed in the Lessons Learned questionnaire. You may wish to add additional questions if they fit your particular audience. If time permits, you may be able to address additional questions beyond the four to five.

   Option 1: Use a computer to project the topic and questions onto a screen. Have participants write on their own papers a response to the question. Give them a few minutes to work through this question. Direct the participants to move around the room sharing their reflections and listening to others. This is a reflective listening challenge for the participants. Call time after about three minutes (five to seven shared reflections). Have participants return to their seats and write down as many of the reflections as they can remember. Ask them to find common themes on their notes page. Table groups share common reflections, find common themes, and then share with the whole group.

   Option 2: Use flip charts to capture the input. Have members in a round-robin fashion share their responses. Record each response as you go along. Report the process with each question until all the questions have been addressed.

4. Save the consolidated list for future review as needed.

Tool: Lessons Learned Questionnaire

1. What tools did we use that were helpful and should be used again for future leadership practice reviews?
2. What should become routine?
3. What were the biggest challenges we faced in reviewing leadership practices?
4. What unique skills did our team bring to the explorations that are applicable to future reviews?
5. What design structures helped us do this leadership review?
6. What have we learned from addressing those practices?
7. In retrospect, what would we have done differently—scheduling, time commitment, people at the table, etc.?
8. What are the most important diagnostic and design concepts we learned as a result of participating in the leadership practice review?
9 What steps could we take to share the lessons we have learned with others?
10. What leadership dimension should we give further consideration to as a result of the leadership practice review?

Notes:

Template: Page 240

ADDITIONAL REFLECTIVE AND PROCESSING TOOLS

Reflection Worksheet

Use as a reflection tool for a dimension or practice. What can your team celebrate and what concerns might they have?

Template: Page 241

Leadership and Classroom Practice Worksheet

Use this tool as a reflective tool of a dimension of practice. Teams use the tool to reflect or brainstorm new classroom and leadership practices. Teams are able to see a side-by-side relationship between the two practices. By identifying an effective classroom practice, can a team find correlational leadership practices that enhance the classroom practice? What classroom practices are enhancing and changing or could enhance and change student learning (dimension of practice)? What leadership practices are enhancing and changing or could enhance and change teachers' classroom practices (dimension of practice)?

Template: Page 242

Systems of Tools: Circle Reflection

Use this as a reflective tool. Reflect on each tool your team used, whether adopted from the toolbox or created by the team. Reflections might include strengths, values, lessons learned, new insight, future actions, random thoughts, and things to remember. Write inside each circle a reflection on the tool used. This tool can be used as you go through the framework for each tool. Upon cycling through a dimension of practice or after a set of tools, respond to the center statement: Place **positive** reflections on the *systems of tools* within this inner circle space. Then respond to the outer circle statement: Place reflections on the **cons** of the *systems of tools* outside of the circle of circles.

Template: Page 248

Shaping Our Reflection

Use this as debriefing tool. The tool promotes reflection of things you learned and things you are going to take and implement right away. Ask what is still on your mind that has gone unanswered. The tool implies learning did take place, that action will be taken based on that learning, and that learning will continue as a result of identifying what you do not know. I have used this tool in several different situations as it has served me well for years.

Template: Page 239

Notes:

Reproducible
Blank Templates

LEADERSHIP IMPACT SURVEY

Use the five-point scale from **Continually (4)** to **Rarely/Never (1)** to describe how regularly the following statements apply to your school leadership practices. Select **Insufficient Information (−1)** if you do not have sufficient information to respond. Circle your responses in the columns. Add subtotals and totals scores.

	Continually	Frequently	Sometimes	Rarely/Never	Insufficient Information	What were your thoughts that contributed to your score?
Setting Direction						
Formal leaders sell and sustain the school's *collaboratively* developed vision and mission through a number of means (i.e., ongoing staff conversations, collaborative development, achievement student data reviews, and school improvement plans collaboratively developed and monitored for student performance results).	4	3	2	1	−1	
Formal leaders get cooperative commitment for school goals (i.e., ongoing staff conversations, collaborative development, achievement student data reviews).	4	3	2	1	−1	
Formal leaders maintain high expectations of staff and students alike. This is visible through the leader's actions and interactions with instructional staff.	4	3	2	1	−1	
Add up subtotals for each column						
Human Development						
Leaders monitor instructional progress (i.e., regularly engages [several times a week] in learning walkthroughs or classroom visits, student work evaluation; multiple formative and summative data sources are shared and analyzed with staff).	4	3	2	1	−1	
Leaders develop teachers' *content knowledge* (i.e., recognized as an instructional leader in the school, consistently sought out for content knowledge, offer professional development with extensive classroom practice and support, provide direct classroom support by modeling lessons).	4	3	2	1	−1	
Leaders develop teachers' *pedagogical skills* (i.e., recognized as an instructional leader in the school, consistently is sought out for instructional teaching strategies knowledge, offers professional development with extensive classroom practice and support, provides direct classroom support by modeling lessons).	4	3	2	1	−1	
Formal leaders provide encouragement, recognition, and support (i.e., teachers with expertise are encouraged to share with others, incentive systems exist to reward teacher progress toward schoolwide goals).	4	3	2	1	−1	
Add up subtotals for each column						

	Continually	Frequently	Sometimes	Rarely/Never	Insufficient Information	What were your thoughts that contributed to your score?
Organizational Development						
Formal leaders adapt and modify procedures, policy, and tools as needed to improve instruction with collaborative input from staff (i.e., has a method for engaging the entire staff in analyzing and designing new practices based on prior initiatives, as well as a way to monitor the results of the school improvement effort; has cross-disciplinary faculty committees with decision-making responsibility).	4	3	2	1	−1	
Formal leaders support and maintain high expectations of collaboration among teachers (i.e., design opportunities for staff participation in curricular design and school improvement; provides time for faculty, grade, and/or department meetings; encourages cross-disciplinary efforts, faculty committees with decision-making responsibility, and professional learning communities).	4	3	2	1	−1	
Leaders procure resources for teachers (i.e., supportive teacher induction programs are maintained within the school; subject matter instructional tools are distributed and mirror the school improvement efforts; differentiated support for teachers based on need, feedback, and observations).	4	3	2	1	−1	
Leaders distribute resources to teachers (i.e., base decisions about budget, school improvement, and professional learning on schoolwide goals for student learning).	4	3	2	1	−1	
Leaders handle disturbances that interrupt teaching practices (i.e., teachers, students, and leaders work together to ensure fair enforcement of rules; they identify and maximize student talents when offering assistance both academically and behaviorally; they use mentors and community support; nonacademic announcements that might interrupt instruction are extremely rare).	4	3	2	1	−1	
Leaders create and maintain an orderly work environment (i.e., teachers, community, and leaders use data on student conduct and achievement to review and adjust policies; leaders maintain a visible presence during passing and instructional times; uninterrupted instructional time is provided for core instruction; collaborative efforts are continually made to improve attendance, student engagement, dropout, and graduation rates for students).	4	3	2	1	−1	
Add up subtotals for each column						
Add up scores from each column Total(s):						
Add the totals from each column together _____ and divide by 14. **Total Score:** _____						

LEADERSHIP IMPACT SURVEY: SCORING SHEET (1 OF 3)

Transfer subtotal scores from the Leadership Impact Survey for each leadership function into the score columns. To do so you will need to add the scores from each function and then divide the total by the number of questions for each: Setting Direction (*3 questions*); Human Development (*5 questions*); and Organizational Development (*6 questions*).

Leadership Function	Individual Score	Team Average	Comments
Setting Direction			
Human Development			
Organizational Development			
Total:			

In which of the three leadership functions did you score the *highest*? What might be the factors associated with the *high* score?

In which of the three leadership functions did you score the *lowest*? What might be the factors associated with the *low* score?

What is the single most alarming aspect of your score? Why?

What is the single most rewarding or pleasing aspect of your score? Why and what would you want to keep the same to ensure your successes?

What one change could you make to help the school perform even more effectively to enhance student performance? *Caution: This is a hypothetical question. More analysis should be given to leadership practices prior to jumping to a new design.*

LEADERSHIP IMPACT SURVEY: SCORING SHEET (2 OF 3)

Transfer and highlight your score from the Leadership Impact Survey to the numbered score bars at the top and the bottom of the scoring sheet. Draw a highlighted connection between the top and bottom scores. Draw a highlighted connection on either side of the previous scored line.

1.0	1.2	1.4	1.6	1.8	2.0	2.2	2.4	2.6	2.8	3.0	3.2	3.4	3.6	3.8	4.0

Leadership Aspect

Limited noticeable leadership	Leader Superhero aspect	Leader-Plus aspect	Leadership Practice aspect

Leadership Type

Manager	Turnaround leader	Practitioner	Cohesive maturity

Awareness of Leadership Impact on Student Performance

Nonacademic management	Unconscious leadership	Mindful leadership	Focused leadership

Essential Leadership Question

Who	Who and *what*	Who, what, and *why*	Who, what, why, and *how*

School Improvement

Status quo	Structure-driven practice	Adaptive practice	Infinity of practice

Improvement From a Leadership Practice Perspective

Design	*Analysis*; design	Analysis; design; *monitors results*	Analysis; design; *new practice*; monitor results

Organizational Culture

Continual flux	Stable standard practice	Professional learning community	Community of practice

Professional Development Criteria

Hit and miss	*Content*	Content and *context*	Content, context, and *process*

Leadership Communication

Nonexistent	Directive	Discussion	Dialogue

Instructional Focus

Instruction and learning should be the central focus (*Reality: not likely*)	*Instruction* and learning are the central focus	*Teaching* and learning are the central focus

Structure

Management practice (orderly)	Comprehensive reform	Situational: Leadership practice is paramount

School Decision Making

Respect for teaching	Ambition to try	Courage to put student learning first	Perseverance for each child	Wisdom of all stakeholders for each child

Leader Decision Making

Interest in education	Involves followers	Engages followers	Convinces followers to take action	Inspires followers to lead

1.0	1.2	1.4	1.6	1.8	2.0	2.2	2.4	2.6	2.8	3.0	3.2	3.4	3.6	3.8	4.0

LEADERSHIP IMPACT SURVEY: SCORING SHEET (3 OF 3)

Which impacting factor (i.e., school improvement, structure) did you find to be the *most alarming*? Why?
Which impacting factor did you find to be the *most accurate* in describing your school's present status? Why?
What is the single most alarming aspect of your score? Why?
What is the single most rewarding or pleasing aspect of your score? Why and what would you want to keep the same to ensure your successes?
How might the score change if we didn't address leadership within the school across all content areas? For example, if you had taken the survey for leadership associated with the content reading only or mathematics or another content area?
What one change could you make to help the school enhance student performance even more effectively? *Caution: This is a hypothetical question. More analysis should be given to leadership practices prior to jumping to a new design.*
What question(s) would you like to have answered?

POST-LEADERSHIP ROUTINE REFLECTION

What am I doing and why?
How is what I am doing enhancing and changing teachers' classroom practice?

Successes Experienced	Problems Encountered
How do I know?	**How do I know?**
What does my gut tell me?	**What does my gut tell me?**
What have I observed or heard?	**What have I observed or heard?**

Interesting insight:

Feedback, if any:

What will I change for the next time?

A VERTICAL LEADERSHIP COMPONENT MAP

Umbrella issues	
Focus area (content) • Reading • Writing • Mathematics • Science • Social studies • Other academic areas as needed	
Dimension of practice • Content • Standards • Pedagogy • Components • Engagement • Knowledge of learner	
Leadership practice • Routines • Tools • Leaders and followers • Interactions • Functions	
Classroom practice	
Routine microanalysis	
Dimension of practice:	

SHAPING OUR REFLECTION

Directions: Place reflection topics in shaded rectangles.

Square = four things you learned.

Triangle = three things you are going to take and implement right away.

Circle = one thing that is rolling around in your mind, that you want to give more thought to or about which you need additional answers.

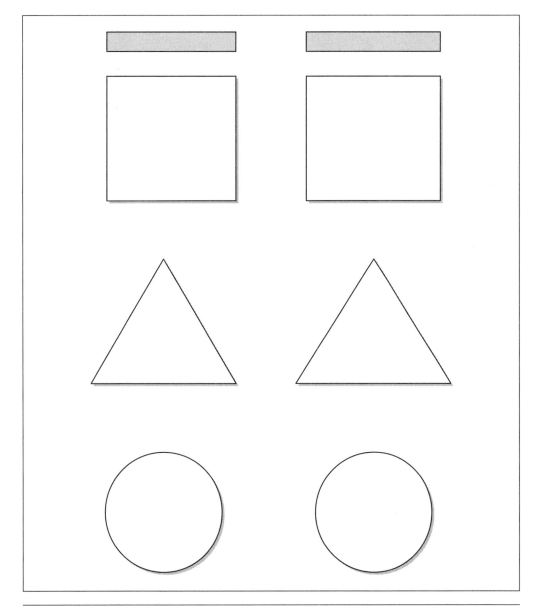

LESSONS LEARNED QUESTIONNAIRE

1. What tools did we use that were helpful and should be used again for future leadership practice reviews?

2. What should become routine?

3. What were the biggest challenges we faced in reviewing leadership practices?

4. What unique skills did our team bring to the explorations that are applicable to future reviews?

5. What design structures helped us do this leadership review?

6. What have we learned from addressing those practices?

7. In retrospect, what would we have done differently—scheduling, time commitment, people at the table, and so forth?

8. What are the most important diagnostic and design concepts we learned as a result of participating in the leadership practice review?

9. What steps could we take to share the lessons we have learned with others?

10. What leadership dimension should we give further consideration to as a result of the leadership practice review?

REFLECTION WORKSHEET

Dimension of practice:	
Concerns	**Celebrations**
•	•
•	•
•	•
•	•
•	•
•	•
•	•
•	•
•	•
•	•
•	•

THE DISTRIBUTED LEADERSHIP TOOLBOX
LEADERSHIP AND CLASSROOM PRACTICE WORKSHEET

Dimension of practice:	
What classroom practices are enhancing and changing or could enhance and change student learning?	What leadership practices are enhancing and changing or could enhance and change teachers' classroom practices?
•	•
•	•
•	•
•	•
•	•
•	•
•	•
•	•
•	•
•	•
•	•

ADVICE NETWORK MAP

Dimension of practice:			
Who are the leaders?	How do you know the people you identified are leaders? *Actions and interactions*	What makes each of the people you identify a leader? *List more than their personal attributes*	Who are the followers for each leader? *Defined by interactions*

How were these leaders assigned to leadership positions?

How do leaders (teacher-leaders) in your school know what's expected of them?

Where did they get their leadership skills?

What kind of support do your leaders (teacher-leaders) get?

How do we make sure the appropriate leaders and followers are engaged in the enhancement and changing of teachers' classroom practices?

Reflective questions based in part on Camburn's work (2005):

IDENTIFIED LEADERSHIP PRACTICES (1 OF 2)

Dimension of practice:			
Routine	Functions	Tools	Leaders/Followers

IDENTIFIED LEADERSHIP PRACTICES (2 OF 2)

What did I discover as a result of reflection on this dimension of practice (celebrate or concern)?

I was surprised with . . .

What were some of the key points that I want to share with others?

How do these leadership routines connect to teaching and learning?

As a whole, do the routines in the dimension of practice enhance and change classroom practice? How do I know?

What don't we know at this point that I would like to know?

ROUTINE MICROANALYSIS CHART

Routine:		
Dimension of practice:		
Microtask	**People**	**Tools**

MICROANALYSIS CHART REFLECTION

From the analysis of your microanalysis chart(s), what should we be *pleased* with or feel good about? *(For each statement, indicate what microtask, person, or tool you are referencing.)*	From the analysis of your microanalysis chart(s), what should we be *concerned* about or need to discuss more in-depth. *(For each statement, indicate what microtask, person, or tool you are referencing.)*
• • • • •	• • • • •

A. What can we learn about our current practices that will enhance the quality of teachers' classroom practices?

B. Are there specific routines, microtasks, or tools we should overhaul, modify, retool, or discontinue that would better help leaders enhance and change teachers' classroom practices?

C. What should we consider for our next steps (i.e., perform deeper analysis of dimension of practice, identify gaps in practice, identify alternative solutions, analyze multiple leaders)?

SYSTEMS OF TOOLS: CIRCLE REFLECTION

Reflect on each tool your team used, whether adopted from the toolbox or created by the team (strengths, value, lessons learned, new insight, future actions, random thoughts, to-remember).

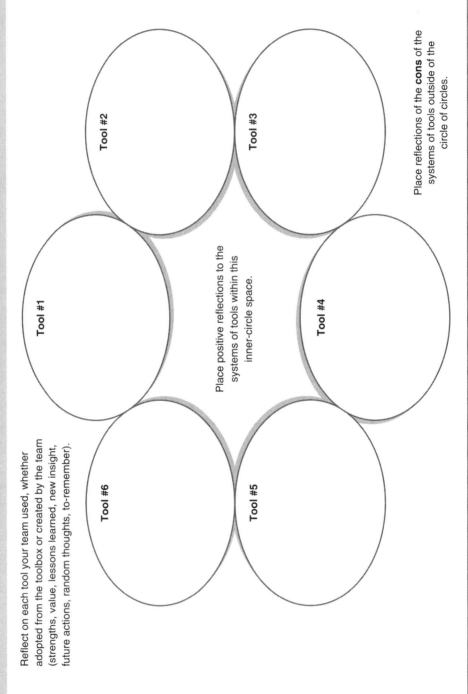

Tool #2

Tool #1

Tool #3

Tool #4

Tool #6

Tool #5

Place positive reflections to the systems of tools within this inner-circle space.

Place reflections of the **cons** of the systems of tools outside of the circle of circles.

SYSTEMS OF PRACTICE

Routine

| District |

1 _____

2 _____

3 _____

4 _____

| Instructional Leader |

5 _____

| Teacher | Teacher | Teacher | Teacher |

| Classroom | Classroom | Classroom | Classroom |

Routine

| District |

1 _____

2 _____

3 _____

4 _____

| Instructional Leader |

5 _____

| Teacher | Teacher | Teacher | Teacher |

| Classroom | Classroom | Classroom | Classroom |

MULTIPLE LEADERS PRACTICE DIAGNOSIS

Leadership Dimension:				
Routine	**Functions**	**Leaders Followers**	**Leadership Distribution**	**Practice Description**
			Collaborated Collective Coordinated	
			Collaborated Collective Coordinated	
			Collaborated Collective Coordinated	
			Collaborated Collective Coordinated	
			Collaborated Collective Coordinated	
			Collaborated Collective Coordinated	
			Collaborated Collective Coordinated	

PRACTICE-TO-PRACTICE: VERTICAL

Classroom Practice: • What is the classroom routine? • Why does it exist? • What tool(s) helps mediate the interactions between the teacher and the students? • What content area(s) does this routine target? • What leadership support exists, if any?	
Leadership Practice: • What is the leadership routine? • Why does it exist? • What tool(s) helps mediate the interactions between the leader(s) and followers? • What content area(s) does this routine target? • To what classroom routine does this routine give support?	
Structures: • What structure(s) exist? • What structures exist that support one or both of the above practices?	
Function: • What leadership functions have you identified?	
Other:	
Dimension of Practice:	

PRACTICE-TO-PRACTICE: HORIZONTAL

Classroom Practice	Leadership Practice	Function	Structure	Comments: Intentions, Practices, Purpose, and Big Picture

Dimension of practice:

Answer the following questions:
- Do I have a better understanding of the differences in each component?
- What did you discover about your issue?
- With this discovery, what is my next step?
- What do I need to change?
- What do I need to keep?

SHAPING OF LEADERSHIP FUNCTIONS FORM

Dimension of Practice: Leadership Routine:						
Directions: Record your responses in the columns of the Shaping of Leadership Functions Form. Use the five-point scale from **Continually (A)** to **Rarely/Never (D)** to describe how regularly the following statements apply to your school leadership routines. Select **(E)** if you do not have sufficient information to respond to the statement.	Continually	Frequently	Sometimes	Rarely/Never	Insufficient Information	**Who is this leader?** Identify the leader(s) that fulfill these functions during the implementation of the routines. Are they formal (F) or informal leaders (N)?
Setting Direction						
Leaders sell and sustain the school's vision and mission during this routine	A	B	C	D	E	
Getting cooperative commitment for the goals	A	B	C	D	E	
Maintain high expectations	A	B	C	D	E	
Human Development						
Monitor instructional progress	A	B	C	D	E	
Develop teachers' content knowledge	A	B	C	D	E	
Develop teachers' pedagogical skills	A	B	C	D	E	
Provide encouragement, recognition, and support	A	B	C	D	E	
Create a sense of accountability for performances	A	B	C	D	E	
Organizational Development						
Adapt and modify tools as needed to improve instruction	A	B	C	D	E	
Support and maintain high expectations of collaboration among teachers	A	B	C	D	E	
Procure resources for teachers	A	B	C	D	E	
Distribute resources to teachers	A	B	C	D	E	
Handle disturbances that interrupt teaching practices	A	B	C	D	E	
Create and maintain an orderly work environment	A	B	C	D	E	

(Continued)

(Continued)

Which of the three functions is this routine or dimension of practice adequately addressing?
How do the functions address the intended purposes of the routine or dimension of practice, and/or how do they not?
How do the followers shape the leaders' engagement of the routine or dimension of practice?
Do these routines need enhancement or change? Is there a need for different or additional routines?
Are there other routines within the same dimension of practices that address the same functions? If so, what routines do we need? Is there a need to enhance or change this or other routines?
Does this routine, if combined with other routines, effectively address all three functions and, in turn, create a healthy system of practice? If not, what needs to happen?

SIDE-BY-SIDE CONTENT COMPARISON

	Reading	Math	Similarities	Differences
Who are the leaders?				
Leadership routines				

ESSENTIAL SIDE-BY-SIDE CONTENT COMPARISON QUESTIONS

How do you know these people are leaders?

Why did you choose these people?
- Inherent in leadership is influence. Academics often define leadership in terms of social influence relationships. Are the leaders listed on the paper there because they influence practice in specific areas?
- It is important to note that just because something influences us does not mean that it is leadership. If your dog barks to be taken outside, is that leadership?

What might we conclude from the list of identified leaders and their similarities and differences?

What might we conclude from the list of routines and their similarities and differences?

What can we conclude about the side-by-side content comparisons?

What should our team do with this information? Is there anything we have identified that could be replicated or practiced in another content area?

Were any tools identified? If so, what were they and were they common across the content? If not, why not? How might a tool identified in one content area be used in another content area?

Adapted in part from Spillane's presentations at the 2004–2005 Kansas Distributed Leadership Academy meetings.

SIDE-BY-SIDE BUILDING COMPARISON

Leadership dimension:				
Routine	Building 1	Building 2	Similarities	Differences

PRACTICE GAP SUMMARY

Leadership dimension:		
Identified Gaps	**Current**	**Desired**
Identified Gaps	**Current Routines**	**Desired Routines**
Identified Gaps	**Current Tools**	**Desired Tools**
Identified Gaps	**Current Structure**	**Desired Structure**

PRACTICE BRIDGE DIALOGUE QUESTIONS

What might be some of the pros and cons of staying with our *present* routine, tool, or structure?

Pros:	Cons:

What might be some of the pros and cons of staying with our *desired* routine, tool, or structure?

Pros:	Cons:

Do the pros outweigh the cons on either of the first two questions? If so, would it be best to stay with our present practices or to proceed with our desired practices? What do you have as evidence to support your response?

Next steps:

FORECASTING LEADERSHIP INITIATIVES GRID

New routines, tools, structures, or systems of practice:

Potential Consequences	Essential Questions	Team Response	Impact on Leadership Initiative	Likelihood	Total
Ripple Effects	How might this practice create additional problems for other practices?				
	How might this practice eliminate other leadership practice gaps in other leadership dimensions?				
	How might the implementation of this practice require additional resources?				
Resource Allocation	Will this practice require additional human resources beyond present capacity? If so, describe it.				
	How might this practice produce a strain on other academic areas and other work groups?				
Interdisciplinary Relationships	How might this practice strengthen relationships with other academic teams?				
	How might this practice involve temporary disruption of the present classroom practices?				
Teacher Classroom Practice	Once in place, how might this practice enhance or change classroom practice in a positive manner?				

ALTERNATIVE SOLUTIONS APPLIED CHART

Routine:				
Microtask	**Solution A**	**Solution B**	**Solution C**	**Solution D**

LEADERSHIP FUNCTION SUPPORT ANALYSIS FORM

Leadership dimension:				
Who can lead? Identify leaders who might be able to contribute to the functions associated with our identified dimension of practice.				
Setting Direction				
Sell and sustain the vision				
Get cooperative commitment for the goals				
Maintain high expectations				
Human Development				
Monitor instructional progress				
Develop teachers' content knowledge				
Develop teachers' pedagogical skills				
Provide encouragement, recognition, and support				
Create a sense of accountability for performances				
Organizational Development				
Adapt and modify tools as needed to improve instruction				
Support and maintain high expectations of collaboration among teachers				
Procure resources for teachers				
Distribute resources to teachers				
Handle disturbances that interrupt teaching practices				
Create and maintain an orderly work environment				

INTENTION VERSUS ACTION (1 OF 2)

Leadership Practice Improvement Area	Intentions	Actions

INTENTION VERSUS ACTION (2 OF 2)

Can you identify what structures, routines, and tools will shape this new action?

○ Structure:

○ Tool:

○ Routine:

Can you identify what functions your action will address and by whom?

○ Setting Direction:

○ Organizational Development:

○ Human Development:

Is there a clear delineation between your intentions and actions? Actions are meaningful and purposeful.

NEW PRACTICE ACTION-PLANNING CHART

Dimension of practice:

New practice to implement	Leader responsible for action	Intended interactions	Beginning date	Review date	Desired outcome	Evaluation of impact on classroom practice	What tools will be used to mediate these interactions?
Additional information that will support this practice:							
Additional information that will support this practice:							

DATA COLLECTION CHART

Questions	Answers
What dimension of practice are we addressing?	
What leadership practice will be monitored and evaluated?	
What do we want to accomplish?	
What exactly will we be measuring?	
What do we hope to learn from this information?	
Who will collect the evaluation data?	
How frequently and over what period of time will information be collected?	
How will the information we gather be documented?	
How will this information be formatted for review?	
How and when will this information be shared?	
Other routines	

STAKEHOLDER ANALYSIS SUPPORT CHART

Name of new leadership practice:				
Type of stakeholder	Identify stakeholders	When during implementation will we encounter these stakeholders?	Why would they support or resist our new practice?	What action can we take to secure support for the new practice?
Supporters				
Skeptics				

EXAMPLE SIX-PERSON PLACEMAT

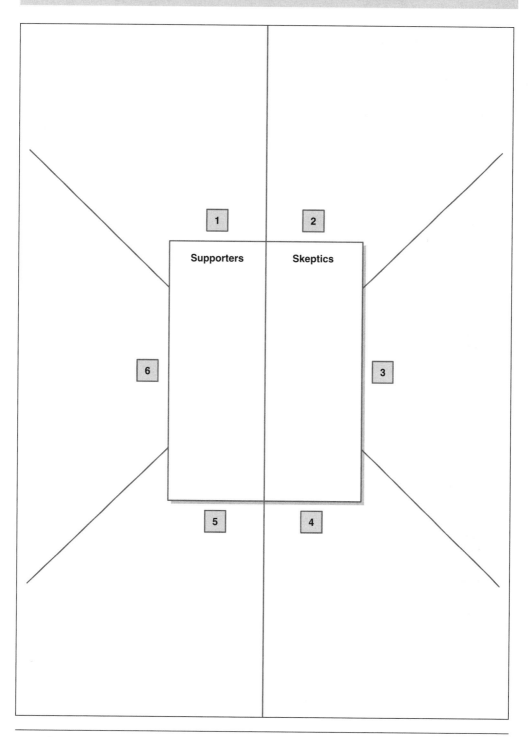

DIRECTIONAL INTENTIONS OF LEADERSHIP PRACTICES

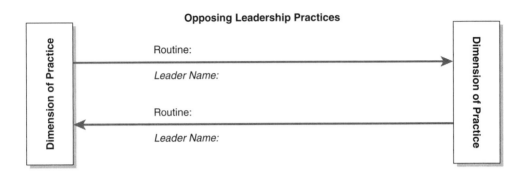

Opposing Leadership Practices

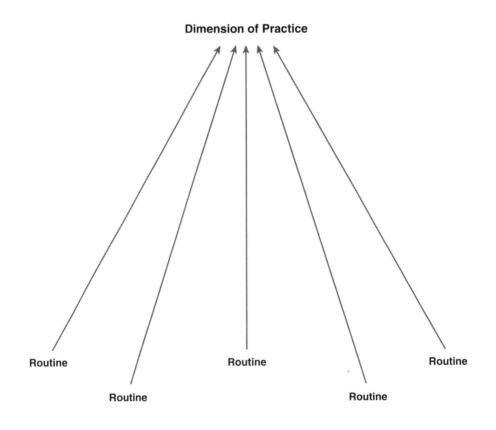

COMPETING DIMENSIONS OF PRACTICE DIAGRAM

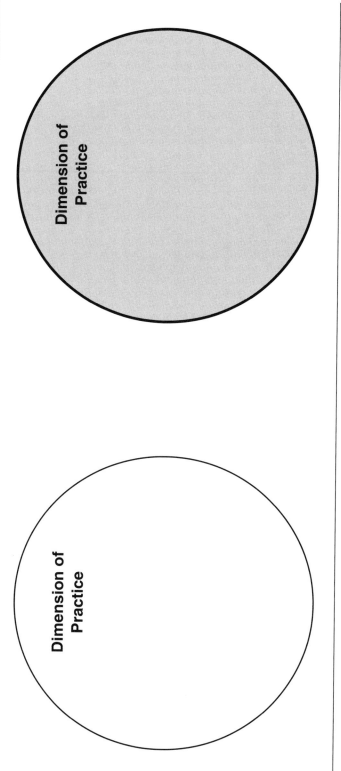

Dimension of Practice

Dimension of Practice

COMMON DIMENSIONS OF PRACTICE DIAGRAM

Dimension of Practice

Dimension of Practice

Reproducible Resources

PRINTABLE FIELD GUIDE TERMS FOR DISTRIBUTED LEADERSHIP

Term	*Definition*
Analysis	A process of dividing a situation into its components
Breakthrough Routine	A culture defined by its repetitive system of practices of using and changing knowledge within a cohesive environment
Bridging the Gap	When a relational connection is made from one component to another
Classroom Practice	The interactions among the teacher(s), students, and materials stretched over time (Cohen & Ball, 1998)
Cohesive Leadership	Leaders and followers unified through designed interactions based on the situation
Collaborated Distribution	*Collaborated* denotes that the leadership practice involves leaders coperforming a leadership routine together at the same time and in the same place (Spillane, 2006a)
Collective Distribution	Those leadership practices that are stretched over the practice of two or more leaders who work separately, but interdependently, in the coperformance of a leadership routine (Spillane, 2006a)
Coordinated Distribution	Those situations in which leaders work separately or together on different sequentially arranged leadership tasks that are necessary for the performance of a particular leadership routine (Spillane, 2006a)
Correlational	A causal, complementary, parallel, or reciprocal relationship, especially a structural, functional, or qualitative correspondence between two or more comparable entities (Dictionary.com Unabridged)
Debriefing	A guided reflective process of the experiences participants had during an activity
Design	Shaping objects to purposes (Spillane, 2006b)
Diagnose/Diagnosis	An exchange of words. The art of thinking together and embracing different points of view. Conversation with a center and no walls. A way of conversing about a topic while suspending judgment (Wellman & Lipton, 2004)
Dialogue	Identify nature or cause of something (Spillane, 2006a). A use of instruments that draws attention to particular dimensions of practice
Dimensions of Practice	A connection between educational content and a situation that crosses both leadership and classroom practice. Routines, tools, and structures help to define a "Dimension of Practice"
Distributed Leadership	A framework for diagnosing and designing leadership from a practice aspect (Spillane, 2006a)

Term	Definition
Enhance or Change Classroom Practice	When a leadership practice has influence on a teacher's classroom practice, it in turn has a positive effect on student academic performance.
Feedback	A form of supportive communication with other people
Focus Area (Content)	The process of designating a single content area (i.e., mathematics, reading, writing, science)
Focused Leadership	To know the precise strengths and weaknesses of each teacher at the point of classroom practice; to know the appropriate practices, in particular, when and how to use routines, tools, and structures to enhance teachers' classroom practice; to strategically distribute leadership by design based on situations and enhanced networks; and to have large repertories of leadership practices to deliver differentiated instructional and focused support to followers on a regular basis
Follower	Someone who knowingly or unknowingly is influenced by another person to change his or her motivation, knowledge, or practices
Framework	A fundamental structure and support system
Front-loading	A term used for highlighting, or loading, the learning prior to, or in front of, an activity (Priest & Gass, 1997)
Infinity Model	An eternal problem-solving and decision-making teaching and learning mentality; a never-ending practice cycle of school improvement; an unbounded, perpetual sequencing of improvement effort
Infinity of Practice	A tool that provides an ongoing, systemic, thinking, and processing professional learning leadership practice framework
Leader	Someone who knowingly or unknowingly influences and changes the motivation, knowledge, or practices of another
Leadership	Those activities that are either understood by or designed by organizational members to influence the motivation, knowledge, affect, and practice of other organizational members in the service of the organization's core work (Spillane, 2006b)
Leadership Aspect	A phase of leadership based on quality, character, and key features
Leadership Functions	Gives purpose and meaning to routines of practice. There are three functions that shape leadership practices: Setting Direction, Human Development, and Organizational Development

(Continued)

(Continued)

Term	*Definition*
Leadership Practice	The interactions between the leader(s), followers, and the situation stretched over time (Spillane, 2005a)
Mapping	A form of creating outlines or charts with the intention of making connections from one topic to another
Microtask	A subtask that, with other subtasks, defines a larger task or routine
Mindful Leadership	Analytical observant and heedfulness of leadership practices upon the organization's improvement factors including those of student performance
Practitioner	A person engaged in the profession of education at the school level
Processing	An activity that is structured to encourage individuals to plan, reflect, describe, analyze, and communicate about experiences
Routine	"Repetitive, recognizable patterns of interdependent actions carried out by multiple actors" (Feldman & Pentland, 2003)
	"Multi-actor, interlocking, reciprocally-triggered sequence of actions . . . " (Cohen & Bacdayan, 1996)
School Improvement	A positive, measurable increase in student performance
Situation	The context that defines the interactions and is defined through the interactions
Structures	A component, property, or relation. Examples: class schedule, 55-minute class time period, preparation-time arrangements for teachers, meeting frequency, and so forth
Systems of Practice	A network of routines, tools, and structures comprising a single dimension of practice to influence the practice of others
Task	A routine or mediated tool. An enterprise of multiple subtasks
Tool	A mediating device that shapes interactions among leaders, followers, and the situation. Tools often tend to be a tangible and can be an external representation of ideas, such as a constant set of expectations
Umbrella Issue	School improvement generalizations or goal statements such as "we want to improve student assessment scores"

LEADERSHIP FUNCTIONS FROM A DISTRIBUTED PERSPECTIVE

Setting Direction

- Constructing, selling, and sustaining a *vision*.

- Getting cooperative commitment for organizational *goals*.

- Setting and maintaining *high expectations*.

Human Development

- Monitoring instruction and progress.

- Developing teachers' knowledge and skill, both individually and collectively.

- Providing encouragement, recognition, and support.

- Developing a sense of accountability for performance.

Organizational Development

- Adapting and modifying standard operating procedures (routines, tools, structure) to support instructional improvement.

- Building a culture that de-privatizes classroom practice, supports collaboration among teachers, and maintains high expectations.

- Procuring and distributing resources.

- Handling disturbances and creating and maintaining an orderly work environment.

Source: From *How Leadership Influences Student Learning,* by K. Leithwood, K. Seashore, S. Anderson, and K. Wahlstrom, 2004, Wallace Foundation Report, retrieved 7, 2007, from http://www.wallacefoundation .org/KnowledgeCenter/. Copyright 2004 by the Wallace Foundation. Adapted with permission.

CRITICAL QUESTIONS

Knowledge Questions
- What are we doing? (routines)
- How does it happen? (tools or process)
- Who is involved? (leaders and followers)
- What do they know?

Comprehension Questions
- What is the purpose?
- Why was this done? (initiated from who, when, why)
- How would you describe it?
- What identifies these as routines?
- Why do they follow . . . ?

Analysis Questions
- Is it meeting its purpose?
- What is the teaching practice response?
- How do you know?
- Compared to the goal, is this routine meeting the needs?
- What evidence supports the continual use of . . . ?
- What are the parts or features of. . . . ? (routines, tools)
- Can I map this to the enhancement or changing of classroom practices?
- How do you know they are a leader or a follower in this situation?

Synthesis Questions
- Is there another way?
- What changes would you make to solve?
- How could this be improved?
- What would happen if . . . ?
- What would the future look like if . . . ?
- What could be retooled, redesigned, reworked?
- Can a model be constructed?
- How would we know this would enhance or change classroom practices?

- Are there alternatives?
- What could be done to maximize . . . ?
- What should we keep?
- What might it look like?
- Could you model it?

Application Questions
- What is our priority?
- How do you propose we implement it?
- How could we organize . . . to show or model?
- What approach should we take?
- Are you committed to . . . ?
- How do we apply what we have learned today?
- What are our new goals?
- What do we know?
- Are we ready to make a decision?

Evaluation Questions
- How do you know?
- How will this be monitored?
- Who is going to hold who accountable?
- How could you determine the need?
- How would you evaluate?
- What data supports our final decision?
- What are the tools we will use to support . . . ?
- Who are the key characters?
- What would you recommend?
- Who do we need to get approval or support?
- Can you assess the value or importance of . . . ?
- How will you know you have enhanced or changed classroom procedures?
- Do we have the resources for . . . ?
- Do we have the time . . . ?
- Do we have the tools or routines?
- Does our present structure enable us to . . . ?

DISTRIBUTED LEADERSHIP TRIPLEX

Systemically More Complex ↓ | More Comprehensive ↓

Leader Superhero Aspect

- **Leadership Focus:** Designated formal leader
- **Research:** Primarily principal—focused on actions, attributes, styles, behaviors of the individual
- **Instructional Focus:** Teaching and learning should be the central focus (reality: this is not likely)
- **Teacher–Leader:** Positional or veteran teacher—opportunities should be situational (reality: it may be role-oriented)
- **Practice:** Highly prescriptive—most likely traditional in approach
- **Structure:** Supports management practices (orderly)
- **Questions**: Who? What?

Leader-Plus Aspect

- **Leadership Focus:** Leadership deployment framework
- **Research:** Multiple leaders—focused on actions of multiple leaders
- **Instructional Focus:** Teaching and learning should be the central focus (reality: more likely than above focus)
- **Teacher–Leader:** Shared and collaborative responsibilities—opportunities should be situational (reality: this is encouraged)
- **Practice:** Prescriptive—adoption most likely of an existing model or prototype
- **Structure:** Comprehensive reform is the forerunner focus to leadership practice
- **Questions**: Who? What?

Leadership Practice Aspect

- **Leadership Focus:** Leadership practice
- **Research:** Leader(s), followers, and situation focused on actions and *interaction* of leaders, followers, and situations
- **Instructional Focus:** Instruction and learning is the *central focus*
- **Teacher–Leader:** Leadership and classroom practice—actions and *interactions* are among leader(s), followers, and situations (reality: this is critical)
- **Practice:** Descriptive before prescriptive—*analysis* drives design
- **Structure:** Situational, but leadership practice is paramount
- **Questions:** Who? What? and *How*? Leadership practice and classroom practice connections identified

Bottom Line:

Although the Leader Superhero aspect and the Leader-Plus aspect may have impact, only when the Leadership Practice aspect is effectively used will the energy and resources of the organization be fully utilized. Only then will true systemic innovation take place to meet and to exceed federal policy expectations.

Source: McBeth & Wheeles (2005a). Revised by McBeth for this book.

THE DISTRIBUTED LEADERSHIP IMPROVEMENT FRAMEWORK

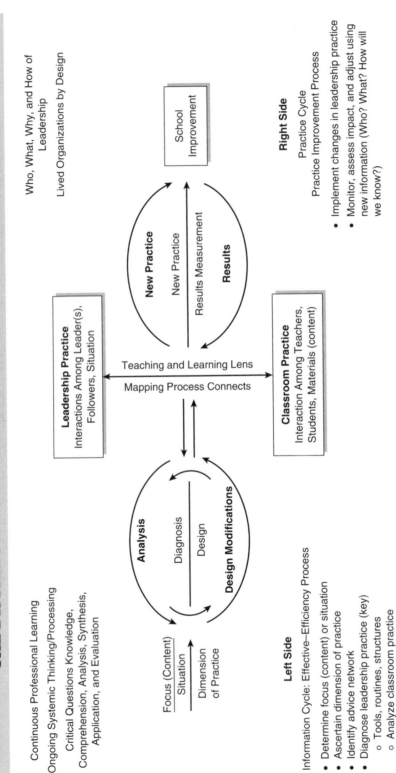

Who, What, Why, and How of Leadership

Lived Organizations by Design

Continuous Professional Learning

Ongoing Systemic Thinking/Processing

Critical Questions Knowledge, Comprehension, Analysis, Synthesis, Application, and Evaluation

School Improvement

New Practice

New Practice

Results Measurement

Results

Leadership Practice

Interactions Among Leader(s), Followers, Situation

Classroom Practice

Interaction Among Teachers, Students, Materials (content)

Teaching and Learning Lens

Mapping Process Connects

Analysis

Diagnosis

Design

Design Modifications

Focus (Content)

Situation

Dimension of Practice

Right Side

Practice Cycle

Practice Improvement Process

- Implement changes in leadership practice
- Monitor, assess impact, and adjust using new information (Who? What? How will we know?)

Left Side

Information Cycle: Effective–Efficiency Process

- Determine focus (content) or situation
- Ascertain dimension of practice
- Identify advice network
- Diagnose leadership practice (key)
  - Tools, routines, structures
  - Analyze classroom practice
  - Establish connections between classroom practice and leadership practice (mapping)
- Design leadership practice modifications (working, retooled, or created)

Source: Created by McBeth & Wheeles (2005b). Revised by McBeth for this book.

SYSTEM SCHOOL IMPROVEMENT INITIATIVE

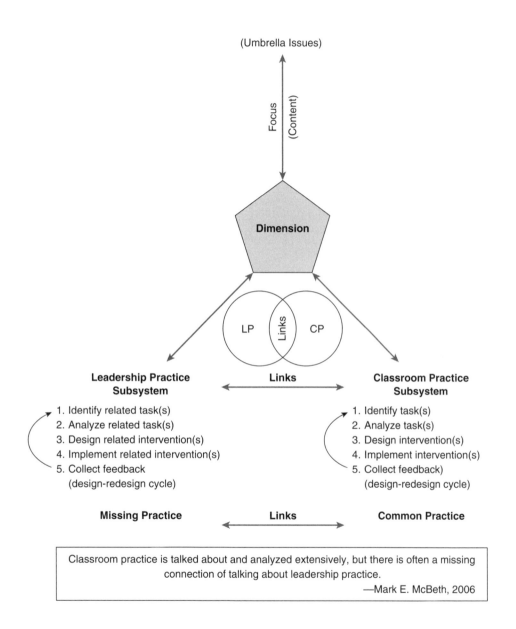

Source: Created by McBeth & Wheeles (2005b). Revised by McBeth for this book.

LEADERSHIP PRACTICE DIAGNOSIS CARD

Definitions

Routine	A repetitive, recognizable pattern of interdependent actions carried out by multiple actors (Feldman & Pentland, 2003). Multi-actor, interlocking, reciprocally triggered sequence of actions (Cohen & Bacdayan, 1996).
Leadership Functions	Gives purpose and meaning to routines of practice. There are three functions that shape leadership practices: Setting Direction, Human Development, and Organizational Development
Follower	Someone who knowingly or unknowingly is influenced by another person to change his or her motivation, knowledge, or practices.
Leader	Someone who knowingly or unknowingly influences and changes the motivation, knowledge, or practices of another.

Leadership Functions

Setting Direction
- Constructing, selling, and sustaining a *vision*.
- Getting cooperative commitment for organizational *goals*.
- Setting and maintaining *high expectations*.

Human Development
- Monitoring instruction and progress.
- Developing teachers' knowledge and skill, both individually and collectively.
- Providing encouragement, recognition, and support.
- Developing a sense of accountability for performance.

Organizational Development
- Adapting and modifying standard operating procedures (routines, tools, structure) to support instructional improvement.
- Building a culture that de-privatizes classroom practice, supports collaboration among teachers, and maintains high expectations.
- Procuring and distributing resources.
- Handling disturbances and creating and maintaining an orderly work environment.

—Ken Leithwood and colleagues (2004)

Coperformance

Collaborated Distribution
- Tasks are completed at the same time and in the same place.

Collective Distribution
- Tasks are completed separately, but interdependently.

Coordinated Distribution
- Tasks are completed in sequential order.

Leadership Distribution Definitions

Collaborated denotes that the leadership practice involves leaders coperforming a leadership routine at the same time and in the same place.

Collective distribution refers to those leadership practices that are stretched over the practice of two or more leaders who work separately, but interdependently, in the coperformance of a leadership routine.

Coordinated distribution refers to those situations in which leaders work separately or together on different sequentially arranged leadership tasks that are necessary for the performance of a particular leadership routine.

—(Spillane, 2006a, 2006b)

References

Ball, D., & Cohen, D. (1996). Reform by the book: What is—or might be—the role of curriculum materials in teacher learning and instructional reform? *Educational Researcher, 25*(9), 6–8.

Barabasi, A. (2003). *Linked: How everything is connected to everything else and what it means for business, science, and everyday life.* New York: Plume.

Bennett, N., Wise, C., Woods, P., & Harvey, J. (2003). *Distributed leadership.* Nottingham, UK: National College of School Leadership. Retrieved August 1, 2006, from http://www.ncsl.org.uk/media/7B5/67/distributed-leadership-literature-review.pdf

Bernhardt, V. (1999). *The school portfolio: A comprehensive framework for school improvement.* Larchmont, NY: Eye on Education.

Bernhardt, V. (2002). Beyond instructional leadership: A framework for shared leadership. *Educational Leadership, 59*(8), 37–40.

Blase, J., & Blase, J. (1999). Implementation of shared governance for instructional improvement: Principals' perspectives. *Journal of Educational Administration, 37*(5), 476–500.

Bryant, M. (2003). Cross-cultural perspectives on school leadership: Lessons from Native American interviews. In N. Bennett, M. Crawford, & M. Cartwright (Eds.), *Effective educational leadership* (pp. 216–228). London: Paul Chapman Publishing.

Camburn, E. (2005, September). *Teacher leadership from the perspective of distributed leadership.* Presentation at the Kansas Distributed Leadership Academy Statewide Meeting.

Camburn, E., Rowan, B., & Taylor, J. (2003). Distributed leadership in schools: The case of elementary schools adopting comprehensive school reform models. *Education Evaluation and Policy Analysis, 25*(4), 347–373.

Chenoweth, K. (2007, April). It's being done. *Education Week, 26*(32), 32–33.

Cohen, D., & Ball, D. (1998). *Instruction, capacity, and improvement* (CPRE Research report series, RR-42). Philadelphia: Consortium for Policy Research in Education, University of Pennsylvania.

Cohen, D., & Ball, D. (2000). *Instructional innovation: Reconsidering the story.* The Study of Instructional Improvement working paper, University of Michigan, Ann Arbor.

Cohen, M. D., & Bacdayan, P. (1996). Organizational routines are stored as procedural memory: Evidence from a laboratory study. In M. D. Cohen & L. S. Sproull, (Eds.), *Organizational learning* (pp. 403–429). Thousand Oaks, CA: SAGE.

Cuban, L. (1986). *Teachers and machines: The classroom use of technology since 1920.* New York: Teachers College Press.

Cuban, L. (1988). *The managerial imperative and the practice of leadership in schools.* Albany: State University of New York Press.

Cuban, L. (1990). Reforming again, again, and again. *Educational Researcher, 19*(1), 3–13.

Dahl. R. (1961). *Who governs? Democracy and power in an American city.* New Haven, CT: Yale University Press.

DePree, M. (2004). *The art of leadership.* New York: Random House.

Dictionary.com Unabridged (v 1.1). (n.d.). *Correlational.* Retrieved August 7, 2007, from http://dictionary.reference.com/browse/Correlational

DuFour, R., Eaker, R., & DuFour, R. (2005). *On common ground: The power of professional learning communities.* Bloomington, IN: National Education Service.

The Education Trust. (2006).

Elmore, R. (2000). *Building a new structure for school leadership.* Washington, DC: The Albert Shanker Institute.

Elmore, R., Peterson, P., & McCarthy, S. (1996). *Restructuring in the classroom: Teaching, learning, and school organization.* San Francisco: Jossey-Bass.

Feldman, M., & Pentland, B. (2003). Reconceptualizing organizational routines as source of flexibility and change. *Administrative Science Quarterly, 48*(1), 94–118.

Firestone, W. A. (1989). Using reform: Conceptualizing district initiative. *Educational Evaluation and Policy Analysis, 11*(2), 151–165.

Fullan, M. (2001). *Leading in a culture of change.* San Francisco: Jossey-Bass.

Fullan, M., Hill, P., & Crevola, C. (2006). *Breakthrough.* Thousand Oaks, CA: Corwin Press.

Garmston, R., & Wellman, B. (1999). *The adaptive school: A sourcebook for developing collaborative groups.* Norwood, MA: Christopher-Gordon.

Gass, M. (1993). *The evolution of processing adventure therapy experiences.* Dubuque, IA: Kendall/Hunt.

Goleman, D. (2002). *The new leaders: Transforming the art of leadership into the science of results.* London: Little, Brown.

Gronn, P. (2000). Distributed properties: A new architecture for leadership. *Educational Management and Administration, 28*(3), 317–338.

Gronn, P. (2002a). Distributed leadership. In K. Leithwood, P. Hallinger, K. Seashore-Louis, G. Furman-Brown, P. Gronn, W. Mulford, & K. Riley (Eds.), *Second international handbook of educational leadership and administration.* Dordrecht, Netherlands: Kluwer.

Gronn, P. (2002b). Distributed leadership as unit of analysis. *Leadership Quarterly, 13*(4), 423–451.

Halverson, R. (2003). Systems of practice: How leaders use artifacts to create professional community in schools. *Education Policy Analysis Archives, 11*(37). Retrieved August 21, 2007, from http://epaa.asu.edu/epaa/v11n37/

Halverson, R. (2005a, November). *A distributed perspective on how leaders use artifacts to create professional community in schools.* Paper presented at the 2005 Annual Conference of the University Council of Educational Administration, University of Wisconsin, Madison.

Halverson, R. (2005b). *Systems of practice and the situational distribution of leadership practice.* Working paper, University of Wisconsin, Madison.

Halverson, R. (2006). *A distributed leadership perspective on how leaders use artifacts to create professional community in schools.* WCER working paper, University of Wisconsin, Madison.

Halverson, R., & Clifford, M. (2005). *Evaluation in the wild: A distributed cognation perspective on teacher assessment.* Manuscript submitted for publication.

Halverson, R., & Gomez, L. (2001). *Phronesis and design: How practical wisdom is disclosed through collaborative design.* Paper presented at the 2001 American Educational Research Association Annual Meeting, Seattle, Washington.

Halverson, R., Grigg, J., Prichett, R., & Thomas, C. (2005). *The new instructional leadership: Creating data-driven instructional systems in schools.* WCER working paper, University of Wisconsin, Madison.

Hargreaves, A., & Fink, D. (2004, April). The seven principles of sustainable leadership. *Education Leadership, 63*(8), 8–13.

Harris, A. (2002, September). *Distributed leadership in schools: Leading or misleading.* Leadership, Policy and Development Unit University of Warwick Keynote Paper presented at the British Educational Leadership, Management, and Administration Society Conference, Birmingham, England.

Harris, A., & Chapman, C. (2002). *Effective leadership in schools facing challenging circumstances.* Final Report, National Conference of State Legislatures.

Kolbe, K. (2004a). *Powered by instinct: 5 rules for trusting your guts.* Phoenix, AZ: Monumentus Press.

Kolbe, K. (2004b). *Pure instinct: The M.O. of high performance people and teams.* Phoenix, AZ: Monumentus Press.

Kouzes, J., & Posner, B. (2006). *A leader's legacy.* Indianapolis, IN: John Wiley & Sons.

Leithwood, K., & Jantzi, D. (2000). Principal and teacher leadership effects: A replication. *School Leadership and Management, 20*(4), 415–434.

Leithwood, K., Louis, K., Anderson, S., & Wahlstrom, K. (2004). *How leadership influences student learning.* Wallace Foundation Report. Retrieved August 7, 2007, from http://www.wallacefoundation.org/KnowledgeCenter/

Leithwood, K., & Riehl, C. (2003). *What we know about successful school leadership.* Philadelphia, PA: Laboratory for Student Success, Temple University.

Lipton, L., & Wellman, B. (2004). *Mentoring matters: A practical guide to learning-focused relationships.* Sherman, CT: Mira Via, LLC.

Louis, K., & Kruse, S. (1995). *Professionalism and community: Perspectives on reforming urban schools.* Thousand Oaks, CA: Corwin Press.

McBeth, M. (2005, April). *The practitioner's field guide to leadership from a distributed perspective.* Kansas Distributed Leadership Academy Statewide Meeting, Topeka.

McBeth, M. (2006, August 29–30). *Enhancing student engagement from a distributed leadership perspective.* Presentation at Kal-Tech Academy 10: Statewide Kick-Off, 2006, Topeka, Kansas.

McBeth, M., & Wheeles, L. (2005a, June). *Distributed leadership diagnosis: Central Middle School case study, Kansas State Department of Education.* Kansas Distributed Leadership Academy Statewide Meeting, Topeka.

McBeth, M., & Wheeles, L. (2005b, June). *The distributed leadership perspective's impact on classroom practice, Kansas State Department of Education.* Kansas Exemplary Educators Network Conference, Topeka.

McBeth, M. and Wheeles, L. (2005c, October). *The Distributed Leadership Perspective's Impact on Classroom Practice.* Rural and Small Schools Conference Manhattan, Kansas.

McLaughlin, M., & Talbert, J. (1993). *Contexts that matter for teaching and learning.* Stanford, CA: Stanford University, Center for Research on the Context of Learning.

Merriam-Webster Online. (n.d.). *Intention*. Retrieved August 29, 2007, from http://m-w.com/cgi-bin/dictionary?book=Dictionary&va=intention

Nathan, L. (2004, April). A day in the life of a school leader. *Educational Leadership, 61*(7), 82–84.

No Child Left Behind Act of 2001, Public Law 107-110 (2001).

Ogawa, R., & Bossert, S. (1995). Leadership as an organizational quality. *Educational Administration Quarterly, 31*(2), 224–243.

Peters, T. (1986). *What gets measured gets done*. Retrieved August 21, 2007, from the Tom Peters Company Web site, http://www.tompeters.com/col_entries .php?note=005143&year=1986.

Phipps, M., & Claxton, D. (1997). An investigation into instructor effectiveness. *The Journal of Experiential Education, 20*(1), 40–46.

Portin, B. (2004, April). The role that principals play. *Educational Leadership, 61*(7), 14–18.

Powell, A., Farrar, E., & Cohen, D. K. (1985). *Shopping mall high school: Winners and losers in the educational marketplace*. Boston: Houghton-Mifflin.

Preuss, P. (2003). *School leader's guide to root cause analysis using data to dissolve problems*. Larchmont, NY: Eye on Education.

Priest, S., & Gass, M. (1997). An examination of "problem-solving" versus "solution-focused" facilitation styles in a corporate setting. *The Journal of Experiential Education, 20*(1), 34–39.

Reeves, D. (2006a, April). *Leadership for learning: Transforming research into action, Center for Performance Assessment*. Kansas Laboratory for Educational Leadership Statewide Meeting, Wichita.

Reeves, D. (2006b). *The learning leader: How to focus school improvement for better results*. Alexandria, VA: Association for Supervision and Curriculum Development (ASCD).

Reeves, D. (2006). Of hubs, bridges, and networks. *Educational Leadership, 63*(8), 32–37.

Schön, D. (1983). *The reflective practitioner: How professionals think in action*. London: Temple Smith.

Senge, P., Kleiner, A., Roberts, C., Ross, R., & Smith, B. (1994). *The fifth discipline fieldbook: Strategies and tools for building a learning organization*. New York: Doubleday.

Silva, D. Y., Gimbert, B., & Nolan, J. (2000). Sliding the doors: Locking and unlocking possibilities for teacher leadership. *Teachers' College Record, 102*(4), 779–804.

Spillane, J. (2004a, October). *A distributed perspective on school leadership, Northwestern University*. Kansas Distributed Leadership Academy Statewide Meeting, Topeka.

Spillane, J. (2004b, October). *Instructional improvement: The role of leadership practice, Northwestern University*. Kansas Distributed Leadership Academy Statewide Meeting, Topeka.

Spillane, J. (2004c, November). *Taking a distributed perspective in practice, Northwestern University*. Kansas Distributed Leadership Academy Statewide Meeting, Topeka.

Spillane, J. (2005a, September 17). *About distributed leadership*. Retrieved October, 15, 2005, from http://www.sesp.northwestern.edu/dls/about/

Spillane, J. (2005b, Winter). Distributed leadership. *Kappa Delta Pi.*

Spillane, J. (2005c, June). *Leadership practice: Taking a distributed perspective in practice, Northwestern University.* Kansas Distributed Leadership Academy Statewide Meeting, Topeka.

Spillane, J. (2005d). *The distributed leadership study: About distributed leadership.* Retrieved from the Northwestern University School of Education and Social Policy Web site on August 19, 2007, http://www.sesp.northwestern.edu/dls/about/

Spillane, J. (2006a). *Distributed leadership.* San Francisco: Jossey-Bass.

Spillane, J. (2006b, February). *School leadership: A distributed perspective, Northwestern University.* Kansas Laboratory for Educational Leadership Statewide Meeting, Topeka.

Spillane, J., Diamond, J., & Jita, L. (2003). Leading instruction: The distribution of leadership for instruction. *Journal of Curriculum Studies, 35*(5), 533–543.

Spillane, J., Diamond, J., Sherer, D., & Coldren, A. (2004). Distributing leadership. In M. Coles & G. Southworth (Eds.), *Developing leadership: Creating the school of tomorrow* (pp. 37–49). New York: Open University Press.

Spillane, J., Hallett, T., & Diamond, J. (2003). Forms of capital and the construction of leadership: Instructional leadership in urban elementary schools. *Sociology of Education, 76*(1), 1–17.

Spillane, J., Halverson, R., & Diamond, J. (2001). *Towards a theory of leadership practice: A distributed perspective* (Institute for Policy Research Working Paper WP-99–3). Evanston, IL: Northwestern University.

Spillane, J., Halverson, R., & Diamond, J. (2004). Towards a theory of leadership practice: A distributed perspective. *Journal of Curriculum Studies, 36*(1), 3–34.

Thompson, S. (2004, April). Leading from the eye of the storm. *Education Leadership, 63*(8), 60–63.

Tyack, P., & Cuban, L. (1995). *Tinkering toward utopia.* Cambridge, MA: Harvard University Press.

Valentine, J. (2005). *The instructional practice inventory: A process for profiling student engagement learning for school improvement.* Missouri University–Columbia, Middle Level Leadership Center.

Waters, T., Marzano, R., & McNulty, B. (2004). *Balanced leadership.* Denver, CO: Mid-Continent Research for Education and Learning (MCREL).

Wenger, E. (2000). Communities of practice and social learning systems. *Organization, 7*(2), 225–246.

Wellman, B., & Lipton, L. (2004). *Data-driven dialogue: A facilitator's guide to collaborative inquiry.* Sherman, CT: Mira Via, LLC.

Index

CORWIN PRESS

The Corwin Press logo—a raven striding across an open book—represents the union of courage and learning. Corwin Press is committed to improving education for all learners by publishing books and other professional development resources for those serving the field of PreK–12 education. By providing practical, hands-on materials, Corwin Press continues to carry out the promise of its motto: **"Helping Educators Do Their Work Better."**